VOICES OF
RUSSIAN SNIPERS

ALSO AVAILABLE

Eastern Front Sniper
The Life of Matthäus Hetzenauer
Roland Kaltenegger

Red Army Sniper
A Memoir of the Eastern Front in World War II
Yevgeni Nikolaev

Lady Death
The Memoirs of Stalin's Sniper
Lyudmila Pavlichenko

Snipers at War
An Equipment and Operations History
John Walter

The Sniper Encyclopaedia
An A–Z Guide to World Sniping
John Walter

Voices of Snipers
Edited by John Walter

VOICES OF RUSSIAN SNIPERS

EYEWITNESS RED ARMY ACCOUNTS FROM WORLD WAR II

Editors
Artem Drabkin & Andrey Ulanov

Foreword
John Walter

Translation
David Foreman

Greenhill Books

Voices of Russian Snipers
This English-language edition
first published in 2022 by
Greenhill Books,
c/o Pen & Sword Books Ltd,
47 Church Street, Barnsley,
S. Yorkshire, S70 2AS

www.greenhillbooks.com
contact@greenhillbooks.com

ISBN: 978-1-78438-782-2

All rights reserved.

Stalkers of the Enemy © Andrey Ulanov, 2022
Russian text © Artem Drabkin, 2022
David Foreman Translation © Greenhill Books 2022
John Walter Foreword © Greenhill Books 2022

The rights of Andrey Ulanov and David Foreman to be identified as the editor and the translator of this work have been asserted in accordance with Section 77 of the Copyrights Designs and Patents Act 1988.

CIP data records for this title are available from the British Library

Printed and bound by CPI Group (UK) Ltd, Croydon, CR0 4YY
Designed and typeset by Donald Sommerville

Typeset in 11.6/16 pt Minion Pro

Contents

	List of Plates	vii
	Foreword by John Walter	ix
1	Stalkers of the Enemy	1
2	Top Ten Soviet Snipers	22
3	Fedor Dyachenko	27
4	Aleksandr Romanenko	77
5	Klavdia Kalugina	95
6	Antonina Kotlyarova	104
7	Victor Shcherbakov	110
8	Rem Altshuller	120
9	Petr Belyakov	145
10	Nikolay Nadolko	177
11	Vasiliy Korzanov	184
12	Boris Godov	199
13	Maria Bondarenko	206
14	Anatoly Nevara	213
15	Mikhail Budenkov	220
	Notes	239

Plates

1. A pair of cheerful Soviet snipers, counting recent successes.
2. Rem Altshuller; Maria Bondarenko; Petr Belyakov; Anatoly Nevara; Mikhail Budenkov; Klavdia Kalugina; Fedor Dyachenko; Victor Scherbakov.
3. Snipers in training, with a portrait of Hitler as a firing target; an instructor explains how to adjust the PEM sight.
4. Five high-scoring female snipers of Third Shock Army, ; Fedor Dyachenko ready for action.
5. Nikolay Nadolko in a studio image with an unidentified but well-decorated comrade.
6. Mamed Ali Abasov, credited with 187 kills; a sniper with the Order of the Red Star; Antonina Kotlyarova.
7. A pair of snipers each wearing the Order of Lenin; Vasiliy Korzanov; Boris Godov, in later life.
8. Aleksandr Romanenko as a young soldier and later as a highly decorated veteran.

Foreword

OPERATION BARBAROSSA, the German invasion of the USSR that began on Sunday 22 June 1941, was to be a game-changer – but not in the way the invaders assumed. For Hitler and his generals, like Napoleon before them, the Road to Moscow was to be a road too far. Even so, the Germans made rapid incursions into Soviet territory at first, their Panzers and Stukas easily overcoming the hesitant resistance of forces hamstrung by a faulty deployment, political interference, and inadequate training.

The Winter War with Finland in 1939–40 had been difficult for the Red Army in many ways, and some of the lessons were still being learned when the Wehrmacht surged over the border. Something clearly had to be done as casualties mounted rapidly and vast areas of the western USSR were devastated. One solution was to relocate industry in a way unmatched before or since.

Ever-growing manufacturing capacity was exploited by producing weapons in large numbers. Losses in combat continued to be high, but were overcome increasingly rapidly. Red Army soldiers then began to turn the tide, forcing the German Sixth Army to surrender at Stalingrad at the beginning of February 1943; burgeoning Soviet war production meant that with overwhelming numerical superiority Soviet airmen were gradually able to wrest aerial superiority from the Luftwaffe; and after the titanic battle of Kursk, ever more powerful armoured and artillery forces led the advance that would reach Berlin in the spring of 1945.

There were many reasons why German dominance faded, but among them was a resurgence of Red Army morale that began with a genuine desire for revenge for Nazi atrocities. Politically inspired propaganda made the most of this of course, but the performance of individuals was well worth praising. Russian snipers were often very effective, individually, in pairs or in squads. Consequently, in 1942, the Soviet government sent Vladimir Pchelintsev and Lyudmila Pavlichenko on a tour of North America and Britain to raise awareness of what was happening on the Eastern Front.

Individual stories published in military periodicals such as *Krasnaia Zvezda* ('Red Star') and the leading newspapers drew attention to snipers such as Roza Shanina – not among the high-scorers, but photogenic and outspoken. Among wartime memoirs published in recent years have been those of Lyudmila Pavlichenko, Vasiliy Zaytsev, Iosif Pilyushin and Yevgeni Nikolaev, all of whom, recruited in the early days of the war, went on to achieve high scores through dedication and first-class marksmanship in spite of wounds of varying severity.

Yet Soviet snipers' success has always been controversial. Their tallies have always been disputed outside the USSR, the inference being that the numbers were inflated either for personal gain or by political dictates, and the inaccessibility of official records has done little to reveal a basic truth.

Artem Drabkin has gathered the testimonies of ten men and three women, who, by and large, have been ignored by history even though Mikhail Budenkov and Fedor Dyachenko (credited with 449 and 425 kills respectively) were among the highest-scoring Red Army snipers.

The snipers whose accounts are included here had diverse and perhaps surprising backgrounds; some were very young. Rem Altshuller was Jewish, Nikolay Nadolko had been born in the Bashkir Republic; Vasiliy Korzanov came from farming stock while Fedor Dyachenko's family had been deported to Siberia after being denounced as *kulaks* (landowning farmers whom Lenin had characterised as 'plunderers of the people and profiteers'); Aleksandr Romanenko had been conscripted before his seventeenth birthday, but only after initial rejection despite possessing a Voroshilov marksmanship badge.

The individual stories remain fascinating, often with a personal dimension and humility lacking in the sometimes self-promotional works of better known snipers who published their accounts during the Communist years.

Voices of Russian Snipers begins by summarising the development of marksmanship in the Tsarist army, a story all but unknown in the West even today. It is still widely assumed that the Russians did not employ snipers in the First World War, even though they were facing German snipers in much the same way as the British and French were doing along the Western Front.

The reality is that specialists were recruited into the Tsarist army prior to 1917, but only in small numbers and lacking the specialist equipment commonly encountered in the West. Though optical sights had been fitted to several of the Federov auto-loading rifles issued in 1915 for trials with the 187th Infantry Regiment, the Russians had relied too greatly on importing optical equipment prior to 1914 – particularly from Germany – and lacked the facilities to make lenses in large quantities. Hence the introduction of specially created sniper rifles could not be undertaken, forcing the impressment of sporting rifles wherever possible.

The book also relates how the rise of marksmanship training prior to 1941 created a pool of potential snipers, thanks to the involvement of agencies such as Komsomol, Osoaviakhim and Vsevobuch. Consequently, though losses of equipment in the opening stages of war were initially difficult to restore, men and women with proven shooting skills could be trained effectually once officially sponsored sniper schools had largely replaced in-service training, whose quality varied appreciably from unit to unit. The advent of optical sights that were compact and easier to make than their conventionally styled predecessors soon made sniping equipment easier to procure.

Andrey Ulanov questions the way in which individual tallies were created, citing instances where claims made on behalf of snipers failed to tally with losses reported by the German units they were facing. This remains a grey area. Though the top ten snipers are duly listed, there is still no real evidence to support individual tallies. It is by no means clear if the 702 kills attributed to Mikhail Surkov are supported by evidence sufficient to convince sceptics of their validity – even though, at least after the introduction of the Order of Glory in November 1943, each kill supposedly had to be verified.

Yet achieving more than 500 kills was by no means impossible. Many Red Army snipers served from the early days of the Great Patriotic War until the German surrender in May 1945. If they had achieved no more than a single kill each day, five hundred kills would have been reached within eighteen months. And though no comparable Soviet record has ever been publicised, the logbook kept by German sniper Bruno Sutkus and highlighted in *Sniper Ace* (2009) recorded in detail no fewer than 207 kills obtained between 8 May 1944 and 7 January 1945.

One of the most interesting aspects of *Voices of Russian Snipers* lies in the details that draw attention to the highs and lows of everyday life on the Eastern Front. These can relate to sniping techniques and the way in which the differing types of cartridge could be used – continual use of armour-piercing or tracer rounds rapidly wore rifling to a point where accuracy was compromised – or highlight unbelievably meagre diets in which canned stew supplied from the USA was regarded as a delicacy! Rem Altshuller even had a female partner, use of women in front-line combat being unique to the USSR.

Reading *Voices of Russian Snipers* will let you see the Red Army's snipers in a different light, focusing more on their day-to-day lives than propagandists' exaggeration. So enjoy these pages as much as I did!

John Walter

# Stalkers of the Enemy

WHEN THE SUBJECT OF SNIPERS IN WORLD WAR II comes up, even those barely familiar with military history may well be able to recall a few names. Although criticised for a multitude of inaccuracies, the film *Enemy at the Gates* reminded the viewer of the most legendary Soviet sniper – Vasiliy Zaytsev. Also well known in the West is the most lethal woman in history – 'Lady Death', Lyudmila Mikhaylovna Pavlichenko, whose memoirs were recently published by Greenhill Books.

For most readers, this is where their knowledge of Soviet snipers ends. The names of many eminent marksmen in the USSR, who had hundreds of dead enemies to their credit, have not become widely known in the West. It is even less well known how the USSR prepared for a sniper war. For the achievements of Soviet snipers were not due simply to the exclusive talent of individuals. As was the case with the astronauts, they were the result of lengthy efforts by a multitude of people – weapon design teams, systems for the mass-training of snipers, and so on.

In this sense the dozens, or even hundreds, of top-class snipers were only the tip of the iceberg. A major war inexorably chews up people and technology, and snipers were no exception. On attack, the life of a sniper was very brief; on defence, perhaps a little longer. On average, snipers managed to carve a few dozen notches on their rifle butts as a record of their personal tally, before heading off to a medical centre or a common grave. But it was the snipers whose names remained unknown to correspondents, and whose feats were not always recognised by decorations, who bore on their shoulders the principal burden of this special sniper war.

Beginnings

Attempts to set up teams of sharpshooters were undertaken by the Russian Army in the course of the Russo-Japanese War of 1904–5. There are references to officers who successfully employed optically sighted hunting rifles which they had acquired in their private lives.

During peace time, efforts were made within the Russian Army to single out and encourage top marksmen. In 1909 special badges in three classes *Za otlichnuyu strelbu* ('for exceptional shooting') were introduced. Other incentives were considered, including financial ones. Paragraph 530 in *Nastavlenii dlya strelbi izh vintovok, karabinov i revolverov* ('Instructions for rifle, carbine and revolver shooting') provided for the presentation of prizes for competitions in shooting and estimating distances by eye, and, in addition, provision was made for 10 rubles to be granted to every rifle and Cossack infantry company, 20 rubles to military colleges, and 5 rubles to a number of cavalry and other detachments to encourage marksmanship. All in all, great efforts were made to devote more attention to training for shooting, including sharpshooting, in the Russian Army.

However, further progress was held back by the lack of technical facilities at the required level – in particular, a highly developed optical industry. Only in 1914, on the shooting range of the officer rifle school at Oranienbaum,[1] were tests carried out on an optical sight made by C. P. Goerz (a German firm with branches throughout the Russian Empire). In 1916 the first – and the last – twenty optical lenses manufactured at the Obukhov plant in St Petersburg were delivered to a company of the 189th Izmailskiy Infantry Regiment.[2] But against the background of the First World War twenty lenses were absolutely negligible. At the front, Russian riflemen were compelled to fight German and Austrian snipers using rifles with just ordinary sights.

Meanwhile, in the course of the First World War, the sniper's art on the Western Front was being raised to a new level. Now it was not just a few individual riflemen who had optical sights. Impressed by the performance of German snipers, and by the introduction of the Mauser Scharfschützen-Gewehr 98 with an optical sight, the French and British began to train their own snipers. In 1915 Major Hesketh Prichard of the British Army set up a sniper school in France. He and his pupils developed numerous methods of sniper warfare, many of which are still current today.

Hesketh Prichard summed up his experience of World War I in the book *Sniping in France*, the first edition of which came out in 1920. After the Revolution the USSR paid keen attention to innovations in warfare. *Sniping in France* was translated into Russian by 1924, the information it contained arousing great interest in the Red Army high command. But the absence of home-grown sniper experience and the lack of the required material facilities continued to exert a negative influence. The Red Army wanted to have its own snipers but did not know how to instruct them properly and could not arm them with sniper rifles equipped with optical lenses made in the USSR.

The results of the Red Army's first attempts to recruit its own snipers are described in the foreword which Sergey Kamenev, People's Commissar for Military and Naval Affairs and Deputy Chairman of the USSR Revolutionary Military Council, contributed to the 1929 brochure *Snayping* ('Sniping'):

> The question of sniping was first raised three or four years ago. It aroused the interest of many people in the Red Army and in the ranks of sports shooters.
>
> Without perhaps having adequately investigated it back then, we set about creating a force of Red snipers, but were unable to carry out the operation in a systematic way. We had to use primitive methods and, because we did not know what was actually required, we did it poorly. We grasped the idea, as it were, but did not fully understand what snipers were for. Some went further and raised the question as to whether they were necessary at all.

The year 1929 saw not only the publication of the initial brochure, entitled *Snayping*, by the rifle section of Osoaviakhim,[3] but also the organisation of a first sniping course at the Vysshey strelkovaya shkola ('Senior Rifle School'). Grigory Morozov, who was in charge, summed up his experience in 1931 in the handbook *Podgotovka otlichnikh strelkov-nablyudateley* ('Training top-class snipers'). It is noteworthy that the author himself remarked that 'I interpret the word "sniper" as meaning a rifleman equipped with a telescopic sight and operating along with an observer who is also armed with a good pair of binoculars or telescope, as well as a field periscope.' Acknowledging that there was at the moment no possibility of supplying these in the desired quantities, Morozov proposed sniper training for those 'top-class riflemen' who would become snipers after they had received the necessary equipment. Another book which saw the light in the same year was *Takticheskoe primenenie snayperov* ('The tactical deployment of snipers') by Evgeniy Menchukov, a senior instructor on that same *Vystrel*[4] course.

However, although at that time the USSR had no experience in training snipers or producing the necessary equipment, the very fact that the country's leadership acknowledged the problem and made efforts to solve it was important.

First and foremost, huge efforts were made to train the civilian population in marksmanship. The Voroshilovskih Strelkov ('Voroshilov marksman') scheme became the Soviet equivalent of the US Civilian Marksmanship Program. According to hearsay, it was sparked off by an incident during rifle training, when a young officer who was unable to hit the target began trying to excuse his failure by blaming the poor quality of the weapons. The People's Commissar for Military and Naval Affairs (Minister of Defence), Kliment Voroshilov, who happened to be there at the time, took the officer's Nagant revolver and, with seven shots, scored 59 points out of a possible 70. Returning the weapon to the embarrassed officer, Voroshilov said: 'There are no bad weapons, only bad marksmen.' This incident was widely covered in the press and sparked off a mass movement to improve rifle training. Successful shooters who reached the required standard were presented with special badges, depending on their results. The thirst for training gripped not just the adult population but also young people, for whom a special 'Junior Voroshilov Marksman' badge was established.

With time, the best marksmen began not just to be taught to shoot accurately, but to be trained as military snipers. They were trained in the army and also on special sniper courses run by Osoaviakhim. Those who successfully completed sniper courses received the title *Snayper Osoaviakhima* ('Osoaviakhim Sniper') as well as a special badge.

The precise number of marksmen trained through the Osoaviakhim system is not known but, according to some figures, the total of those who received Voroshilov Marksman badges could be in the range of six to nine million. Their contribution was widely recognised even in the USA, where, in 1942, a well-known poster was published with the legend 'This man is your friend: Russian, he fights for freedom': the Soviet sniper has a Voroshilov Marksman badge on his breast.

No less constant attention was paid to creating the 'material facilities' for Soviet snipers. For the Soviet leadership this objective was rendered easier by budding military cooperation with Germany. After its defeat in World War I Germany became a pariah country and the Versailles Treaty imposed severe limits on the development of its army and navy. In their search for a solution, the German military and firms connected with arms production embarked on active collaboration with a number of countries where it was possible to avoid the Versailles limitations – notably Finland, Sweden, Switzerland and the Soviet Union.

The first Soviet purchases of optical sights took place at the beginning of the 1920s, when, following an order from the artillery committee of the Red Army artillery administration, optical sights for rifles and machine guns were bought in Germany. Another small batch of sights from various German firms was purchased in 1925 for trials to select the best model. The final choice was the Zielvier ('Four times', referring to magnification) from Carl Zeiss of Jena, 500 being ordered in 1927. At the same time, work proceeded on the manufacture of Soviet sights. The first result of this was the appearance of the Opticheskogo vintovochnogo pritsela obraztsa 1930 goda ('Optical rifle sight, model 1930'), also known as the 'PT'. However, the plans for turning out these sights in large numbers were not to be realised owing to the huge complexity of the sight's mechanical components. More successful was the 'Model 1931' variant, which became known as the 'PE sight'.

The optical design, involving nine lenses, was similar to the above-mentioned Zielvier, whereas the construction of the adjusting mechanisms and dioptre regulation depended on another German sight which was referred to in Soviet documentation as the 'Vizar-5' (*Zielfunf*, 5× magnification) made by Emil Busch of Rathenow. Nevertheless, even this sight was still quite complex and expensive to produce. In 1937, after the transfer of PE production from Factory No. 69 in Krasnogorsk[5] to the No. 357 'Progress' factory in Leningrad, the sight was simplified further by removing the focussing mechanism to become widely known as the 'PEM'.[6] The PE and PEM became the principal optical sights used by snipers in the Red Army.

The Red Army's main sniper rifle at that time was a special version of the Model 1891/30 'Three Line' Mosin.[7] Although there had been proposals to develop a special magazine rifle for snipers, it was decided, initially at least, simply to select the most accurate rifles to receive optical sights.

However, optical sights had been installed on experimental Fedorov rifles as early as 1916 and the Soviet military leadership retained the desire to develop sniper variants of the self-loaders approved in the 1930s.[8] Like many US Army generals, the Red Army chiefs supposed that the magazine rifle was obsolete and ought to be replaced as soon as possible. Moreover, it was considered that for the rank-and-file army sniper there were adequate opportunities to use a self-loading rifle, and its automatic features would enable him to hit his target quickly in combat.

The adoption of the Tokarev self-loading rifle (SVT-38) raised the question of producing a sniper variant. At its own initiative the Kharkiv Factory No. 3 manufactured a compact sight duly adopted as the Opticheskogo vintovochnogo pritsela obraztsa 1940 goda ('Optical rifle sight, model 1940') though better known as the 'PU' or Pritsel Ukorochenniy ('Shortened sight'). Originally designed for installation on an SVT, because it was simpler and more convenient, it became within two years the main sniper sight used in the Red Army.

The scale of work done before the war is impressive, especially if one remembers that, as distinct from other military fields, sniping in the

Red Army was actually developed from scratch. In just over ten years a method for the mass training of not only snipers, but instructors too, was established and developed and several variants of completely modern sights and appropriate brackets were devised. This made it possible for the army to recruit a large number of snipers. Confirmed after the beginning of the war, on 29 July 1941, article No. 04/601[9] provided for two snipers in an infantry reconnaissance platoon and two in every rifle company. It was for them that 'sniper rifles with optical sights' were provided – 74 per regiment.

Sniper Warfare

The first months of the German Blitzkrieg offered the snipers very few opportunities to show what they could do. During the first half year of war the Red Army lost a huge amount of military equipment and trained personnel. Especially problematic for snipers was the loss not only of a large number of riflemen and rifles with optical sights, but of lower-ranking officers too. Those who replaced them often had a poor understanding of how snipers should be deployed.

For example, an order from the general staff of the 33rd Division dated 4 December 1941, began with the words: 'During peace time, considerable attention was paid to the training of snipers. Since the beginning of the war the attention of command personnel to this question has diminished to an unacceptable degree.'[10]

Nevertheless, by the end of 1941, the Red Army leadership had already begun to make efforts to reinvigorate sniper recruitment. It proceeded best where the front-line was stable. A good example is provided by the biography *Lady Death*. Back before the war Lyudmila Pavlichenko had completed a two-year Osoaviakhim course in Kiev. During the first days of the war, she volunteered for the Red Army and became a sniper in the 25th 'Order of Lenin' Chapaev Rifle Division of the Red Army. Because the southern sector was attacked by Romanian forces, which were less battle-ready than their German allies, the defenders of Odessa were able to hold out for a lengthy period. The same story was repeated at Sevastopol against the forces of General Erich von Manstein. Another focus of positional war was Leningrad.

The stationary line of defence quickly taught the warring sides to value snipers and make good use of them. Nevertheless, even on peaceful sectors of the front, not all commanders knew how to deploy snipers correctly. One report contains a description of the way an infantry officer demanded that a sniper assigned to him fire at the armour plating of a German pill-box – so that he could listen to the 'zing' of the bullets striking it. However, this was not the worst case, as it is possible that this officer simply wanted to be sure of the sniper's qualifications.

In the 391st Rifle Division it was a much less encouraging story.[11] From the moment of its formation in September 1941 the division had neither snipers nor sniper rifles – only individual riflemen engaging in stalking at their own initiative, and using ordinary rifles with open sights. Finally, in August 1942, the division received ten sniper rifles, of which five were handed over to the 1,024th Rifle Regiment. Having completed an Osoaviakhim sniper course in Leningrad before the war, Sergeant Buzelin trained a sniper team from six former hunters, who had already begun to 'operate' against the enemy in sniper pairs. However, at the end of September, according to the document, the snipers were sent to fight with a company and after four days of combat only two of them were left. At the initiative of the regimental commander a new sniper team was formed, this time with fifteen men, and their training was directed by the same Sergeant Buzelin.[12] Because there were only two sniper rifles, training was inclined to drag, and speeded up only in November, when the division received another thirty sniper rifles. The new sniper teams set off for the forward line in the middle of December 1942 and, as the report indicates, 'their impact was significant'. The Germans really began to conceal themselves and 'ran about like hares', while movement in the Soviet lines became freer, because the enemy riflemen and machine gunners rarely took the risk of opening fire by daylight.

In February 1943, on the orders of the divisional commander, the regimental sniper teams were disbanded before an offensive and the snipers sent in pairs to rifle companies. In 10–15 days of fighting seven of nine snipers were killed and all the sniper rifles were put out of commission. There were no new rifles – and correspondingly no new snipers in the division until July.

The sniper conference held in April 1942 by the political section of the 76th Rifle Division declared,

> that this valuable personnel resource has been cast aside, not taken into consideration, and snipers are not being deployed in accordance with their intended purpose. Sniper weaponry has been incorrectly distributed and, as a consequence, sniper rifles and associated devices are to be seen in the hands of cart drivers, horse attendants and other soldiers employed in the rear.[13]

Eighteen months later, in November 1943 an inspection carried out in the 19th Army on the Karelian Front revealed that, in particular, snipers of the 77th Motorised Rifle Brigade had been put in a brigade team which was being deployed like an ordinary line company and that in the 104th and 122nd Rifle Divisions 'Weapons have not been calibrated and are mostly dirty and out of order.'

As a rule, similar situations arose in the case of snipers who had been trained on the spot in military units. In spite of menacing commands from 'above' and numerous instructions, admonitions and other guidelines, it was extremely hard to overcome deficiencies in the training of the Red Army's lower and, to some extent, middle command structure. These problems had arisen before the war as a consequence of the explosive growth in numbers at the end of the 1930s and were significantly complicated by the losses in the initial war period. This did not of course just affect sniping. The standard of training on the spot also varied widely. Not every unit, to be sure, had an instructor who knew the theory of sniper shooting and was not simply a sniper who had become a 'senior' figure after heavy fighting experience.

The Red Army high command was also well aware that talented riflemen and, in particular, competent instructors for them were to be found in all detachments. Along with orders for snipers to be trained and deployed directly within units, a lot of work was done to centralise sniper training. The main centres were schools of sniper training for top-class marksmen in military districts in the rear. New recruits who had had shooting training prior to call-up headed there and, following a course of instruction, went to the front as trained snipers.

The training was conducted not just by purely army structures, but by civilian ones as well – in particular by Osoaviakhim, by the Komsomol[14] or by youth detachments of Vsevobuch,[15] which were set up to train 'snipers, sub-machine gunners, medium machine gunners, tank destroyers and mortar crews'. The best known were the Central School for Sniper Instructors and, in particular, the Central Women's School for Sniper Training, which was an institution unique both in Russian and Soviet history and the history of the world.

Considerable attention was also given to publicising snipers and their operations. Both the central organs of mass information and newspapers in front-line units regularly published articles about sniper activities, stressing their contribution to the struggle against the enemy.

Portrait of a Sniper

At the end of 1944 the Red Army rifle tactics committee sent a questionnaire out to the active army entitled *Ispolzovanie snayperov v boyu po opytu Otechestvennoy voyny* ('The deployment of snipers in combat based on the experience of the Great War for the Fatherland'). It is difficult to exaggerate the significance of this document, especially the responses from the front-line units. It presented in essence a cross-section of Soviet sniping at the moment of its greatest florescence, when the problems of the initial war period had been resolved to a significant degree and Soviet snipers had become one of those instruments which the Red Army was using to drive the front-line further and further westward.

As the poll indicated, the majority of Red Army snipers operated within the framework of a set routine, in rifle companies. However, there were also special sniper teams attached to higher structures. For instance, the general staff of the First Baltic Front noted that in some divisions there were special teams of women-snipers sent from the Central Women's School for Sniper Training.[16] Unfortunately, in 1944, fighting on the offensive cost the Red Army snipers dear. Some replies noted that the prescribed sniper numbers were only to be found before an offensive began; the majority were eliminated in the course of the fighting. Thus the 22nd Army responded that:

As a result of protracted fighting by army units on the offensive the majority of snipers were put out of commission because they were not always deployed properly and they received almost no reinforcements. In the units and formations sniper training is also at a low level. As a result of all this there are very few snipers at the moment.

Experience shows that snipers are best removed from detachments because, as a rule, they are not deployed for the right purpose (e.g., as observers, signallers, etc.), while on the offensive they are used as rank-and-file riflemen, which leads to rapid and pointless sniper losses.[17]

In many units the commanders had independently arrived at the idea that snipers were better deployed in special detachments created for them rather than in companies. For example, the 13th Army responded that there the regimental and battalion commanders were setting up small teams from the 5–10 best snipers as a personal reserve. Many contributors to the questionnaire spoke out in favour of this approach – the creation of special sniper teams under the control of a rifle division or regiment.

The overwhelming majority of Red Army snipers in 1944 operated in pairs. As a rule, the more experienced sniper was the main shooter, and the other was the observer, although pairs of experienced snipers often swapped roles depending on their degree of exhaustion. Very rarely did snipers operate on their own and, as a rule, this was determined by the personal preference of the snipers themselves. Generally, when the number of snipers in a detachment was uneven, efforts were made to find an assistant for the spare sniper. For example, the 13th Guards Rifle Corps responded that because of the shortage of sniper rifles 'a sniper is paired with a good shot who is armed with an ordinary rifle'.[18] On the First Baltic Front, 'In those cases when a second sniper could not be found, someone going out stalking on the forward line would have a sub-machine gunner assigned.'

Soviet snipers were most effective when firing from distances of between 300 and 600–800 metres. The closer the marksman, the greater the probability of him or her being detected. As for longer distances, up to 1,000 and even 1,200 metres, any mention of them is usually accompanied by expressed reservations like 'if the sniper is well trained and the rifle is well adjusted', 'firing from a long distance is not very effective', 'in practical terms it doesn't pay to fire at targets further than 700 metres away', and 'hitting the target from distances greater than this should be considered an exception'. Interestingly, the enemy had a good picture of most Soviet snipers' capabilities. One reply pointed out the desirability of increasing the range of firing certainty because in the depths of the German defences 'the enemy are often seen, individually or in groups, on observable sectors during daylight hours'.

To some, the cited figures may possibly seem on the low side, for some marksmen now achieve more impressive results even when using rifles from those times. However, it should not be forgotten that such firing is generally conducted on a shooting range where the distances to the targets are known and modern devices are used: laser range-finders, ballistic calculators, and hand-held weather stations. During the war years snipers at the front had to rely purely on their own experience – that is, if they succeeded in gaining any.

The Germans came to similar conclusions with regard to operating distances for front-line snipers. For example, in *Merkblatt für die Ausbildung und den Einsatz vom Scharfschützen*, 'Leaflet for the training and deployment of snipers',[19] the basic directions recommend distances up to 600 metres, and only at the end are distances up to 800 metres mentioned.

The main problem at that time was that of precisely measuring distances to the target. Up until the advent of compact laser rangefinders this was only possible with the aid of quite large and conspicuous stereoscopic rangefinders. It goes without saying that these could not be used in the majority of the situations in which a sniper was able to operate. Practically all snipers reported that they estimated the distance to the target by eye. Moreover, an error of 'no more than 10 per cent' was regarded as satisfactory, even for trained snipers. Very many of those who replied stated that training in determining distances was insufficient 'especially in the case of young snipers'. The most reliable method of determining distances was through preliminary weapon-testing: 'before going off to their hide-out, experienced snipers checked the distance to the target by firing tracer or armour-piercing bullets, which sparked on contact with a hard object'. These tests also prompted adjustments in response to meteorological conditions such as wind, humidity, atmospheric pressure, and so on. The most experienced marksmen determined the strength of a side wind from local signals – for example, the swaying of tree tops – but, as was pointed out: 'All this comes from the personal experience of each sniper, for the theory of this area of ballistics is, as a rule, poorly mastered by snipers.'

Firing too many tracer or armour-piercing bullets, of course, led to increased wear and tear on rifling. A separate section of the questionnaire was devoted to this phenomenon, some snipers responding that after 150 shots the impact on the rifle was such that it needed to be rebarrelled or at least readjusted, though others suggested as many as 200–300 shots.

For a long time, it was considered that, although the SVT (Tokarev self-loading rifle) was not accepted by the majority of Red Army soldiers owing to its complexity, snipers loved and valued it. However, the results of the 1944 survey present a different picture. Although some snipers really did speak out in favour of a self-loading sniper rifle, their opinion of the SVT was mostly negative: 'It has a substantial defect – great sensitivity to sand and mud.' 'The SVT is more prone to jams and hiccups.'

In addition, trials undertaken with self-loading sniper rifles in 1942, both on firing ranges and in the field, revealed that erratic ignition not only increased bullet dispersion but also that one or two 'fliers' were often encountered.

Owing to deficiencies in the construction of the rifle and its optical-sight mount, the Red Army's central artillery board decided to discontinue issuing SVT sniper rifles once a mount suited to the PU had been developed for the bolt-action Three Line. According to current information some SVT rifles were released later, but in 1944 most participants in the survey responded that there were no self-loading sniper rifles in their units.

It might be added that work was on-going in the USSR at that time to produce a special self-loading sniper rifle. In particular, as early as February 1945, the technical council of the People's Commissariat for Armaments examined a plan by the young designer Gherman Korobov. Also working in this sector were Sergey Simonov and Vladimir Degtyarev, son of the eminent machine-gun designer. But it was only several decades later that Evgeniy Dragunov managed to come up with a self-loading weapon which the military authorities were completely happy with.

As for the 1891/30 sniper rifle and the PU/PE optical sights, by 1944 most snipers acknowledged that they were of good quality. Criticism of their quality was confined mainly to items produced in 1942, at a time when disruption of manufacturing industry was at its greatest, and, much less frequently, 1943.

It is worthwhile at this point to make a comparison with the situation in the enemy camp. Up until the Second World War the German high command paid little attention to sniper training, considering that greater priority should be given to thoroughly equipping the forces with easily removable sights of small magnification to raise the effectiveness of rifle fire. In a sense this was close to the 'Scout Rifle' concept proposed by the celebrated American marksman Jeff Cooper at the beginning the 1980s. This resulted in the short and light $1.5 \times$ Zielfernrohr 41 (Zf. 41) sight. However, the Zf. 41 was too low-powered to be effective at long range, and German snipers preferred rifles equipped with the $4 \times$ Zf. 39 (the general name for the four-fold magnification sights of various firms) and then the newly introduced Zf. 4 sight.

The Zf. 39 and Zf. 41 were tested in the USSR and evaluated as follows:

> At the scientific testing range for rifle and mortar arms under the Red Army central artillery board tests were carried out on two German optical rifle sights in 1943: an optical sight of small dimensions and one of large dimensions, which were found in German arms supplies.
>
> In terms of optical characteristics, the smaller German optical sight is significantly inferior to the Soviet PU and PE models,

but in terms of weight, dimensions and compactness it has advantages over the sights mentioned above.

In terms of optical characteristics, the larger German optical sight has advantages over the PU and PE models, but these were not borne out by actual firing tests.

It is worth mentioning that the German optics industry was significantly more developed than its Soviet equivalent and optical sights for the Wehrmacht were produced under brands well known even today, like Carl Zeiss, Kahles, Swarovski and a number of smaller manufacturers. Besides, the Germans encountered a shortage of optical sights during the course of the war and began to take optical sights of suitable specifications from civilian rifle owners. Under this programme, which was given the name 'The huntsman's gift' (*Jägerspende*), the gun owner was compensated for the cost of the sight and the mounting was returned to him – while the gunsight went off to the front, usually the Eastern Front. As a result, from 1942 Soviet snipers were possibly facing adversaries with high-class sights of high magnification – 6× upwards and even as much as 8×.

Soviet marksmen rated their adversaries, the German snipers, quite highly. Suffice it to say that by the winter of 1941–2 the German snipers had already forced Soviet officers to abandon the fur coats which distinguished them from the ordinary soldiers. For example, in the course of one offensive, the 327th Rifle Division lost 58 men killed and 631 wounded in the course of a single day, 13 January 1942.

Among the dead was the commander of the 1,098th Division, Colonel Petr Yakovlevich Komarov, who was killed by a bullet to the head. The nature of the wound indicated that he had been struck by a sniper who had picked out the commander because of his distinctive good-quality white fur jacket and beaver lamb cap. The commander of the 1,100th Rifle Regiment, Colonel Fedor Egorovich Kovshar, was wounded in the head on 19 January and died four days later. However, for personally leading soldiers into attack during the capture of the village of Kolomno,[20] the brave commander was posthumously awarded the Order of Lenin. After a number of such deaths the officers' uniforms in the division were replaced and they stopped wearing shoulder belts.

The German snipers were still very dangerous adversaries at the end of 1944. Soviet marksmen noted that, although there had been fewer enemy snipers 'of late', the Germans were training them in large numbers and quite thoroughly. Thus, the 136th Division reported: 'They quickly spot their targets and shoot quite accurately.' It was also noted that personal carelessness on the Soviet side 'has even sometimes cost the lives of battalion commanders'. A report from the 19th Rifle Corps read: 'It must be acknowledged that the enemy still holds the initiative with regard to sniper fire owing to the insufficient number of snipers in our units and their lack of experience.'[21]

A separate section of the questionnaire was devoted to the organisation of sniper and sniping-instructor training and the passing on of experience from the best snipers. And, judging by the size and volume of responses, even at the end of the war these questions were very important for front-line snipers. The replies often contain criticism directed at the lack of handbooks; articles about the top snipers in the 'Red Army Press' – newspapers at divisional and army level – were clearly not an adequate replacement. There was a demand for reference and instruction books and also a suggestion to 'introduce a section entitled 'Sniper advice' into one of the military magazines' and 'to put out a handbook under the title *Polnyy kurs teorii snayperskoy strelby* ('A complete course in the theory of sniper shooting').

Many who responded also commented on the lack of instructors. Usually, they were selected from available snipers or former snipers who had been promoted to officer rank. If such were not to be found, the best trained and most experienced officers were drawn from rifle platoons and companies. There was also a proposal to solve the question of insufficient instructors in particular through special training of sniper instructors on front-line and army courses.

Sniper Tallies – Myth or Reality?

The question of the reliability of sniper results is one of the most difficult faced by a military historian. As a rule, the circumstances surrounding the destruction of expensive military equipment – naval shipping, aircraft, armoured vehicles – are quite well documented. Therefore, in comparing the claims of one side with data about losses from the other, it is possible at least to attempt to track down who is able to claim what. Of course, even here there are complexities stemming from both banal exaggerations of results and the principle: if we were firing at the time, the victim must be ours.

However, in the case of snipers, the question of results is significantly more complex. Documents very rarely specify the reason for the loss of low level, rank-and-file service personnel. As a rule, this data is only available in the overall total, which simply gives the numbers of dead and wounded for a recorded period – with no indication as to who fell victim to a sniper bullet, who perished from a mortar or shell splinter during artillery bombardment, and who was blown up by a mine. It is impossible to separate out the victims of sniper fire, if there was active combat on a particular sector.

As an example, one might quote the recent research of the Russian historian from Saransk, Igor Chernyaev. On analysing the records of the 257th Independent Rifle Brigade, he discovered a report about a sniper company from the 7th Motorised Rifle Division of the NKVD forces for the period 21–24 August [WHAT YEAR?]. The total NKVD tally came to 642 enemy soldiers and officers. However, according to German data, the German 296th Infantry Division, which happened to be operating on this sector, lost only 227 troops dead and wounded. Moreover, on 22 August the Germans actually beat off an assault by the Soviet 110th and 257th Independent Rifle Brigades supported by the 192nd Brigade.

An even more interesting picture emerges if you compare Soviet and German documents for a more tranquil section of the front – like the case of the German 112th Infantry Division, which was facing the Soviet 356th and 60th Rifle Divisions. On 17 August [YEAR??] snipers of the 356th Rifle Division reported seven kills, and the same number on the 18th. According to the German records, however, losses on 17 August comprised one dead and three wounded and on 18 August two dead. The picture was similar for the subsequent days – on the 19th Soviet snipers reported five enemy kills and the Germans three wounded, and on the 20th the Soviet claims of six enemy dead were countered by German reports of three wounded and two dead.

The picture changed radically in September with the arrival of a 'seconded sniper team'. On 7 September the snipers of the 356th Rifle Division reported fifteen kills and the 'guest' troops came up with 200 (!), while the German documents for this day mentioned ... three wounded. The round figure of 200 dead probably gave rise to doubts even within the local Red Army units because the following day the figure given by the seconded troops was a 'modest' forty-five. Snipers of the 356th Rifle Division reported thirteen dead Germans, while the German division noted ... two wounded. On 9 September the German division lost one man killed and seven wounded, while the snipers of the 356th Rifle Division made claims of six German dead and the seconded troops reported seventy-two enemy destroyed.

It is also worth mentioning that a lull on a tranquil sector of the front did not by any means signify that only snipers were firing at the enemy. For example, on 8 September the gunners of the 918th Artillery Regiment claimed to have killed ten troops and destroyed one dug-out.

However, documentation from the other side became accessible to historians only after the end of the war. Way back in 1942, nobody carried out a daily check on reports to see how far claims corresponded with real losses. After viewing the figures cited above, we can only note that even in 1942 front-line snipers evaluated their achievements more realistically. It is possible that checking was stricter – documents mention that some snipers did not even bother to fire if they thought that there was nobody to confirm their strike. However, in a best-case scenario observers were able to establish that the targeted victim had fallen and lain for a while or had disappeared into a trench and not been seen again. It can also be assumed that subsequently, as more combat experience was accumulated, the gap between snipers' claims and actual enemy losses significantly narrowed – ascertaining this is even more difficult, because separating them out from the enemy losses in the second half of the war is more complex.

It is worth mentioning that attempts by Russian historians to check on even single episodes from the combat record of enemy snipers produce no less interesting results. For instance, in his article '*Simo Khyayukha: chelovek-legenda ili chelovek-mif?*' ('Simo Häyhä: man of legend or man of myth?') the historian Oleg Kiselev attempted to analyse the claims of one of the best-known snipers in the West – the Finn Simo Häyhä. This created a number of difficulties because official documents linked to the legendary sniper are surprisingly few. In fact, all that exists is a certificate awarded to Häyhä along with a presentation rifle on 17 February 1940, by the commander of the 12th Infantry Division. This document indicates that Häyhä wiped out '219 enemy with rifle fire and approximately the same number with a sub-machine gun'.

How anyone in the heat of battle could count up even an approximate number of those killed by a sub-machine gun is a very interesting question. Although there are claims that some of his officers or fellow servicemen totalled up his strikes in a more regular fashion, no official documents testifying to this total have ever been published. However, even comparing certain well-known facts with Soviet documents also gives a very remarkable picture.

From 18 to 25 December 1939, the Finnish sniper was responsible for roughly a hundred claims of success (21 + 25 + 51), whereas the losses in the Soviet units facing him, the 213th Rifle Regiment and the 1st Battalion of the 184th Rifle Regiment, came to no more than 40 dead and 165 wounded. In other words, a sole Finnish sniper was laying claim to half the casualties inflicted not only by his own battalion, but by the one next to it, which was also fighting against the Soviet 213th Rifle Regiment.

Moreover, as Kiselev points out, the word 'sniper' or its synonyms was only mentioned once in the operational reports of Häyhä's battalion's adversaries in the month of December: in the report of 22 December, it is specifically noted that two members of the regiment had been wounded as a result of sniper activity. Moreover, these same reports regularly mentioned artillery, mortar and machine-gun fire, rifle crossfire and other enemy activity.

It is significant that, in the reports of other units, the activity of Finnish snipers is given more attention. But because neither Finnish nor Soviet commanders conducted daily checks, it is quite possible that Finnish snipers who achieved a higher correlation between claims and actual achievements than Simo Häyhä remained unknown even in their own country.

It can be seen that collating documents from both sides makes it possible to give some indication of the upper limit of correspondence between sniper claims and established losses. But because losses from sniper activity were quite rarely separated out into a distinct category, it is extremely difficult to obtain a more detailed break-down. There is even less chance of being able to determine the actual achievements of a particular sniper in cases where several men from the same detachment were active on the same sector.[22]

However, it is worth remembering that, against the background of a major war, increases in personal tallies by individual snipers were scarcely able to play much of a role. Of much more significance, even on a tactical level, were several pairs of attentive eyes identifying any enemy activity on a particular sector of the front and also curbing the activity of enemy observers. And in this sense the timely destruction of a single plain or stereoscopic periscope might not have added a notch to a rifle stock, but would signify much more in the scales of war than a hundred dead enemy.

Summary

An enormous amount of work had undoubtedly been carried out in the USSR in the inter-war period. Industry developed an up-to-date optical instrument manufacturing capability from absolutely nothing, and a system was implemented for the mass training of not only 'top-class marksmen' but also snipers as a special military field.

This peacetime bonus enabled the USSR to compensate for its early losses during the Great War for the Fatherland and renew sniper recruitment, training new snipers both on a centralised basis and on-the-spot in front-line units. Moreover, during the second half of the war, the issues of proper training and effectual deployment of snipers directly in front-line units were largely solved, although even at the end of 1944 the lack of instructors with a good theoretical background – and even handbooks – was acutely felt.

The war period brought huge experience in the practical and systematic deployment of snipers. But, regrettably, such experience was not required in anything like full measure during the peaceful days after the war. Within the framework of preparations for a 'third world war', which was viewed as a conflict employing mass-scale strike weapons and mechanised manoeuvres, the concept of sniping appeared surplus to requirements and was actually reduced to the idea of a 'sharpshooter section' armed with the SVD (Dragunov sniper rifle).

But the dismissal of sniper experience, and absence of a sniper school, cost the Soviet Army and subsequently the Russian Army dear in a string of local conflicts. Only at the beginning of the new millennium did it become necessary once more to revive sniping within the fighting forces of the Russian Federation.

Ironically, this was achieved by turning to Western experience – with regard to modern sights and specialist equipment and to issues of training and application. And yet that path had already been traversed by the Red Army snipers!

Andrey Ulanov

Sources

Davydov, B., Savenko, S., *Sovietskie opticheskie pritsely, 1920–1940* ('Soviet optical sights, 1920–1940'), *Mir Oruzhiya* ('World of Weapons'),2005

Gabitov, A., *Stanovlenie snaiperskoi podgotovki v SSSR 20-ykh godov* ('The advent of sniper training in the USSR in the 1920s'),2019

Kamenev, Appoga, Sozontov, Denisov, *Snaiping : Iskusstvo strelby naivysshei metkosti: Sbornik statei* ('Sniping : the art of shooting with maximum accuracy: a collection of articles'),1929

Morozov, G. *Podgotovka otlichnykh strelkov-nablyudatelei* ('Training of top-class marksmen-cum-observers'), 1931

Petrakova, V. *Podgotovka zhenshchin-snaiperov v gody Velikoi Otyechestvennoi voiny* ('The training of women snipers during the Great War for the Fatherland'), 2013

# Top Ten Soviet Snipers

Editors' comment: It should be noted that other snipers have been recognised in some sources as having more than the 429 kills credited here to tenth-ranking Fedor Okhlopov. They include Ivan Nikolaevich Kulbertinov (487), Vladimir Nikolaevich Pchelintsev (456) and Ivan Mikhaylovich Renskov (437).

1: Mikhail Ilich Surkov (1921–55)
Personal tally – 702

The most successful sniper in the Red Army. Prior to army service, Surkov lived in Krasnoyarsk Territory and hunted in the taiga. In January 1941 he was called up into the army. He served initially in the 1,341st Regiment, 319th Rifle Division, and then in the 39th Rifle Regiment, 4th Rifle Division.

By the beginning of 1942 Surkov had been awarded his first decoration – the medal 'For Valour'. The accompanying citation noted that in twelve days of fighting he had killed sixty-five Germans (twenty-five of them in one day, 3 March), wounded five more, and also trained three snipers. For this Surkov was promoted to the rank of sergeant-major and he became a sniping instructor.

Surkov's fame was so great that the Soyuzkinotekhnika cine-operator Arkady Levitan visited the unit specially to film him and, according to his recollections, filmed not only the sniper himself but also the moment when a slain enemy soldier fell.

There is information that suggests that Surkov's actual score might have been even greater. On account of conflicts with his superiors his decorations were down-graded; in particular, the regimental commander's recommendation of the title Hero of the Soviet Union was changed to the Order of Lenin.

In two years of warfare Surkov was wounded seven times and after the last wound he was commissioned as an officer with the rank of junior lieutenant.

2: Vladimir Gavrilovich Salbiev (1916–66)
Personal tally – 601

Called up into the army in September 1941, Salbiev served in the 3rd Rifle Battalion, 117th Rifle Regiment, 23rd Rifle Division. It is noteworthy that the citation accompanying his first decoration in September 1943 mentions that, 'After every breakfast and dinner, as soon as he has seen to the soldiers' food, Sergeant-Major Salbiev goes off stalking.'

Suffice it to point out that at the end of 1942, when Salbiev was already a well-known sniper and sniper platoon commander, he was appointed commander of an anti-tank gun platoon. In this capacity he knocked out three enemy tanks.

At the presentation to him of the Order of the Great War for the Fatherland in June 1944 it was noted that the platoon of snipers trained by Salbiev had wiped out up to 200 enemy soldiers and officers – for which seven of his charges had already been awarded orders and medals.

In 1943 Salbiev was also recommended for the title Hero of the Soviet Union, but received instead the Order of the Red Banner.

3: Vasiliy Shalvovich Kvachantiradze (1907–50)
Personal tally – 534

Called up into the army in August 1941, becoming a sniper of the 179th Rifle Division, Kvachantiradze was recommended for his first decoration in November 1943. At that point his claims amounted to eighty-one dead enemy soldiers and officers

His tally continued to grow subsequently. In particular, in September 1944, Kvachantiradze came across two German 75-mm guns and completely obliterated their crews, as well as those who attempted to take their place. The first recommendation for the title Hero of the Soviet Union for Sergeant Kvachantiradze was put forward by his unit command in 1943. However, he actually received the star of the Hero award in 1945, after a second recommendation.

4: Akhat Abdulkhakovich Akhmetyanov (1918–76)
Personal tally – around 500 (sometimes given as 502)

Initially called up into the Red Army in 1938, Akhmetyanov took part in the Soviet–Finnish war. In 1940 he was demobilised but called up for a second time in June 1941. At the front from July 1941, in August 1942 he joined the 260th Rifle Regiment, 168th division, at the Oranienbaum bridgehead. As early as November 1942 Sergeant Akhmetyanov was awarded the Order of the Red Star for his personal tally of eighty-three enemy soldiers and officers, and also for training twenty-five snipers. During the war he was wounded four times, and after the fourth – a serious stomach wound – he was demobilised.

5: Ivan Mikhaylovich Sidorenko (1919–94)
Personal tally – around 500

Served in the Red Army from 1939. His first decoration was the medal 'For Valour', awarded to Lieutenant Sidorenko in his capacity as deputy commander of the mortar company in the 1,122nd Rifle Regiment, 334th Rifle Division. The main reason for the award was a successful counter-attack that resulted when the lieutenant got the soldiers to follow his personal example. The order also mentioned that by this time Sidorenko had wiped out fifteen Germans with his own weaponry.

Sidorenko subsequently became deputy chief of staff for the 1,122nd Rifle Regiment and organiser of sniper recruiting in his unit. On top of his independent operations as a sniper, Sidorenko trained 250 snipers. In June 1944 he was awarded the title Hero of the Soviet Union.

6: Nikolay Yakovlevich Ilyin (1922–43)
Personal tally – 494

Ilyin served in the 50th Guards Rifle Regiment, 15th Guards Rifle Division, and received his first decorations as a sub-machine gunner. His recommendation for the Order of Red Banner in 1942 mentions that Ilyin wiped out thirty enemy sub-machine gunners, when the enemy burst through towards the staff headquarters on 3 November 1941.

Ilyin's operations as a sniper are reflected in a later recommendation for the title Hero of the Soviet Union, which indicates that on 16 October 1942, he was presented with the sniper rifle of another eminent sniper, Husen Andrukhaiev. With it Ilyin wiped out ninety-five Romanian soldiers in less than two weeks. His tally at the moment of his award came to 215.

Nikolay Ilyin was killed in action on 25 July 1943. His rifle no. KE-1729 was handed over to another Soviet sniper, Afanasy Gordienko.

7: Nikolay Evdokimovich Kazyuk (1922–90)
Personal tally – 446

In 1939 Kazyuk entered the Lviv infantry college and he served at the front from July 1941. As an accurate marksman, he was enrolled in the 'hunters for snipers' programme. At the beginning of 1942 he was seriously wounded and, after recovery, appointed to a mortar sub-unit.

He received his first decoration, the Order of the Red Banner, in 1942 when he was already deputy commander of the 451st Independent Mortar Battalion, 369th Rifle Division. The accompanying citation states that Kazyuk wiped out ten enemy soldiers 'with infantry weapons'.

8: Petr Alekseevich Goncharov (1903–44)
Personal tally – 441 (sometimes given as 445)

Goncharov worked at the 'Red October' metallurgical factory in Stalingrad. In September 1942 he left for the front as a volunteer. According to his recommendation for the title Hero of the Soviet Union, on 25 July 1943 his personal tally amounted to 380 dead enemy soldiers and officers, and he had personally instructed nine snipers. He lost his life on 31 January 1944.

9: Mikhail Ivanovich Budenkov (1919–95)
Personal tally – 437

A member of the Red Army since 1939, Budenkov was at Brest when the war started on 22 June 1941. He began his sniper operations as commander of a mortar squad. He was transferred at his own request to a rifle company and later fought again as a sniper. According to the citation accompanying his award of the title Hero of the Soviet Union, by 1 September 1944, he had in his tally 412 Germans, including five snipers and two observers.

10: Fedor Matveevich Okhlopkov (1908–68)
Personal tally – 429

A Yakut by ethnicity, Okhlopkov was employed as a hunter before the war. He was sent to the front in December 1941. Initially he was no. 1 in a machine-gun squad. From October 1942 he was a sniper in the 234th Rifle Regiment, 179th Division. In January 1944 he became commander of a sniper platoon section in the 259th Rifle Regiment in the same division (serving under his command among others was Vasiliy Kvachantiradze). According to his decoration certificate, by June 1944 he had wiped out 420 enemy soldiers and officers. Over the war period he was wounded twelve times, the last occasion in June 1944, after which he was not discharged from hospital until April 1945. On 24 June 1945, he took part in the victory parade.

During the course of the war his recommendation for the title Hero of the Soviet Union was reduced to the Order of the Red Banner. He received the gold star of the 'Hero' award in 1965 on the twentieth anniversary of victory.

3 Fedor Dyachenko

I HAIL FROM THE POLTAVA REGION,[1] from the village of Betyaga, which is not far from Khorol. Our family was deprived of its holdings as *kulaks* and deported to Krasnoyarsk Territory.[2] I was called up in May 1942; a narrow strip of paper with a lilac stamp arrived from the Norilsk recruiting office – my call-up papers. I bade farewell to my job as a plasterer, the construction site where I was working and my fellow-builder friends, and set off the following day for the district recruiting office. My knapsack contained my entire wealth: a couple of changes of underwear and a new 'cowboy' shirt.

A narrow-gauge railway took us to Dudinka, and then we set off on a veteran steamship up the Yenesei River, which had only just been cleared of ice. Along the way I got to know a former Norilsk barber, Ivan Denisenko, who was originally from a district next to my own.

There was another Ukrainian among the recruits, a miner called Nikita Derevyanenko from Kharkiv. He was ten years older than us. The skin of his strong, gnarled hands was impregnated with black specks of coal dust. He took special pride and pleasure in his luxuriant, Cossack-style, moustache, which had turned a ginger colour from tobacco.

At the end of May our travels concluded in the small, ancient Siberian town of Kansk.[3] Before the war it had been a quiet, provincial place, but now its narrow streets were bustling with masses of evacuees and military personnel. Several military colleges and units were based in the town itself and around it. The 120th Reserve Rifles, to which we had been allocated, were camped outside the town. The tents, dugouts and sheds occupied a significant area on the edge of a pine forest, which was growing on sandy soil. The slightest breeze raised clouds of sand, which would remain crunching on your teeth for ages. Our heads were shaved, we were issued uniforms, and we became so alike that, for a while, we had trouble recognising one another.

The senior commanders we rarely saw, so I do not remember their names, and I have already begun to forget their faces. The only thing that has remained in my memory is that our battalion commander had the rank of captain; his tabs included a single bar and he had two medals jangling on his chest. It was said that he had distinguished himself in the first battles at Vyazma or Smolensk.[4] I have clearer memories of the political education officer, although I cannot recall his name either. He was from Leningrad, a teacher by profession. He had volunteered for the front, been seriously wounded, and limped slightly as a result. When he spoke, he was always very pleasant and courteous.

The military training in my platoon section was the responsibility of Sergeant Ivan Mishchenko, a smart and cunning lad with broad Mongol cheek bones. According to what he said, he had been in Belorussia when the war broke out. In the first month of the war, he had been taken prisoner at Smolensk. The Germans had herded him and other soldiers into a barbed-wire enclosure like a farm pen, where they suffered from thirst and hunger. But Mishchenko did not remain a prisoner for long. While his group was being herded into another pen, there was an aerial attack and, in the ensuing confusion, he and several others threw themselves into the nearest bushes and from there escaped into the forest. After wandering through the Smolensk forests for a few weeks, they rejoined their own side. Mishchenko was appointed commander of a regimental reconnaissance platoon section. He was wounded in the battles for Moscow and ended up lame. But he was declared fit for non-combat service and sent to our reserve regiment.

On account of his heroic record, we forgave him his irascibility and fault-finding and even took pride in him before soldiers from other sections, who were not commanded by officers with front-line experience. Mishchenko drove us till the sweat dripped, making us crawl on our elbows. One time we played a trick on him; he had just arrived from somewhere, and we threw ourselves on the ground and crawled to meet him.

At training sessions, he strove to create what he called a 'tactical atmosphere'; he would devise various tests for us. Thus, he would point to some object and give the command: 'Attack that machine gun! Forward!' And we would crawl on our elbows towards this 'machine gun', or something else. If anyone did not press close enough to the ground, he would send them back, letting them know that, if they failed to do so, they would be 'pressed' by a German bullet.

But even worse than the 'tactical situations' were the forced marches with full kit. They were held at least twice a week. We were roused from our beds at night by an alarm sounding, and then the company commander, sometimes the battalion commander, set us a combat objective, for instance: 'There's an enemy parachute drop in the vicinity of Kruglaia Hill. The 7th Company is ordered to wipe it out.'

We might have a five-kilometre run, followed by a forced march, and then some crawling on our elbows, then another run before the marching resumed. The sand raised by our feet dried our throats and insides. Finally, we would reach our shooting range, where we attacked plywood targets. You could not lag behind, or else you would be sent to the kitchen, where our querulous cook Mikheyich would make you peel potatoes – insisting, moreover, that the peel be removed in delicate rings and every single eye dug out.

The thing I liked most was shooting, although at first my short stature made it difficult to handle a rifle: a Three Line of the old type was almost as tall as I was. Ivan Denisenko urged me to demand a partner who would carry it for me.

If I peeled potatoes reluctantly, I polished my rifle till it shone. The combination of gun oil and dust got into every chink and I would work it out, even though it took up a lot of time. One day Mishchenko noticed how many matches I had expended on cleaning my rifle just once and showed me a set of tiny wooden sticks which he used for that task. Some were sharpened like pencils for cleaning the bolt and others were flat, like tiny shovels, for the magazine. There were five of them and they were kept in a special rag. That evening I found a stick of oakwood which I shaved into smaller sticks and gave them the same shapes as in the sergeant's collection and, during my entire army career from then on, there was not a single occasion when my weapon refused to function.

We eagerly awaited the shooting exercises, but a neighbouring company was always first to use the range and of this we were very envious. Finally, our turn came. The night before, the *starshina* [sergeant-major] gathered together a whole brigade of carpenters and they put the targets together. I was entrusted with removing the dust from the sighting devices. In the evening, activities were called off earlier than usual because, prior to shooting practice, the boundary lines had to be marked out and the targets set up. Getting all this done in time meant being at the shooting range before first light and therefore we were woken a bit earlier.

In the morning a bugle played the call for reveille. We sprang up, got dressed and set off in ranks to the canteen. There we quickly gulped down our thin millet porridge and were force-marched to the range. On arrival there, two of the three platoons stacked their arms and set about the necessary preparations. One platoon formed a barrier, so no outsider would wander in during shooting. Finally, those controlling the targets took up their positions in the trenches. We remained where we were, the red flag floated slowly up the flagstaff, and the bugle played – that signified that shooting could commence.

When the first shift had finished shooting, the signal for 'all clear' was sounded and they advanced to view their targets. When they came back, we discussed their results. Then the following shift took over, while we waited our turn. Finally, our section was able to take their place on the firing line, rifles in hand. We fired three cartridges each, and ran up to bring back the targets. I hit the bullseye three times out of three. The bullet holes could be covered with a single five-kopeck piece. But only a few of us achieved that level of accuracy. The company as a whole fired poorly the first time. When he found out about this, the battalion commander prescribed extra shooting practice instead of physical training. Mishchenko made me a kind of instructor and Nikita Derevyanenko and another man were my first trainees.

We now tended to spend less time on the parade ground, performing punishment tasks or acting as sentries, but the number of tactical activities increased. I remember to this day the way the platoon commander would kick away the camouflaging on a foxhole if he could discover it from a distance of twenty or thirty metres. How grateful we were for these lessons when we found ourselves later in the trenches of Leningrad.

Almost every day the reinforcement companies and battalions were drawn up on the parade ground. The soldiers were in their new uniforms with fresh ammunition. The quartermasters laid out on tables fat folders containing lists which the soldiers signed, sometimes without realising what for. Then followed a formal meeting and, raising the dust, marching columns set off for the railway station. In July 1942 we too were despatched to the front in the same way.

At first, we did not know where we were going but after Vologda it became clear; it was the Leningrad Front. We disembarked at Tikhvin.[5] The town greeted us with not very summery gloomy skies and drizzle. The countless bomb craters and shell holes were filled with water. Everywhere there was evidence of recent fighting: the twisted frames of burnt-out vehicles and carriages, buildings destroyed. Cascades of artillery fire rumbled away somewhere far to the west. But what surprised us most of all was that nobody apart from us paid the slightest attention to it.

Our marching company disembarked and set off westward. That night we came to a large stretch of water; it was Lake Ladoga. There were dozens of launches, self-propelled barges and tugs rocking by the piers, and many of them carried anti-aircraft machine guns and cannons. We were lined up and counted. A sailor in a black pea-jacket approached the political education officer and spoke to him briefly, after which he pointed to a moored launch to the left of a half-sunk barge. This was the floating craft in which our company was about to cross the lake.

The long line of solders headed for the pier. On embarking we accommodated ourselves where we could and pressed close to one another because, even though it was summer, it was chilly on the water at night. Derevyanenko and I found a place next to an AA machine gun set up on a small steel tower. Then the naval gunners came, put on their steel helmets and took the covers off the machine gun with the words: 'Don't be scared, infantry!'

There was a muffled rumbling in the bowels of the launch. Our frail vessel – as it appeared to us – cast off from the pier and, leaving a trail of foam behind it, headed westward, into a frightening pitch-dark expanse enfolded in light smoke. We were followed by another launch casting off from the pier, and another after that. Soon there was a whole squadron of barges and boats packed with people heading westward one after another.

After several hours the first rays of sunlight in front of us illuminated a narrow strip of land covered by dark green forest. We were coming to the final destination of our journey of many days. But before reaching it, we would have to endure one more minor adventure. My ears caught the deep rumbling of aircraft engines. The alarm sounded on the launch and two planes with crosses on their wings appeared in the sky. They flew over us in the direction of the shore, where AA guns were pounding, leaving clouds of exhaust fumes in the sky. The enemy 'vultures' rose higher, as if looking for quarry. The sailors next to us also opened fire from their machine gun.

In the meantime, the launch had approached the shore and stopped about twenty paces from the shoreline shingle. The command was given to disembark and the soldiers from our company poured over the side. The water came up to our waists or chests and we waded through it to the shore, where we ran towards the wood, seeking the protective cover of trees.

I had never been to Leningrad and now, as we marched from the Finland Station along the gloomy streets, I was stunned by its stern exterior. I had imagined a quite different kind of city – beautiful and majestic. But instead of this, I saw barricades blocking off streets, barriers wrapped with barbed wire, reinforced concrete pyramids, pillboxes at crossroads with menacingly staring gunports, and the burnt-out shells of battered buildings. There were no shop windows left. They were concealed by sandbags and some were blocked up with fresh brickwork with narrow slits in it. Leningrad was preparing for street battles.

Every scrap of land free from asphalt and paving was being cultivated and green with onion shoots, potato plants and swelling cabbage heads. Women and children were scurrying around the plants, weeding and watering.

By evening we had been led to the outskirts of the city, where the company was accommodated for the night in a five-storey building. In the morning we learnt that we were in the rear of the 55th Army, from where we would serve as reinforcements for its active units. In the meantime, we would be employed on auxiliary work. We were taken to some storehouse. I was confused by the even sound of a metronome which reached us through speakers set up at all the city intersections. Then suddenly the beat ceased. The calm voice of an announcer warned us of the start of an artillery attack. A shell exploded several blocks away from us, and then another, and another. A girl told us where the nearest bomb shelter was and we took refuge there.

I was soon enrolled in the 187th Rifle Regiment under the 72nd Rifle Division and my life at the front began. The division had been badly knocked about in the fighting at Uritsk[6] and it was withdrawn to the second line for reinforcement (including our marching company) and rest and recreation. We were lodged in the buildings of the No. 4 Vegetable Combine and the Aleksandrov farm. The soldiers compensated for the lack of space by constructing dugouts. We were surrounded by patches of waste ground, quarries, ditches, vegetable gardens and small groves of trees. Here and there the ground was scarred by the remains of trenches.

Our company occupied a long barrack with empty window openings. The rooms contained clothing and straw brought in by our predecessors, who were soldiers just like us. There were about fifty men from the marching company here and my Norilsk Ukrainian friends, Nikita Derevyanenko and Ivan Denisenko ended up in my platoon. We began to get ready for bed. To our right were the troops who had already tasted trench life and they talked about their most recent engagements.

It turned out that, for almost the entire previous week, the regiment had alternately attacked, withdrawn and gone on defence. After fierce fighting barely thirty men remained from the company in which we were now enrolled. The division had been originally established on the basis of the 7th Naval Infantry and there were still a few in it who had kept their pea jackets under their tunics and went into battle with the cry '*Polundra!*'[7] rather than 'Hurrah!' But there were very, very few of them; the majority had either departed for the rear and medical treatment or lay in the ground. I got to know one of the 'veterans', who was called Nikolay. He stood out from us because he used different words for such things as dugout, toilet, and kitchen. This former sailor made himself conspicuous by his reckless, at times even ostentatious daring, which is characteristic of Baltic mariners.

In the second line we did not sit idle; we set up armoured shelters, and dug trenches. Up in the skies we often saw 'frames' – double-fuselage enemy reconnaissance planes',[8] and several times there were real aerial battles.

On those warm summer mornings, we left our 'glassless' barracks, had breakfast, and went to tactical exercises. Occasionally they involved two sides, and a few times, when the 'attacking' side and the 'defenders' clashed 'hand to hand', it almost turned into a mass brawl. I could never get used to the practice whereby, in order to avoid confusion while reporting the situation on the battlefield to a platoon commander, I was supposed to use the official designations: 'reference point 1' or 'reference point 2' and, instead, I would bellow out to our Lieutenant Teplov in a mixture of Russian and Ukrainian: 'Comrade Lieutenant, there's a Nazi crawling out of the pipe! I can see a machine gun near those stones!' Teplov got very upset at my incomprehensibility.

Our company was under the command of Senior Lieutenant Ivan Dmitriyevich Nikiforov. He had been promoted from the ranks, having begun his military career the previous autumn as a rank-and-file scout, and therefore he commanded our respect as a very intelligent, fair and – the main thing – astute commander. He had been promoted to platoon commander for his daring assault on a German airfield, which resulted in his reconnaissance group managing to blow up an enemy aircraft. In the spring he was entrusted with a company and, from being the most incompetent company in the regiment, it quickly became the most proficient.

During a smoking break at tactical exercises one day my friends Ivan Denisenko and Petr Kholodny noticed a kite high up in the sky. I decided to show off my prowess in sharpshooting, took aim and, in response to a bet, brought the bird down with a single shot. At this point I heard an angry shout from Nikiforov: 'Who was firing?' I was frightened, thinking that I would get a reprimand, but instead I received a rapturous response from our company commander; in the entire regiment up to now only Simanchuk had been able to shoot with such accuracy. Such was the name of a sniper well known on the Leningrad Front, whose rifle had been presented to him personally by Andrei Zhdanov,[9] member of the military council of the North-West Sector and the Leningrad Front. Simanchuk was one of the first to open a sniper tally at the front and by this time he had already been awarded the Order of Lenin. He never left the forward line and constantly increased the total of Fritzes he eliminated.

A few days later the company commander called me up and handed me a sniper rifle. He showed me how to use the optical sights. I was surprised how convenient it was; up until then I had not come across anything like it. The only thing I was unable to master at first was setting the range with a revolving drum, but Nikiforov assured me I would get the knack.

Soon after, Denisenko, who thanks to his hairdressing abilities was shaving and cutting the hair of half the battalion's officers and therefore up with the latest gossip, brought the news that we were being sent to the forward line. Before that, there would be another re-formation within the company – the third in a week. Nikita Derevyanenko was being taken away from us and put in charge of transport – he was very fond of horses – and Vasya Avdeyenko, who had come with us from Kansk, had been appointed a deputy platoon commander in the battalion's mortar company. I was appointed to the same platoon section as Petr Kholodny.

Before departure we were formed up and taken to the battalion's quartermaster section to obtain cartridges, grenades and boxes of emergency supplies. The *starshina* exchanged our old uniforms for new ones. Following the advice of front-line veterans, I stuffed not just my ammunition pouches but even my pockets with cartridges and also stuck several packs down my tunic. We moved up to the forward line in the early morning twilight.

It was still dark when we drew near to the outskirts of Kolpino[10] and the huge hulk of the Izhora factory[11] loomed up in front. First light found us striding past its buildings. The sun's morning rays illuminated the factory chimneys, which had been pierced by shells, and the ruins of the workshops. We came to the canal which divided the town into two. Along its left bank almost nothing remained of the pre-war buildings. They were mainly wooden and most of them had burnt down. Only the stoves remained as reminders of the conflagration.

We were permitted to make a stop by a dam, after which the company moved off towards the forward line, platoon by platoon. It took us about an hour to get to our positions. Petr Kholodny and I selected a separate trench, a foxhole. From there to the dugout was a distance of roughly twenty metres. It was thirty metres to the nearest foxhole, where Ivan Sery had established himself, while Denisenko was further away. According to the Border Patrol lieutenant, who was in charge of the detachments we were relieving, the enemy unit defending the area in front of us was the 250th Spanish Division. The platoon commander, Lieutenant Teplov, warned us to look out, especially at night; it was quite possible the enemy reconnaissance would poke their noses in.

There had earlier been a settlement in this spot, but now only ruins remained. Beyond it the road ran through to Moscow. Our trenches now lay on one side of it and the Spaniards had theirs on the other side. Right in front of my foxhole was a small hill and, on it, an enemy pillbox with a gunport. At times it even seemed to me that I could see a machine gun sticking out of it. It was silent in the daytime but at night it spat fire.

I spent a long time watching the enemy positions. Nothing was happening there – until a couple of soldiers appeared. They were arguing about something and vigorously waving their arms. Then one of them crawled out onto the parapet and began digging. I carefully took aim, pulled the trigger and fired . . . The Nazi waved his arms in the air and hid from view. I had missed. Immediately bullets began rattling against my parapet and the revolting screech of a mortar bomb followed. I dropped down to the floor of my foxhole. Somebody fell on top of me and I wondered: 'It's not a German, is it?' I opened my eyes. It was Petro. He had been barely awake and was dreadfully scared. In actual fact there was plenty to be scared of; the enemy mortar bomb had exploded a mere metre and a half from our trench.

The company commander soon came by and asked the reason for the 'spree'. Had we wiped out some enemies, or at least frightened them? 'We were more frightened ourselves,' I replied. Nikiforov had a good laugh. He advised us to be more certain of our targets and to tidy up the foxhole; after the explosion its walls had partially collapsed.

It looked as if the Germans were in the same situation because, on their side, they were brandishing their shovels without a break. Several days later I nevertheless succeeded in shooting one of them. I chose a spot further away from our foxhole in an old machine-gun trench, stuck in some strands of heather and began to wait. The time dragged slowly, but finally two figures appeared from behind the ruins of a brick house.

Somebody fired from our side and they fled. I was upset, thinking that they had been frightened off too early and would now go away. I wanted to fire after them, but the Germans had now settled down and again set off walking towards me in their normal fashion. I took careful aim and fired. One of them fell, clutching his side. The other fled and jumped into a trench.

I did not stay around to tempt fate and quickly changed my position. As it turned out, I was just in time; the enemy immediately dropped ten mortar bombs on the spot where I had only just been lying.

Growing bolder, I quickly began to raise my tally. My platoon commander, Lieutenant Teplov, patiently assisted me in this. He taught me to observe all the changes in the landscape on the enemy side. He would turn up and ask me to show him what new features I had noticed. I would tell him: nothing, and he would frown and instantly point out newly dug soil or an osier bed that was not there before. That meant that something was going on there and that probably there would soon be a target there for me. And indeed, if you kept a watch on this spot, you would be bound to get somebody.

One day our company political education officer, Trunov, called at our foxhole. He said that in the next company the Komsomol members had announced a competition in honour of the twenty-fifth anniversary of the Great October Revolution; it involved killing as many Nazis as possible. He asked if we agreed to take part in it.

It occurred to me that the Germans were still pottering about on their forward line; only the previous day I had shot four of them in one day. It was quite possible to 'score' two per day. Trunov replied that he would record a pledge on my part to take my tally up to seventy by 7 November. I did not object.

After this the political education officer kept calling on us; he was interested in how things were going and one day he invited me to the company command post. There I was shown a copy of the Leningrad Front newspaper *Boyevaia krasnoarmeiskaia* ('The Red Army Military Bulletin') dated 30 September 1942. Printed on the front page were the following lines:

> The initiator of the October competition in his detachment, Red Army soldier Fedor Dyachenko, is increasing his combat tally with every passing day. On 26 September Dyachenko shot nine Fritzes in the course of a single day. Yesterday he tracked a group of Germans proceeding along a trench and through accurate shooting felled six of them without a single miss. 'If I have failed to kill a single Nazi in a day,' says Dyachenko, 'that means that I have not fulfilled my duty to the Motherland.' In the last ten days Fedor Dyachenko has wiped out thirty-two Nazi bandits.

Hundreds of men and officers took part in the October competition. Even my fellow Ukrainian friend Ivan Denisenko wanted to eliminate some Nazis. He complained to me once that if he told the girls after the war that he had fought with a brush and razor rather than a rifle, nobody would marry him. I had an enemy firing point on my radar and I offered him the chance to wipe it out.

Just in front of the area where our company and the neighbouring one linked up, the Germans had erected a machine-gun pillbox. You could not get past it day or night. Its gunport was well camouflaged, so that it could not be spotted during the day. The only solution was to detect it from the sparks at night but, as if to spite us, the enemy machine gunners would not open fire. Finally, when our patience was almost exhausted, the Spanish machine gun started up and the sparks from the firing slit indicated where it was. We immediately put in pegs as a guide. With their help we finally managed to see the artfully camouflaged gunport in the pre-dawn mist.

Now we had to wait till somebody appeared there. Again, the agonising minutes went by. Three hours passed, but the pillbox showed no signs of life. I was already thinking they might wait till the brightest part of the day was over, and we would have to watch till evening. Ivan was in a dreadful state; he really wanted a smoke, but we were lying in no-man's land and that would have given us away instantly.

But then someone appeared to open the door to the pillbox, and a silhouette in a helmet was distinctly visible in the gunport. Not far from the pillbox the head of a soldier wearing a blue Spanish forage cap rose cautiously above the trench – we still called the 250th Division the 'Blues' because of the caps – and Ivan's bullet felled him. Without waiting for return fire, we inconspicuously crawled away and threw ourselves into our own trench. The enemy bullets were too late. Denisenko merely swore at them in response and gave them a derisive whistle with two fingers. Now he had something to tell his future sweethearts in Poltava after the war.

During this time, I succeeded in wiping out an enemy sniper. For about three weeks he had been stalking with impunity on our sector of the front but, in the end, we trapped him by means of a single cigar. It all began with the appearance of some 'bushes' on the enemy side which had not grown there before. I gave a signal to my partner, Nikolay Kazakov, and he lit up a cigar and began to expel the smoke over the parapet. He then stuck up a stick with a helmet on it, in imitation of a soldier who was excessively absorbed in smoking. The bushes stirred; the enemy marksman had decided that there was easy prey awaiting him and as a result he was struck down by a bullet from me.

Autumn came into its own with lengthy downpours. The foxholes, trenches and dugouts were filled with water, and there was no salvation from it. While we scooped it out, it seeped in again from below. The Spanish were better placed; their positions were elevated, which gave rise to bitter envy on our part. It was on one of these dank days that I almost met my end.

At first light Lieutenant Teplov and I clambered out to the forward line. I crawled into our pits by no-man's land, while the platoon commander remained in the trench to keep watch. Things were relatively quiet in the enemy lines that day. Occasionally a machine gun would start up from one of the second-line trenches. Later on, a couple of soldiers appeared about 400 metres behind this trench. They were pushing some sort of barrow. I shot one of them; he clutched his stomach and collapsed. The other man fell down and disappeared, having apparently crawled into a trench.

I kept watching. I surveyed the enemy forward line and saw something gleam. I gave it a more attentive look and the gleam was repeated. It was like the reflection from the eyepiece of a stereoscopic periscope. Then a helmet appeared. I had to fire. I fired and, instead of changing my position, I stayed where I was. Within five minutes machine guns and mortars had begun to pound this sector, churning it up like a real plough. I survived by mere chance. It became clear that the glinting glass and helmet were a trap I had credulously fallen into. It was a lesson for the future.

The following day I was summoned to the battalion staff headquarters. It turned out that awaiting me was a correspondent from the front-line newspaper *Boyevaia Krasnoarmeiskaia* ('Red Army in Combat'), Senior Lieutenant V. P. Gheorghiyev. He had written the September article about me. After we had introduced ourselves, he questioned me for a long time about my operations and was surprised that I had had no specialised sniper 'education'. Then asked me to take him with me on a sniping sortie. He was not exactly short of stature, which raised certain apprehensions among our battalion staff, for our trenches on the front line were quite shallow. However, Gheorghiyev managed to gain permission and he set off with me for the forward line.

The wind was beating right in our faces, accompanied by heavy rain, so we ran to our company quarters. The senior lieutenant had virtually to double up in order to squeeze into our dugout. Inside our squalid abode the air was foul: a mixture of long unwashed bodies, damp foot wrappings, and smoking cable, strips of which we lit and used for illumination. But the journalist was not discouraged; it was as if it was the first time that he had visited soldiers' quarters like ours. Gheorghiyev lay down to sleep and we, as hosts, freed up the best spot for him. In the morning, I gently shook him by the shoulder.

We climbed out of the dugout. The rain had stopped. Whitish wisps of morning mist hung over the ground. From the enemy's side the sounds of a machine gun firing short random bursts in our direction could be heard. We selected a suitable spot in a trench and began to keep watch. I handed my rifle to Gheorghy, so that he could make use of its optical sights. Several minutes later he returned it to me and pointed to a target – a group of enemy soldiers carrying some kind of long box. We should have fired but, before allowing the journalist to go with me, the battalion commander had given orders that we should not take risks in vain and I dared not disobey his command. So, on this joint sortie with Senior Lieutenant Gheorghiyev we did not kill a single German.

One day Lieutenant Trunov called me up to the command post. He ordered me to take my weapon and gear the following morning and report to the divisional staff headquarters. The next day I was at the northern boundary of Kolpino, where the staff headquarters were located amidst the furnaces and pits of the Krasny Kirpichnik ('Red Bricklayer') factory. The huge furnaces with their arched vaults were like halls and provided excellent cover. Seven or eight of us had arrived, all snipers. It soon became clear that the aim of the invitation was to send us off to a sniper course.

The sniper school of the 55th Army was located on the right bank of the Neva. We reached Ust-Izhora on a passing 1½-tonne truck, crossed the river via a pontoon bridge and arrived at Ovtsyno, which, to our surprise, had hardly suffered any bomb damage at all, even though the enemy were quite close by. At the school we were met by a duty officer who reported our arrival to the head of the school, a young, somewhat foppish, senior lieutenant. His rank surprised us; we considered that a serious institution like this should be under the command of a major at least. Later I found out that he was Grigory Gilbo of Leningrad, a Master of Sport in Shooting, and a former student of the Friedrich Engels Leningrad Institute of Soviet Commerce. He was assisted by Lieutenant V. F. Trashchikov, Master of Sport (Shooting) and Lieutenant N. I. Mironov, a trainee of the Dynamo club.

After the formalities were over with regard to enrolment, we were taken to our quarters – a long and cold barrack room, but after sitting in trenches it seemed like paradise. Lighting was provided by electric bulbs hanging from bare wires. Compared to the smoking cable, they seemed like the height of luxury. Next to me on the bunks was Sergeant Aleksandr Kuritsyn from Leningrad. I also knew that, although he had only just joined the regiment, his name was already well known to the whole division. A Baltic seaman, he had been on active service since the very beginning of the war.

Firing on the range began the following day: distance – 300 metres, a head as a target, three cartridges. I fired three times and got three hits. Shooting practice revealed one unwelcome fact – many snipers had been fighting with poorly calibrated rifles. The school remedied this instantly. Lieutenant Trashchikov taught us the cunning art of adjusting our weaponry. My rifle began to shoot superbly; I was comfortably able to achieve 45 hits out of 50. Having learnt at the school all the intricacies of calibrating a military weapon, I was now afraid even to breathe on it.

Apart from firing practice and tactical exercises we dealt with the theory of marksmanship. For me bullet deviation presented a particular complexity. All I had to do was learn the definition that it referred simply to the tendency of a bullet to drift to the right. I could not understand why I needed to know about the term. With corrections for wind and temperature everything was plain, so what was the point of going on about 'deviation'? It turned out that adjustments for it also needed to be made when shooting over long distances.

Grigory Gilbo directed the training in a very interesting way. He revealed to us one of the secrets of detecting a sniper's position in winter – the cloud that appears above a rifle barrel during hard frosts. In order to avoid it, it is essential to keep the barrel as close as possible to the ground. To conceal your position after firing you needed to smooth out the black stripes that remained on the ground with a stick. Another secret: on a frosty day it was essential to exhale downwards, or else your eyepiece fogged up.

Gilbo and his assistants often went out to the regiments, ventured up to the forward line with snipers, and studied their mistakes and experiences. On returning to the school, they shared with us the knowledge they had gained on the battle front. The instruction period flew by before we realised and it was soon time to return to the regiment.

A 1½-tonne truck got us to Kolpino by evening. A jumble of machine-gun rounds could be heard from the direction of Izhora and flares were soaring up beyond the No. 3 Kolpino hostel, but in the city all was peaceful. I walked up to the boundary and further along the familiar trench, which led to the forward line from the former radio-station, and set off to find my company. Senior Lieutenant Nikiforov was doubly pleased at my arrival; the company's ranks had been badly thinned in recent engagements.

Our section dugout was now located about a hundred metres from the commander's, almost on the company flank. On the way there I met my old friend, the barber Vanya Denisenko, who told me the latest. It turned out that, two days before my return, he and other soldiers from the platoon along with Lieutenant Teplov had gone crawling out on reconnaissance towards the forward-most enemy trench. They succeeded in capturing a prisoner for interrogation, but the platoon commander was wounded in the process and had finished up in hospital, and now it was not clear if he would survive. A new commander had arrived in his place, a Lieutenant Saraiev. Our mate Ivan Sery had ended up in the medical centre as well. It later emerged, to our great joy, that Teplov had survived but not returned to the company. He had been taken in by the divisional staff headquarters, so from then on, we saw him only now and then.

Trench life had become more organised in my absence. The burning cable had been replaced by a lamp made by our own craftsmen from a 45-mm shell case. The soldiers had covered the walls of our quarters with boards and placed a small plank bed in one corner. In the course of conversation, I failed to notice myself curling up upon it. I was wakened by an enemy artillery attack in the morning; it looked as if the foe was preparing to attack.

Through a combination of crawling and short dashes I reached the platoon commander. He was overjoyed to see me and pointed to an old well: there was a machine gun concealed there behind a log and it had to be 'removed'. I worked it out that this would require taking up a position to the right of the target, that is, scrambling over the parapet to the wire itself.

I started crawling. The morning frost had stiffened the lumpy soil. I scraped my hands bloody and regretted ten times over that I had not brought gloves with me. I noticed a shell hole up ahead and went towards it ... and at this point the bullets began to whistle over me, effectively disarming me. I froze, and soon the firing ceased. Apparently, the enemy had decided that they had dealt with me. I tore ahead and with three leaps reached the salvation of the shell hole. The Spanish machine gunner was as visible as my own five fingers. He was firing unhurriedly, in short bursts, carefully selecting new targets. I caught him just as he was taking aim and pulled the trigger ... The machine gunner shuddered and fell still. Hiding behind mounds, I went from shell hole to shell hole while the bullets hummed over me and got back to our trench. The new platoon commander was simply ecstatic at what for me had been a routine success.

Despite the lively crossfire, the Spanish troops were not setting up an attack. Gradually our firing duel began to die down and almost ceased. The silence was broken only by odd rounds and single shots. We set about repairing the broken sections of the trenches.

Soon the company *starshina*, Nikolay Sokolov, arrived. Standing by the thermoses, he filled the soldiers' mess tins placed under his ladle with millet soup. At that time food on our Leningrad Front was served twice a day – at breakfast and dinner. But our *starshina* still contrived to provide our soldiers on the forward line with tea, which meant a lot to us. On this occasion he handed over the bread for our section to me; it was my turn to lay down the law. A loaf could not be evenly divided, so we did as follows: one of us would turn his back to the chunks of bread laid out on a newspaper or cape, and a second man pointed at them and asked who to give the next chunk to. The soldier looking away called out a name, and so it continued until all the bread had been distributed.

This time we were not given the opportunity to eat in peace . . . The artillery started up again. Sand sprinkled down from the ceiling of the dugout and we dived into the trench to protect our soup. 'Why are they acting like madmen today,' growled Leonty Prikhodko, 'the damn bastards, not even giving us time to eat!' but I was unable to continue the conversation. The order came for all snipers to report to the company commander.

We ran along the communication passage to the company observation point. Also present, apart from Senior Lieutenant Nikiforov, was Senior Lieutenant Shchukin, commander of mortar forces, who was continuously observing the enemy through a periscope. Some sort of movement had been detected in the Spanish trenches. It looked as if the foe was planning an attack.

The telephone piped up. Nikiforov had been summoned by the regimental commander; the company had been ordered to get ready to repel an assault. Handing the receiver back to the radio operator, the company commander ordered us to go and join Lieutenant Natalich and the 2nd Platoon; a decision had been made to reinforce the flank of the company, in the expectation that that was where the enemy would try to get through.

Natalich immediately instructed us to go to our foxholes. I ended up beside a young soldier named Slava Golubyev. Having arrived quite recently, he lacked front-line experience and was plainly nervous. His hands, which were gripping the neck of his rifle stock, were white from tension. In an effort to calm him down, I engaged him in conversation. He turned out to be a local lad, from Leningrad. I liked the thorough way in which he was keeping watch. In time Golubyev was to become one of my best pupils.

The Germans launched yet another artillery strike. To the right we could hear the piercing whine of a 'donkey' – that was the name we gave to the enemy's six-barrelled Nebelwerfer rockets. After the volley was over, some human figures clad in blue-green overcoats leapt out of the enemy trenches and charged ahead, with the clear intention of attacking our first platoon. I gave Slava a shout, telling him to occupy the reserve foxhole. Our forward-line artillery unleashed a hail of fire and dampened down the enemy's initial attacking impulse.

An enemy officer in a cap with a high crown emerged from a trench and, flourishing his pistol, began to shout something – most likely trying to get his detachment to follow him into the attack. Firing into the air, he climbed onto the parapet. I fired, and the officer fell back into the trench. My magazine was now empty and at that moment another hulking foe began to rouse the men to attack. Golubyev held his nerve and knocked him over.

The Spanish troops opened a disorganised volley from their submachine guns but they were now hindered from attacking by the machine-gun fire of Nikolay Bazhanov on the flank. In the heat of battle, we failed to notice that several of the enemy had made it to no-man's land, hidden behind some anti-tank obstacles, and were now strafing our communication trench. I shouted to Slava to use his grenades. With the aid of this so-called 'pocket artillery' he forced the enemy out of their refuge and then we wiped them out with our rifle fire. Not a single Spaniard got away.

That day the enemy facing our company did not succeed in advancing any further than no-man's land, but on the neighbouring sector of the 3rd Company there was fighting in the trenches. Our 3rd Platoon had to engage the enemy in hand-to-hand fighting on the flank; they could not withstand our onslaught and fled. There were a number of wounded, but the medical orderlies did their best. In the end, the enemy failed to penetrate our defences that day.

I had a visit one day from Junior Lieutenant Mykola Kochubei, the best known mortarman in the regiment. He was twice my height and my foxhole was too small for him, but somehow he managed to accommodate himself. We got talking. It turned out that we were fellow Ukrainians; he was from the same Lubny district of Poltava Region, but that was not of course why he had come.

The enemy had established themselves in some trenches and were not poking their nose out. However, they had to be removed and Kochubei suggested that we map out together some targets which the mortar squads would wipe out, while I and the other snipers would finish off the enemy who survived and tried to escape. It was an attractive idea. We pin-pointed a dugout in the second trench to start with. The Spanish troops usually assembled there during daylight hours. The dugout was well camouflaged and the communication trench leading up to it was barely visible. Only on the right was there a small defile where snipers could trap their victims.

Kolya Kazakov and I took up our positions while it was still dark. The morning frost chilled us to the bone, but we waited patiently, moving only what we could allow ourselves to move – our fingers – so that our hands would not stiffen up. The day dawned. Kochubei began to give orders by telephone to his own squads. His command post was not far away from us and we could hear everything distinctly.

The mortars whistled and shrieked, and hit the dugout straight away. Then came another volley, and they sprayed the enemy trenches. The Spanish troops dived into the communication trenches to save themselves. I had an excellent view of their helmets through my optical sights. I took the first shot and then Kazakov's rifle followed suit. The crackle of machine-gun rounds and mortar explosions blotted out the sound of our shots and the enemy had still not guessed that they were under fire from a couple of snipers. I shouted to Kazakov not to mess about.

To the right another of our snipers had joined in. He did well in deciding to take advantage of the enemy's confusion. The Spaniards could not hold out, leapt out of the trench and ran in various directions, but our bullets caught them wherever they went. An hour later I gave Kazakov the signal to withdraw. We took a trench to the company observation point, where Nikiforov and Kochubei were happily awaiting us. The company commander took our sniper record booklets and recorded our kills, crediting me with four enemy victims and Nikolay with three.

Kochubei asked to look at my booklet and clicked his tongue in admiration: 'You've dispatched seventy-two Nazis to the other world, a whole company! Some Ukrainian! And that was over how many days?' When he found out that it was only a month, Mykola rapturously squeezed my hand and invited me to visit him in order to discuss further joint operations.

Kochubei was one of the old school, a naval officer. In his quarters he had a stove constructed of brick – a huge asset in our trench existence. The mortarmen treated me to American Lend-Lease canned strew, which we described as 'Second Front', and a captured flask of spirits also appeared. Kochubei recalled a boatswain from his submarine, a stern man at first glance, who could bang in nails with his fist and who, on account of his cooperativeness, enjoyed huge respect, firstly among the sailors in his brigade and then among the soldiers of his division. He had perished in 1941, and now Kochubei was bent on revenge – both for him and for his other mates in the Red Fleet.

Finally, Kochubei came to the business which concerned him and for which he had invited me over: he too wished to master the sniper's art so that he could look his dead foes in the face. I could hardly refuse my heroic fellow Ukrainian.

In the regimental workshop Kochubei managed to procure a sniper rifle. I helped to set it up and, in the early morning of a cold November day, when the day was just beginning to dawn, we set off for no-man's land. Following the October frosts the air was unusually damp, as if the ground was thawing out once again. I thought it must be an autumnal thaw and I was not mistaken.

We had barely established ourselves in our position – in a foxhole by a forward-line trench – when the wind swept a thick fog up from a gully. You could not even see two metres in front of you. I thought we should go back, but Junior Lieutenant Kochubei was not the kind of man to give in so easily.

Nikiforov came up to us. He was worried about the listening post. The Germans could easily creep up to it under the cover of the fog and wipe it out. We had his permission to get through to them and check how they were.

Normally, the 150-metre distance from the forward line trench to the forward post could not be attempted; the enemy would be covering every bump in the ground. Many were the soldiers who had sacrificed their impetuous heads on this stretch and hence it was known as the 'valley of death'. But now we were safely cloaked by fog and, stooping over, we made short dashes from shell hole to shell hole and negotiated the dangerous strip quite quickly. We crawled the final metres on our elbows and almost collapsed into the shallow trenches of our outpost.

The figure of a Red Army soldier with a sub-machine gun in his hands loomed over us: 'Stop. Who goes there?' He was simultaneously afraid but pleased to see us. We passed on Nikiforov's order to the commander of the forward-line platoon to strengthen the watch and headed for a sniper foxhole, which I fitted out for myself. The ground around it hardly crumbled at all, but it was of course a bit tight with two of us in it.

I began to explain to Mykola in a half-whisper where the enemy trench ran, what reference points I had noted and how many metres away they were. He listened attentively without averting his gaze from the Spanish trenches, and then he tugged me by the hand. Beyond the second enemy trench two silhouettes appeared and our optical sights gave us a good view of them. Both of the enemy were in their underwear. One had a kettle in his hand and a towel over his shoulder. The second was carrying a box or bag of some kind. From the braces worn by the second man I realised that he was probably an officer, while the other one was his batman.

I told Kochubei that I would take out the batman and he could take aim at the officer. Following my shot the dead Spaniard dropped the kettle and collapsed as if he had been knocked out, and Kochubei felled his quarry on the spot. For a first attempt it was a huge success. We stayed in the foxhole till it got dark, but the enemy grew cautious and did not show themselves above their trenches. We went back to the listening post trench. When they saw how successful we had been, some of the troops there wanted to become snipers too.

By the time of the Great October celebrations, it had frozen underfoot and there were all the signs of a real winter; there was already snow in the hollows and shell holes, but so far only a light layer. However, the time when we would be snowed in by huge drifts was not far away. The quartermaster staff looked after us, issuing wadded trousers and fur gloves, and half the soldiers received good-quality fur jackets. In my new winter garb I looked like a well-rounded water melon and I struggled to get into a narrow trench but, on the other hand, I did not freeze. However, the Spanish troops were not so well off; they wrapped blankets over their grey-green overcoats and tied woollen scarves round their heads like women. They looked as if they were freezing.

Although the enemy were hiding in dugouts, with the help of the mortar crews my score was soon close to 220. This figure was engraved on the receiver of my sniper rifle. When I first took possession of it, I guessed that I would not rest until I had achieved this number of victims. One day I was summoned by the regimental commander. Major Popov informed me that the following day I would be going to an army rally for snipers. I had been entrusted with representing the regiment in place of the recently wounded Simanchuk. To avoid embarrassment before our neighbouring regiments, the regimental commander had instructed the quartermaster to provide me with some cleaner clothes.

The rally was held not far from the banks of the Neva in the Rybatskoye village school. Located in its basement was the political section of our 55th Army, and on the second floor was an army club. When we sat down in the assembly hall, I met my old acquaintance, the journalist Gheorghiyev. He introduced me to the Leningrad woman sniper Natalia Timkina, who had a medal 'For Valour' gleaming on her chest.

First to speak was Army Commander Sviridov. He was followed on the stage by some well-known snipers: Shcherbakov, Bugaiov, Ilyin and Sarychev. Finally, my name was announced. I lost my nerve at first. I was asked how I became a sniper and I related one episode which had become etched in my memory. We were on our way to the forward line and we saw a woman with a little girl in an old vegetable garden. A shell flew over and exploded just where they were standing. The little girl survived but there was nothing left of her mother. I tried to soothe the child as much as I was able and promised to take revenge on the murderers. What more could I say? And now I was taking revenge. Concluding my talk, I confessed that I had still not seen Leningrad at all, but I asked to be considered a native of Leningrad. How could I have known back then that I would be spending a large portion of my subsequent life in the city on the Neva?

At the rally I got to know the legendary marksman of the 43rd Division Teshboi Odilov. I was stunned by his account of the way three German snipers had once pinned him to the ground with their fire for three whole days. He only had to raise his head or reach for the bag containing his bread and salami, and a shot would follow. The snow under him melted from the warmth of his body and he had already several times said goodbye to this world. The Germans relieved one another in guarding him, but there was nobody to relieve him. But he still managed on the third night to break out of the trap of fire and later to square accounts with the three enemy soldiers. He tracked them down for almost a week and a half, worked out where they would be going and wiped out all three.

In the evening I went back to the company and told Senior Lieutenant Nikiforov about the rally. He was interested to hear that in some divisions there were entire sniper companies. In our company by that time there were twenty-three snipers. Nikiforov wondered: why not make the entire company a sniper company? In order to the get soldiers interested, he proposed a competition. Besides that, he obtained some more sniper rifles and organised a sniper group of five men, including Vanya Denisenko, Slava Golubyev and Kolya Kazakov. The group was headed by me. Apart from eliminating enemy firing points, we were obliged to take the young marksmen under our wing. There began a period of intense work.

More often than not I operated as a pair with Slava Golubyev. We had a special liking for the old German trench in front of no-man's land. It was not easy to reach; the snow covered up footprints. But if you managed to set yourself up there while it was still dark, the entire line of enemy positions lay open to you for 500–700 metres. Firing these distances in winter demanded a good knowledge of the theory behind the sniper's art; apart from making adjustments for the wind and the moving target, you also had to consider the air temperature and the deviation.

One day I detected the glitter of glass amidst some snow-sprinkled ruins. Was it an observer? A sniper? We tried to provoke the 'glass' into firing; we raised a cap on a stick, but no one fired in response. It glinted only in the first half of the day. I informed Nikiforov and laid out my ideas. The company commander agreed with me that it was probably a stereoscopic periscope.

For four days Denisenko and I stalked this mysterious piece of glass. Then one clear frosty morning we took up our positions and began waiting. The 'glass' appeared again, glinting. Ivan fired and through my binoculars I could easily see a double periscope which had fallen onto the ground. A soldier started crawling towards the dead man and I knocked him off too. In the evening we reported to the company commander that we had eliminated the enemy observer.

Perfecting your skills in shooting required constant practice. Not far from our dugout stood an iron girder sticking up vertically from the ground. It was about 300 metres away. We made it a rule that, before venturing out to our positions, we would take a shot at it. It helped us to adjust our settings for the particular cartridges we were using. Over long distances the trajectory of a bullet's flight is strongly influenced by the ballistic properties of the ammunition – the weight of the powder, its dampness, the mass of the bullet, its calibre, and so on. Every batch of cartridges is different and necessitates new calibration, which is why we strove to use cartridges from just one batch at a time. Of course, it's a small detail, but over long distances it is on the calculation of small details that accuracy in shooting depends. Adjustments to their rifles and selection of cartridges helped Soviet marksmen to reduce the spread of bullets in their shot-groups to a third of conventional results.

One day the following incident occurred: we had set about renovating our trench and decided to use the remains of some logs from the ruins of a German dugout near a highway. After our second expedition there, we discovered a trench leading from the dugout to the enemy's side. Denisenko contrived to find out by some cunning ruse that it ran to the Spanish storehouse and kitchen and he suggested that we '*dekulakize*'[12] the enemy. We told our platoon commander about this plan. Lieutenant Saraiev hesitated: on the one hand, he would have to inform the company commander because, if anything went wrong, he would be responsible; on the other hand, if we did inform him, the loot would have to be divided up, or the operation would be entrusted to someone else, and we would not get a look at the loot.

In the end we succeeded in convincing our commander not to inform Nikiforov and at night four of us set off on the raid. First, we crawled up to a ditch. We paused and listened: everything seemed calm. The silence was broken only the occasional shots of bored sentries. We made our way onto the highway, which had been practically stripped of snow by the wind, quickly crossed over to the enemy side and crept into the trench. We proceeded about forty metres along it without meeting anyone. According to Ivan's calculations it was only a little way to the Spanish stores dugout.

Finally, we reached the goal of our operation. Denisenko deftly stuck a steel rod into the lock and tore it off. Ivan dived in through the doorway with Leonty Prikhodko behind him. Slava Golubyev and I stayed outside to cover them. The silence was extraordinary. We could hear the sound of an enemy sentry not far away beyond the bend in the trench line, murmuring some song to himself. I could barely cope with my excitement as our mates appeared from the dugout with big sacks over their shoulders.

At the same time the angry voice of someone's Degtyarev machine gun spoke up on our right flank. A sub-machine gun responded from the German side, then a second one, and a shooting match flared up. There was some commotion in the enemy trench and we tried to get as far away as possible. We ran back across the highway and dived into our own trench . . . and almost on top of the company commander who was waiting for us there.

'So, we decided to cash in, did we? Who gave permission?' he began his rebuke. We kept silent, guiltily lowering our eyes and apparently displaying such unanimous repentance that he couldn't restrain himself at the sight of us and burst out laughing. Coated in mud, shivering, with big sacks on our shoulders, we did indeed present a comical spectacle.

Nikiforov decided to make use of our revelation to seize a prisoner for interrogation but, when he contacted the staff headquarters about it, they sent over divisional reconnaissance rather than entrusting the operation to him. Out of our entire company only Ivan Denisenko was included in the reconnaissance group – as a guide. We were set the objective of 'blinding' the enemy.

On the day of the operation shots from my sniper group rang out along the company's whole forward line. Our principal targets were enemy observers and the gunports of firing points. In the meantime, the sappers were clearing passages through the minefields and cutting the barbed wire. At night the divisional reconnaissance went into action but, unfortunately, they were not successful. Several soldiers were killed and, on top of everything else, the prisoner for interrogation was hit by a stray bullet. They did not succeed in getting him to our trenches alive.

Meanwhile, the sniper recruitment process on the Leningrad Front in general and in our company in particular was growing and broadening. Apart from the specially trained marksmen with sniper rifles on the forward line, ordinary soldiers, signallers and sappers began to emerge with Three Lines. In our mortar company several men besides Kochubei opened their personal scores. One who distinguished himself was Yegor Ushakov, a woodcutter from Archangel.

One day he and I set off on a sniper sortie towards the bridge over the Izhora.[13] I had long been fond of a shooting position there beside the Moscow highway. First, we followed a trench. Then, before crawling out into no-man's land, we stopped for a smoke and he told me how he had killed his first German with a sniper rifle. It happened in the district where we had enjoyed a brief period of rest and recreation. Kochubei and Ushakov had set an ambush in the ruins of a house and waited for quite a long time until some enemy soldiers appeared. On this occasion they were lugging some logs. Yegor took aim and felled one of them. The others dashed up to the fallen man, and Kochubei remained in control of the situation, knocking over another three, one after another, with precise shots, after which he said to his partner: 'We've got to get out of here, Yegor!' The Germans came to their senses and covered the area with mortar salvoes, but too late; our successful mortarmen were already far away.

December 25, 1942, was drawing near – the anniversary of the foundation of the Ukrainian Soviet Socialist Republic – my land and that of Kochubei. Mykola proposed that we celebrate this date by giving the enemy a 'sniper's Christmas', since their Christmas coincided with our anniversary. We occupied our firing positions while it was still dark. The Spanish troops were only firing now and then, but frequently sending up blinding flares which turned night into day. Our hunt did not work out; we expended five cartridges and all to no purpose.

Then we heard the sounds of an accordion, but being played in a style that was not ours. The enemy had had one over the eight on the occasion of 'Christ's birth' and were now relaxing. We waited till they came up the nearby rise. Their silhouettes were distinctly visible against the snow-covered field behind them and we fired almost simultaneously. While confusion reigned on the enemy side, I had time to reload and lay out one more of them.

By the end of the year our company had become wholly a 'search and destroy' unit. All our marksmen and machine gunners had opened their accounts. We wrote about this to our division's legendary sniper, Grigory Simanchuk, who was still under treatment in a hospital in Sverdlovsk. I was awarded the Order of the Red Star and promoted to senior sergeant.

Soon after New Year I met another well-known sniper from our division, Sergeant Aleksandr Kuritsyn. He was in the 14th Regiment, with which we constantly competed in terms of kill numbers. By that time Aleksandr's tally exceeded 200. He told me how he had got the better of one enemy sniper. The latter had gone to ground near an embankment behind a pile of railway sleepers. Kuritsyn tracked him for two days, but the German was extremely cautious. The enemy sniper had devised a simple method of stalking; he tied a helmet to a stick and used that to move it. Aleksandr guessed his cunning ruse straight away. He fired at the helmet and immediately rolled away from the place he had fired from. A second later a bullet struck the spot where he had lain.

The foe was being cautious. He appeared from behind the sleepers only in the evening, not realising that, in his white camouflage suit against the background of the sunset, he was as visible as could be. Kuritsyn wiped him out with a single shot.

All this acquired experience was considered and used when new ways of eliminating the enemy were being worked out. Sniper Vanya Myakshin and his partner Makarov cooperated with the soldiers of Senior Lieutenant Serkov's '45-millimetre' platoon. At a certain time, the gunners would roll out their cannons to a forward trench and conduct direct fire at the gunports of the enemy firing points and dugouts, while the snipers covered the squads against enemy machine gunners and picked off any surviving Nazis who were scattering.

One day in the first half of January an order came through at night to intensify our vigilance. Our company commander stationed extra guard posts and issued the machine gunners with three or four additional cases of full cartridge-belts. The heralds of an approaching artillery attack appeared in the forward trenches – observers with their stereoscopic periscopes, telephones and radio receivers. Kochubei set up his observation post next to me.

In the morning the rumble of artillery could be heard from the Ivanov district on the left flank. It was the beginning of operation 'Iskra [Spark]', to breach the blockades on the Leningrad and Volkhov Fronts. Soon after, Kochubei received the order to open fire. Our artillery, both regimental and divisional, spoke up – howitzers from individual artillery regiments and barking 45-millimetre guns. As soon as the artillery's softening up was over, the enemy forward line came to life, and the work started for us snipers. Nikiforov gave the command – to direct our fire at the gunports of enemy pillboxes with tracer and incendiary bullets in order to illuminate them for the gunners.

There were two firing points in the sector which I was covering. One was swept away, literally with the third shell, tossing logs and boards up into the air along with clods of earth. The other one needed a bit more work. When the pillboxes were dealt with, Ivan Myakshin approached me. Without explaining the reasons, he asked me to go with him along the trench to the junction with that of the neighbouring company. It grabbed my interest, and I followed him amidst the whistling of bullets and shell splinters.

Waiting for us in a foxhole was Ivan's partner, Mikhail Yegorov. The soldiers pointed out to me an enemy squad hidden in a stack of beams from a bridge across the Izhora which had been blown up. On a tripod they had a machine gun which had been painted white. If our infantry had attempted to cross the river over the ice, they would have been wiped out.

It would not be possible to pick off the squad from the river; it was too soundly concealed. Any attempts would merely serve as warning shots. Yegorov was assigned to cross over to the opposite bank at night and silently seize the machine gun. As darkness descended, he left his rifle in the trench, took only silent weapons and crawled off. Long, agonising minutes of waiting followed. We began to be concerned that something might have happened to him, although no shooting could be heard from the opposite side of the bridge. And then Yegorov appeared in front of the trench, breathing heavily, weary but happy. He had brought a trophy machine gun with him – a German MG 34. He had cut the throat of the Fritz guarding it.

One January evening some newspapers arrived along with the thermoses containing hot food. They informed us that, after seven days of intense fighting, our forces had liberated the town of Shlisselburg and a whole list of population centres, and on 18 January the blockade of Leningrad was breached. Our joy knew no bounds; we had waited so long for it! We shouted 'Hurrah!', let off our weapons and hugged one another. Senior Lieutenant Nikiforov appeared in response to the noise. Learning what had happened, he remarked that soon we would be advancing. And indeed, the order came the following morning to prepare for an offensive.

We took up our places in the trenches while it was still dark. I was next to my partner Slava Golubyev. On the enemy's side blinding flares were constantly soaring up into the sky and, now and then, the darkness was cleaved by the blindingly bright trails of tracer rounds. Finally, our platoon commander, Lieutenant Saraiev, turned up looking grumpy and intense. Nobody had ever seen him like that. He summoned the commanders of the platoon sections. He had been told by the battalion staff that the artillery softening-up would commence in two and a half hours, after which the 14th and 133rd Regiments would attack. The 187th would remain where it was in the meantime to cover the divisional flank. That was what was responsible for his bad temper; like all of us, he wanted to move ahead and smash the enemy.

The artillery cannonade began at first light. The remnants of snow in the enemy lines vanished before our eyes and turned them into a zone of earth churned up by explosions. Then the battalions went into the attack. Ordnance fired from the enemy side. There was hand-to-hand fighting in the enemy trenches.

We did not sit idle for very long and our regiment went on the offensive as well. Lieutenant Saraiev kept Slava and me beside him the whole time, constantly pointing out targets which had to be wiped out or quelled. More often than not they were enemy machine-gun posts impeding the advance of the platoon.

The commander set us a new task – to operate on the right flank, covering the advance of our soldiers. There were some ruins there in which we decided to take up a position, but then it turned out that up to a platoon of Germans was approaching from the other side. A little bit more, and we would have walked straight into them. We urgently needed to move onto the enemy flank, open fire and sow panic. We went into a trench that had only just been won from the enemy. Its floor was covered with dead bodies, helmets scattered around and abandoned weapons captured from the other side. Round a corner was a dugout from which voices emerged, but we had no idea in what language. I got a grenade ready just in case, flung the door open and bellowed: '*Hände hoch!*'

'What are you yelling for?' came the reply. They were our own forces. It was machine gunner Kostya with his partner and they had decided to have a bite to eat here. On learning that the Germans were approaching, they grabbed their light machine gun. I directed them towards the nearest foxhole and Golubyev and I ran on further to the right. By arrangement with Kostya we were all to open fire simultaneously when I waved my hand.

Finally, we came to a suitable place to set up a firing position, fell to the ground and prepared to fire. I waved my hand and the machine gun began to mow down the enemy, who were advancing in short rushes. On our side we dispatched bullet after bullet, and almost every one found its target. The enemy panicked under the crossfire, began to flap around, and fled back, leaving several motionless bodies lying on the ground.

The company was given the command to dig in, even though it had succeeded in moving several hundred metres ahead. We put the trenches captured from the enemy in order and set up foxholes. There was water wherever you poked your spade, although it did not appear at first glance to be a marshy area. Judging by the sounds of the guns, our neighbours were approaching Krasny Bor on the left. Fire was raging unceasingly there.

At night I ran into the assistant to the head of the Komsomol divisional political section, Captain Savitsky. He told me how my mate and sniping competitor from the 14th Regiment, Sergeant Kuritsyn, had saved the entire battalion, which had taken the brunt of the enemy counter-strike. The battalion commander had requested help, but it was nowhere to be found. Kuritsyn bailed them out. He took up an effective firing position on the enemy flank and began to dispatch bullet after bullet, killing almost twenty Germans at one blow. The enemy began to panic and he ran back.

The enemy had brought up fresh forces at night and, after a short artillery bombardment, attempted to counter-attack. Our gunners and mortar crews had hung a curtain of fire in front of us, but nevertheless at the critical moment of the battle the enemy Stielhandgranaten[14] began to fly over into our trenches. The troops seized them by their long wooden handles and flung them back. In the end the enemy rolled back from our trenches after sustaining great losses

An hour and a half after hostilities began there was a lull, but we realised that it was temporary. The company commander ordered us to stay in our foxholes and to be on the alert. This warning did not prove vain; in the enemy lines we had noticed the characteristic assembly of infantry that usually occurred before an attack. Our ears also picked up the low-pitched rumbling of enemy tank engines.

Through the optics of my rifle, I spotted a German officer. Perched on the ruins of a brick house, he was scrutinising our positions through binoculars. I was in no hurry to fire: I wanted him to thrust himself further out of his refuge, to make sure of bagging him. Killing the commander of an enemy detachment before an attack guaranteed that it would be deferred if not frustrated. In his impatience Golubyev was trying to hurry me up, but I was in no hurry and I was too experienced to give in to him. I caught the German in my sights, waited till he raised himself a little, and fired. Waving his arms comically, the officer fell. Nikiforov cried out in joy: 'Well done, good lads!'

On the left flank there were sounds of battle. It looked as if the Germans had knocked out our patrol by the bridge over the Izhora and were attempting to get round to the company's rear. Our commander took the decision to use one platoon to distract their attention on their right flank and to strike in the centre with the other two. The plan came off perfectly; the enemy retreated in panic, and on the left flank as well. Similar fierce clashes lasted for almost seven days.

Finally, the offensive came to an end and once again we firmly established ourselves on defence. The 55th Army liberated Krasny Bor, Staraya Myza, Chernyshovo, Popovka station and the edge of the village of Stepanovka. Of these population centres, only the names remained; there were no houses – just continuous ruins. On the last day of fighting, my partner and the Komsomol organiser for our company, Slava Golubyev, lost his life.

He had come to the front as a seventeen-year-old volunteer from the Leningrad blockade and become an experienced sniper within a couple of months. At a regimental Komsomol meeting, which was held one day in Kolpino, a letter from some Leningrad women was read out. They described the barbarous bombardment of the city, the destruction of their school by enemy shells. A teacher had been wounded and children had perished. Slava sat stunned by what he heard; it was his school and his teacher. He soon had the opportunity to avenge them.

My partner on that sortie was Kazakov, while the combination of Golubyev and Denisenko went to ground about a hundred metres from us. We found something to rest our rifles on and took aim at an enemy dugout, from which the sound of an axe was issuing forth. A log appeared behind the parapet and then a forage cap. Kazakov fired and the log and the cap disappeared from our field of vision. Stunned by the death of his partner, a Spanish soldier emerged incautiously from a trench. I gave him a death sentence too.

The enemy were plunged into confusion, dashing around their communication trenches. Mortars started hitting our proposed ambush site. Taking advantage of the noise and bustle, Golubyev and

Denisenko opened fire from positions from which the entire enemy trench was clearly visible. By the time the enemy had worked out what was happening, they had immediately wiped out several soldiers and withdrawn to a safe place. Thus did Slava wreak vengeance for the spilt blood of his first teacher, Anna Nikolayevna, for the school he attended, and for his home town.

And now this extraordinary lad was dead. Only the evening before we had eaten porridge from the same mess tin and he tried to leave more of it for me, claiming that he wasn't hungry. But during the day the company received orders to mount a fighting patrol. Prior to the planned offensive the commanders wanted to clarify what enemy forces lay in front of us and what their firing system was.

We launched an attack on the sector in the district of Yam-Izhora, which formed a junction between enemy detachments. At night regimental sappers dug passages under minefields and barbed wire obstacles and, after a brief artillery strike at first light, we attacked. We quickly dashed over the parapet and crossed no-man's land. The distance to the enemy trenches was next to nothing, 100–150 metres. But then the enemy machine guns started up.

Prikhodko and I quickly silenced one them, but there were still guns rattling away on the right flank of our company. A large-calibre machine gun began spitting fire and our soldiers went to ground. Nikiforov was biting his lips: if we were to be pelted with mortars, almost nothing would remain of the detachment. He ordered that the signaller call up mortar forces, but the line was broken. At this point one of the soldiers overcame his fear, got up and brandished his sub-machine gun. The company rose after him and went into the attack. Our soldiers killed off those they found in the enemy trench, seized a prisoner for interrogation – a German NCO – and withdrew. Along with the captive, who had turned grey with fear, they brought back a cape on which lay the body of Slava Golubyev. It was he, the Komsomol organiser, who had saved the company by sacrificing himself, because the first man to get up in attack generally perished.

And so, finally, the second winter of the war was drawing to an end. The snow had thawed, the rains had come, and the trenches were once again impassable whether by transport or on foot. We were endlessly scooping water out of our damned fortifications and constantly reinforcing their walls. Yet, the advent of warm weather was bound to cheer us up.

Kochubei's trench was beside my foxhole. We now almost constantly operated together. Serving as a spotter for the gunners, he drove the 'beast' out of its 'lair' with his 50-mm mortars, and then together we finished him off with our sniper rifles. Thus, today he had pelted an enemy grouping and, taking advantage of the confusion, I had expunged four enemy soldiers. The Germans responded with fire, and we changed our position, moving to a spare one to get out of trouble.

With the onset of spring the enemy snipers became more active. First and foremost, they came after us – their 'opposite numbers'. News of sniper duels on the forward line began to come in more often. It was in just such a duel that my old Norilsk friend and fellow Ukrainian Vanya Denisenko lost his life. We had gone to ground about 150–200 metres from the enemy. Around ten o'clock in the morning there was some sort of commotion among the Germans – whether a change-over of detachments or the arrival of reinforcements. Some inexperienced enemy soldiers poked their heads out of their trenches, curious as to what was happening on the forward line and we 'silenced' some of them.

However, we too were possessed by an unhealthy curiosity as to what was going on among the Fritzes. Our attempts to get a better view of what was happening in their trenches led to them opening precision fire on us. I ordered Ivan to change his position, but then another group of enemy soldiers came along. Without listening to me, he raised himself above the parapet, fired and then instantly dropped his rifle and fell backwards. He had a tiny bullet wound in his forehead.

We buried Ivan on the edge of Kolpino, let off a triple volley, and swore to avenge him. I felt depressed after the funeral – from the death of a friend on top of many days of accumulating fatigue. I did not want to drink or eat, or talk to anyone. Kazakov and Kochubei tried to cheer me up, but I kept to myself and went off for walks. The company commander, Nikiforov, realised what was happening inside me and relieved me of commitments in the meantime.

I was brought out of this depressed state by the news of yet another loss in our company – on the same sector where Vanya Denisenko had perished. Junior Lieutenant Vasilyev had been fatally felled by an enemy marksman. He carelessly looked out from his place of refuge and a bullet struck him.

In the evening I was called up by the battalion commander, Captain Smirnov, and given the task of eliminating an enemy marksman. We were now facing an SS regiment rather than Spanish troops, so the sniper was most probably more experienced than those we had already encountered. The change in the enemy's behaviour was now comprehensible to me: less noise in the trenches on the forward line, more precise artillery fire, and snipers acting much more professionally. Their bullets had killed not only Ivan Denisenko and Vasilyev, but also sniper Golubkov.

Before going out to stalk him, I needed to study the behaviour of the enemy marksman. For this I called on Lieutenant Petukhov's platoon. He was suffering losses from enemy snipers almost every day. The trenches on this sector were dug in marshy soil; they were shallow and watery. In two or three places they were impassable; just stick your head out and you were bound to attract a deadly bullet.

In my effort to understand how my adversary acted, I ignored no information – even if it was inaccurate. One soldier offered to show me where the enemy sniper was firing from. He was sure that there were five of them operating on this sector and attempted to convince me of this. The longer I listened to his arguments, the more confident I became that I was dealing with a solitary sniper, or with a pair of snipers who were using several different firing positions.

I spent the night in the mortar crew dugout and, before it got light, I set off again for Petukhov's platoon. I stopped by the bend in the trench line where Golubkov had perished. Ahead of me were the ruins of a trench. Here began the 'valley of death' – the sector which the Nazis riddled with sniper fire. I decided to lure my adversary out and provoke him to fire. I put my Cossack fur cap on a stick and cautiously raised it a little higher than the parapet. The Fritz was not tempted by my ruse. I repeated the operation – again without result. I displayed the cap once more. A bullet whistled over my head. I showed the cap a third time, slowly moving it along the parapet, then stopped and repeated the procedure. Bullets whistled over my head. I lowered the cap, and saw there was a hole in it below the star emblem. The wretch had ruined my cap, but at least I now knew how he operated.

Divisional reconnaissance also helped me to gather data about my enemy. They caught a prisoner for interrogation – an SS clerk, who said that there were only three snipers in their battalion. They were all extra-class shots, graduates of the Berlin school.

In order to wipe out one of them, the one who had murdered Vanya Denisenko, I decided to take along the experienced snipers Nikolay Kazakov and Ivan Sery. We engaged in a small military discussion on how to take the experienced 'beast' down. Scratching the back of his head, Kazakov suggested that the adversary needed to be lured by a real sniper; one of us would have to act as 'bait'. Nikolay himself volunteered for this perilous role and made suggestions himself as to the best way of arranging things. We would need to set up a bogus foxhole with a cap peak and a gun-port and, moreover, construct it in such a way that the light from the rear distinctly outlined the marksman's silhouette. Kazakov would take two or three shots and allow the enemy to spot him, and then quickly change his position. We agreed to Kolya's proposal.

The following day we set about preparing our firing positions and were joined by snipers Sarenbai Rustambekov and Leonty Prikhodko. Sarenbai and Kazakov dealt with the bogus position: they dug out a trench and put an armoured shield in front of the gunpoint, as is usually done in good sniper foxholes, and carefully camouflaged it.

We agreed with the commander of the platoon in whose sector we were preparing our ambush, Lieutenant Petukhov, that, when the 'hunt' began, surplus movement along the trenches would cease. We had to give the enemy marksman the impression that we were afraid of him.

In the meantime, the SS sniper continued to operate. One of his bullets smashed the optical sight on the weapon belonging to Aleksey Zaytsev, a soldier in our group, and ricocheted into his arm. Fortunately, he managed to notice that the firing was coming not from the old brick ruins, as he had earlier supposed, but from a second trench much further to the right.

Everything was ready. We spent the time remaining till darkness fell adjusting our weapons. At night we took up our positions: Kazakov in the bogus one and Ivan Sery with me in the main one. At first light we surveyed no-man's land as usual, to check whether anything there had changed overnight. Everything seemed to be the way it was. But where was the enemy marksman hiding? Under the wreck of some tank? A real sniper would never select such an obvious place.

Somewhere to the right somebody let off his rifle from boredom. Then our machine gunner combed the parapet of the enemy trench. Taking advantage of the commotion, Kazakov fired two shots and then another two. However, the enemy marksman did not show himself, even though we waited right till evening. Maybe he was not on the forward line that day?

In the meantime, the company was wearing itself out on earthworks. An order had come to dig out trenches of full depth and equip them with dugouts. The white nights were approaching. The troops would sleep two or three hours but, knowing what an important operation we were engaged on, the commanders gave orders that the snipers should be left in peace. Our mates moaned that they were taking the rap for various 'idlers', but they did not wake us up. After a good sleep we set off again to our firing positions. This time I decided to go to ground with Kazakov.

We began to wonder why our adversary was not showing himself, and then it occurred to me that we had overdone it with the armoured shield. It was very difficult to land a shot in the narrow slit and the German had simply not risked it. We decided to check this. I moved the shield to the side and placed a rifle on the shelf we had made in the parapet and cocked it. Immediately an enemy bullet whistled past my ear. I was as delighted as if I had met an old acquaintance; the German was here, on this sector.

I set off for our main position and began to wait. The minutes dragged by slowly. Finally, Nikolay fired twice, after which he knocked the shield off with the end of his gun barrel and placed a dummy in the gunport in place of himself. The German took his time about it but finally fired at the 'Russian sniper'. I distinctly saw a flash in an area between the first and second enemy trenches. It turned out that our adversary had camouflaged his position under an old tree stump. I took careful aim, pressed the trigger, reloaded and dispatched another bullet just to make sure. Vanya Sery also fired. After this we quickly crawled back; we urgently needed to change our position. Bullets whistled over our heads, but we paid no attention to them and crawled through the mud, stones and bumps in the ground back to our trench. A ditch came to our rescue and we slipped into it and only then paused to get our breath back and put ourselves in order at least to some small degree. The SS marksman did not show up again on this sector.

In the evening Kochubei told me that Grisha Simanchuk had come back to the regiment. On 12 August 1942, during a routine sniper sortie, the Germans had detected his position and pounded it with mortar fire, after which they bombarded us all day, not even allowing us to raise our heads. The medical orderlies only managed to carry the wounded sniper away from no-man's land at night. He was sent off straight away to a field hospital, where the doctor fought a long time for his life. As soon as his situation has stabilised, he was evacuated to Sverdlovsk. However, gangrene set in on one of his legs and, by the time he arrived there, one of Simanchuk's feet had to be amputated. He spent a long time convalescing in the Urals, learned to walk with a prosthesis and finally managed to get himself sent back to the front.

I went to the regimental staff headquarters to make the acquaintance of the hero whose example had prompted me to become a sniper. There were some interesting stories about him.

After a difficult sortie in December 1941 Simanchuk had overheard two soldiers expressing doubts as to whether he had really 'done in' more than a hundred enemy over a few months. He then took them with him to the forward line. 'Let's go out and see if Simanchuk is just boasting,' he told them in Ukrainian, but they both understood him.

After several hours of motionless observation of the enemy forward line both soldiers began to shiver and to wonder how they could get back as soon as possible. But at this point, on the enemy side, a hefty soldier attempted to jump across to a neighbouring dugout. One shot and he was lying face down in the snow. An hour later the sniper finished off another foe. It was said that these two subsequently became almost the best of his pupils.

On 20 February 1942 Grigory wiped out his 121st Fritz and the following day he was taken from the regiment to a front-line sniper rally in Leningrad. Among the dignitaries present was Andrei Zhdanov and the commander of the front, Lieutenant-General Mikhail Khozin. After several speeches Simanchuk was given the floor. He began his address in Ukrainian with the words: 'I haven't much to boast about, with only a hundred and twenty-one kills . . .', which gave rise to laughter in the hall, even from Zhdanov. At that time a total of 121 enemies was a great many, and here he was dismissing it as 'not much'.

My fellow Ukrainian described one cunning ruse he had employed to eliminate an opponent. His optical sights picked up a German cook at a field kitchen. At first, he wanted to shoot him, but then decided that it would be better to leave him alive; for then he would know precisely where the enemy soldiers were coming from and going to. By the time the Germans worked out what was going on, he would be able to knock off a few of them, maybe even a dozen. This plan vindicated itself in full.

In the regimental staff headquarters we finally became acquainted. Outwardly, to my disappointment, Simanchuk was not at all as I had imagined; he was only my height and no Hercules. But he had plenty of desire to get even with the Nazis. We agreed to go out together to the forward line the following day.

In the early morning, before dawn, Simanchuk appeared in our trench in camouflage gear along with his inseparable self-loading Tokarev rifle and its optical sights. We set off along the communication trenches to my foxhole near the bridge across the River Izhora. Along the way my new mate talked about his village, the best in the entire Chernigov region, to which 'some sod' had given the name Navozy.[15] But I could not stop thinking about my own home village of Betyagi and wondering how my mother, sister and brothers were getting on under occupation.

Simanchuk liked my sniper's 'nest' – particularly the armoured shields which Kochubei had quite recently brought in from somewhere.

They had transformed the firing position into a real pillbox. I showed my guest my map, indicating the reference points and distances to them, and set off to my reserve position. We had made a plan beforehand with our machine and artillery gunners with regard to coordinated action.

Two hours later an enemy soldier appeared with a bucket by the river, about half a kilometre away from us. He was only visible for a moment, but that was enough for an experienced sniper to bag him. Struggling to hide his excitement, Grigory asked when I went up to him: 'Did you see it?' That day we shot another couple of Germans. We went back to the company when it became quite dark and only there found out that there had been a panic-stricken search for Simanchuk through all the battalions. The regimental staff were concerned as to what might have happened to him.

Although Simanchuk strove to go out on the forward line, his wound still played up and therefore he became an instructor in our regimental sniper school, which was headed by my former platoon commander, Lieutenant Teplov, now back from hospital. Running ahead of my narrative, I will just say that Simanchuk survived the war, returned to the Ukraine, settled in the republican capital of Kyiv and worked as a mechanic at the Darnitsa silk company.

The nature of our life in May 1943 is well illustrated by the following entries from the diary of my friend, Lieutenant Nikolay Kochubei, which he made during the course of those days:

> *2 May.* Spent a whole day and night at an observation point by the ruins of a church not far from the bridge across the River Izhora. Kept watch on the enemy. Two new dugouts have appeared over there. Early morning smoke came out of them. Also found a trench by which the Germans carried up ammunition and food in thermoses.
>
> *3 May.* Company Commander Shchukin at the observation point. Went out stalking early morning. Chose a spot in no-man's land, beside a deep shell-hole, and began to watch the trench where the Nazis were bringing up food. A soldier appeared with a thermos, walking unhurriedly, as if at home. Trained my sights

and took him out with one shot. Two other soldiers came up to him and I nailed them too. The enemy spotted me and made things hot for me. Just as well the company commander covered me. Managed to get back to our observation point.

4 May. Spent all day in firing positions. Checked the state of the mortars. Calibrated several new weapons against enemy firing points. Couldn't sleep at night . . .

6 May. Went out stalking with Yegor Ushakov. We took up positions in no-man's land. Lots of movement all day on the Nazi side. We managed to wipe out thirteen Nazis, nine of them mine. The company commander congratulated us on a major military strike. Rained cats and dogs all night. Pumping water out of dug-outs and wells from first light.

11 May. Went out to a position in the old place, towards the bridge over the Izhora. Wiped out three Nazis in a shallow trench. But only got out by a miracle. The Germans apparently guessed where my lair was and unleashed a hurricane of mortar fire. Lay in the shell hole right till evening. Soaked to the skin. At night Yegor Ushakov crawled over to me. Incredibly surprised when he saw me safe and sound. Turned out, the company had as good as buried me. Somebody said he saw a direct mortar hit on my lair. This means I'll now survive to the end of the war.

13 May. 'Snipered' with Fedya Dyachenko. Perfect day. Sunny. Warm southerly. Starlings in an old pussy willow battered by bullets and shell splinters. A successful day. Dyachenko bagged six Nazis and I got two.

June 1943 witnessed an event which defined my entire subsequent life; by regimental command I was appointed Komsomol organiser for our battalion. Educational activity and paper work took up all my time. My rifle was abandoned like an orphan in one corner of the dugout with nothing to do.

One day I was called up to the 55th Army political section for a seminar of battalion Komsomol organisers. Before it started the deputy head of the front-line political administration for Komsomol activities,

Lieutenant Ivan Stepanovich Bichurin, decided to have an informal chat with us. We gathered in the house occupied by the Komsomol section of the army political department. Bichurin was interested in the way I had organised activities in the battalion. No doubt all the Komsomol members in the detachment had become snipers, with an organiser like me? I had to confess that I had hardly any time left for sniper matters.

Then we were set the task of demonstrating to Komsomol members through personal example how the Nazis should be wiped out. Returning to the battalion, I made arrangements with the battalion deputy political education officer, Captain Krylov, to commence regular sessions with Komsomol members on the art of the sniper. He charged the commander of the mortar company, Lieutenant Shchukin, with assisting us in this matter by running a session on the calculation of angular values and ways of determining the distance to the target. I was responsible for conducting practical activities on the forward line. The company Komsomol organisers began in time to assist the soldiers of their detachments to learn the science of precision shooting, camouflage, and proper target selection. Our activities soon bore fruit; the number of snipers in the battalion grew significantly and most of the rest became accurate marksmen.

This was a period of rapid development of sniper recruitment in the Red Army. The names of heroic snipers on various fronts became widely known: Vasiliy Zaytsev at Stalingrad, Lyudmila Pavlichenko in the Crimea and in the Caucasus, Inna Mudretsova in the battle for Moscow. The Leningrad Front had its own famous sniper, Vladimir Pchelintsev, who visited the USA and Britain with Pavlichenko. I knew of him, but we became acquainted only after the war. Soviet Information Bureau bulletins included news about snipers. Rallies for them were held on both an army and a front basis. At our Leningrad Front staff headquarters there was a whole group of officers who were responsible for training sniper instructors.

In the meantime, our forces had gained the upper hand in the battle of the Kursk bulge[16] and begun to liberate my Ukrainian homeland region by region. We were undergoing re-formation when I was contacted by the regimental Komsomol organiser and informed that Poltava had been liberated. I could not believe it at first, but the Soviet Information Bureau bulletin announcing this had been transcribed by radio operator Vitaly Bagry. Several days later I sent off a letter to my home village of Betyagi and asked whoever it ended up with (it was a small village and we all knew one another very well) to write back and let me know what had happened to my family.

For the next few days, I lived on tenterhooks, waiting impatiently for the *starshina* to deliver the mail and walking away in disappointment on learning that there were no letters for me. Finally, the long-awaited reply came. It was written by the chairman of our district council. Vladimir Nikolayevich Vatsenko (my mother was illiterate and could not reply herself). As far as she, my little sister Galya and my younger brother Grisha were concerned, everything was alright; they had survived. They lived of course in extreme need, but were coping in the meantime. Things were not so good with regard to the second of my three brothers. The invaders had taken him away for forced labour in Germany. Only after the war was he able to return home. The trials that had fallen to his bitter lot were enough for several biographies. However, he coped, graduated from an institute and went on to work on the district newspaper. But back in the autumn of 1943 I did not know all that and wanted to wreak vengeance for my brother as well.

The Leningrad Front was getting ready for an offensive. Intense preparations went on up to and including December. Our division, which had been rested and reinforced in the rear, was supplied with tanks and taught how to storm fortifications, advance behind a real wall of fire (which often resulted in deadly sacrifices) and to fight in hand-to-hand combat. The soldiers often engaged in practice tussles with the 'enemy' with such passion that the officers had to separate them. These sessions were held in all divisions, not just ours, and in all the armies on the Leningrad Front. Finally, it was our turn to advance.

On 14 January 1944, the guns fired incessantly from morning to evening on the Oranienbaum bridgehead to our right. The 2nd Shock Army then went on the offensive, followed by the 42nd, which included our division. At first, we moved forward in the second echelon. Marching in formation, I was curious to view the traces of recent battles: the burnt-out frames of vehicles, twisted ordnance, bodies of enemy soldiers.

We crossed the Pulkovo heights, striding past the ruins of the celebrated observatory. The entire territory was pitted with trenches and foxholes, artillery positions and machine-gun nests. Something was flashing to the right – a salvo from the long-distance guns of the ships of the Baltic fleet and shore-based fortifications, firing at the limit of their range.

It was not easy to make your way across the crumbly snow, churned up by countless wheels and caterpillar tracks. Besides that, we were constantly yielding the right of way to columns of trucks and tanks and, the closer we got to the front, the more we had to withdraw to the gutters. We passed through Veneryazi, Kokkolovo, Vittolovo – of the villages only the names remained. There was just an endless snow-covered plain where they had once stood. On the Kirkhgof Heights to the right fiery flashes could be seen. There was a fierce battle raging; for the second day running a continuous cannonade could be heard from there.

Winter that year turned out to be quite strange. First the frosts came down and we rejoiced in the warm fur jackets and felt boots we had been issued. Then a thaw began and I exchanged my boots for a pair belonging to a policeman. Then it began to freeze again and the sharp wind lashed my face with snow. The notion of getting rid of my felt boots did not seem quite so sensible now.

I stopped next to Kochubei. His mortar crew was setting up a firing position. Our formation had received orders to relieve the 45th Guards Division marching in front of us and break through the second zone of enemy defences. The enemy's firing system was unknown and the commanders did not allow us time to clarify the matter. Heavy fighting awaited us.

We were sitting at day-break in a former enemy trench and ahead of us lay the German forward-line trenches. I took a nap, snuggling up to my rifle. Although I was now the battalion's Komsomol organiser, I continued to increase my combat tally and was now over the 400 mark. Many of my mates also had three-figure totals. The hands of the clock showed 9:20, flares were soaring up above and a real tornado of fire was descending on the enemy lines. Howitzer shells and rockets were flying over our heads. Operating from camouflaged positions, anti-tank guns and regimental artillery had been set up to use direct fire against the German firing points. Over the forward line hung a pall of black smoke from which bits of debris were occasionally flung up.

The command was given, and the snow-covered plain was covered with masses of men in white camouflage suits running towards the enemy. Firing as we went from machine guns and rifles, we charged on through the passages in the minefields, which had been earlier cleared by sappers, and burst into the first, and then the second, line of enemy trenches, crushing everything in our path. Further along our ranks to the right, a machine gun started up. I threw a grenade into the gunport of a pillbox. There was an explosion and black smoke streamed out. I leapt onto the roof and mounted a small red flag. The soldiers of our battalion had a store of such flags and now they were gleaming scarlet along our whole line of attack.

By morning it became known that the 2nd Shock Army and our 42nd Army had met in the vicinity of Russko-Vysotsky, up to seven enemy divisions had been routed, and a lot of equipment had been captured. And once again we attacked. Ahead of us everything was in flames, the enemy trenches had been literally ploughed up by shells, and the area was piled with enemy corpses. A few surviving Germans were jumping up with their hands already high, clutching their heads and muttering something.

But the Germans still managed to cling on to part of the sector. They had clearly received reinforcements and were now counter-attacking. On the battalion's left flank, where Vanya Myakshin and I ended up, enemy tanks had begun an attack against the battalion. Ivan loaded his rifle with armour-piercing bullets, directed it at the viewing slit of a tank and took aim. I watched for several seconds as his rifle swayed smoothly and the marksman sought the right moment for a precise shot. Finally, he pressed the trigger, and the tank turned to one side, carried on for several more metres and came to a halt. Our gunners seized the moment and finished off the armour-plated beast. After the second or third hit the tank burst into flames. The German sub-machine gunners, unable to stand the sight of the spectacle, turned and fled.

The offensive had already lasted two hours and we were dropping with fatigue. Our division was moving towards the south-east to cut off the retreat of the enemy's Pushkin–Pavlovsk grouping. We spent the night to the accompaniment of artillery fire, but we were so tired that we slept soundly right on the snow, huddling up to one another. And in the morning, there was more fighting.

The commander of our regiment decided to take the enemy by surprise and at dawn the next morning we carried out an assault without the usual artillery softening-up. The rifle companies successfully made it to the enemy's forward trench and engaged in fierce hand-to-hand fighting, but we were unable immediately to get any further towards the settlement of Doni; the enemy mounted a counter-attack. With the fury of doomed men, the German ranks ran towards our positions and then rolled back under machine-gun fire, charged again and again withdrew. The artillery did not die down for a minute and, from the powder fumes, the snow had turned from white to ash-grey.

I turned an old shell hole into a firing point. Slightly to my right were the battalion commander and his liaison. I looked out. Right in front of us were enemy ranks, moving in short rushes. Behind the soldiers a German officer was striding confidently. His contorted face and the raised fur collar of his overcoat were clearly visible through my optical sight. I fired and the German fell; the Wehrmacht now had one officer fewer. Having lost their commander, the enemy soldiers began to drag their feet. Our company on the right flank took advantage of this and crushed the opposition with a dashing bayonet attack.

The fighting died down at night but sparked up with new vigour during the day. The soldiers were nodding off in the trenches, amidst the snow. We commanders walked around the dugouts and surviving pillboxes abandoned by the Germans, getting the men up onto their feet, so the Germans would not catch us by surprise. Some soldiers were clutching their sub-machine guns while still only half awake.

Bursting through on the east, the battalion came across a small river. It turned out to be our old acquaintance, the Izhora. There was a new command to prepare for an offensive and this time there were tanks in support. Within an hour and a half, the T-34s arrived. We hailed the tank crews, sat on the armour plating and advanced as part of a tank assault.

The company was drawn into battle on the edge of some small village. Huge conflagrations were blazing on the horizon and artillery and mortar squads were hammering the enemy forward line without a pause, while machine guns rattled away.

We launched one more attack and at this point an enemy machine gun opened fire at us from some ruins. I felt a heavy, dull blow in my leg and my whole body was transfixed by acute pain. I collapsed into the darkness.

I was wakened by the voice of our senior nurse, Lida Ivanova. She was telling someone that my life was not in jeopardy, but the wound had probably gone through to the bone. I opened my eyes and standing next to her was Kochubei. He bent over and kissed me. He cheered me up, and said that everything would be alright, that I would catch up with him at Berlin. I promised that I would definitely do so. Unfortunately, I was unable to go back to my own regiment.

I was dispatched to a hospital in Leningrad. On the second day the leg swelled up to huge proportions and turned blue, and my temperature rose. The doctor in charge said that the leg needed to be amputated immediately, but I categorically refused. They took an X-ray and it turned out that a small splinter had settled in the wound, struck the bone and introduced an infection. When I found this out, I decided to take it out on my own. I procured a metal spike for packing cigarettes and, when there was nobody in the ward, I rinsed it in a mug of hot tea and thrust it into the wound. I appeared to have moved the fragment because I felt a frightful pain throughout my entire body and passed out from it.

The returning nurses discovered me lying on the floor and told the doctor. I was sent to the operating theatre straight away and both the steel spike and the mortar splinter were extracted from my leg. In the end the doctors succeeded in saving the leg. Three weeks later I was walking, and on the eve of Red Army Day I heard on the radio that I had been awarded the title Hero of the Soviet Union. The edict from the USSR Supreme Soviet was subsequently published in the newspapers and, still incredulous, I read it several times.

After hospital I intended to return to the regiment, but I was called up into the front political administration. My old acquaintance, Lieutenant-Colonel Bichurin, sat me down beside him and asked about my plans. I said I intended to carry on fighting but I had given no thought as to what to do after the war. But it turned out that the political administration decided otherwise and I was sent as a cadet to a front-line course on training and retraining political staff.

A period of intense study began. We worked twelve hours a day and still contrived to fit in another hour or two before bedtime. I had not the slightest understanding of the subjects being studied up until then and I found the textbook on dialectical and historical materialism particularly hard going. So I studied right up until the end of the war. After completing the course, I earned the epaulettes of a junior lieutenant and, following this, I devoted another twenty years of my life to service in the Soviet Army.

4 Aleksandr Romanenko

BEFORE THE WAR WE LIVED in Bolshiye Chapurniki, the centre of the Krasnoarmeisky rural district of Stalingrad Region. I was only able to finish six grades at school. Then, after 1945, I completed my education at evening school and studied for another five years at a technical college. My elder brother Vasiliy, who was two years older than me, was on active service from the very beginning of the war. He worked his way up to becoming the deputy commander of a tank corps, was promoted to lieutenant-colonel, and lost his life in the battle for Berlin on 20 April 1945.

Meanwhile at our school in Chapurniki I took first place for small-bore rifle shooting. Then I won the district championship in the face of competition from boys in all sixteen district schools. I even surprised myself, scoring 50 points out of a possible 50, and I was awarded the 'Voroshilov Marksman' badge. That was how I managed to become a sniper.

When the Germans were approaching Stalingrad, we were evacuated across the Volga. My parents, my little sister Tamara and I set off on the long journey. At the end of 1942 the enemy was routed and we returned to the west bank of the Volga – not to our own village, which had been burnt to the ground, but to Svetly Yar. There we were told that those born in 1925 were being called up into the army, but not those born a year later. I got together with lads of the same age; we decided that this could not be the case and we headed for the recruitment office.

There we said that we had been born in 1925 but had no documents. The commissioner looked for our names in the lists, failed to find them and said we could go through when our documents were found. But at the moment we were too young and the army was no place for us.

What were we to do? I came up with another suggestion – that we tattoo '1925' on our arms and try to join up on that basis. We did so, waited ten days and went back to the recruitment office. The commissioner had left for Stalingrad on business. We approached his deputy and said we had been before, but no more than that. Again, he naturally failed to find us in the lists and once more asked for our documents. We replied that we had been in the evacuation and our documents had got lost and showed him our tattoos. He then gave us blank sheets of paper and asked us to write declarations in accordance with a set format to the effect that we wanted to serve at the front. Our call-up papers arrived several days later.

The recruitment commissioner arranged a meeting with us, said we would be sent off in a few days, explained what clothes we needed, and advised us to take enough food for three days.

We were called up on 6 April 1943, and driven out to the outskirts of Stalingrad. Everything around lay in ruins; all that was left was the old flour mill which the high command had used as its headquarters. A train of heated wagons was run up to the mill, and we were loaded aboard and taken off to Pugachov in Saratov Region.[1] An assembly point was located there, in dugouts on the edge of the town.

The day after our arrival representatives turned up from the junior officers' college, which was then situated in the town of Volsk.[2] Those of us from Stalingrad were lined up and sorted in terms of our fields of expertise, to which we were duly assigned on request. I immediately asked to join the snipers but, because of my short stature (I hadn't fully grown by then), they did not want to enrol me in a cadet sniper company. It was then that I was compelled to produce my 'Voroshilov Marksman' badge and accompanying documents. After that they didn't have the right to refuse me.

The college turned out to be from Belorussia – it had been evacuated along with its teaching staff to Volsk at the very beginning of the war.

As soon as we arrived, we were taken to the bath house. Our civilian clothes were gathered up and we were issued instead uniforms and boots with foot wrappings. On 1 May 1943, the company took the oath of service and at the same time we were accepted into the Komsomol. Training commenced, and went on for six months. We were kept busy for ten hours a day, with no days off.

The commander of our sniper company, a captain by rank, turned out to be a very experienced soldier of the old, pre-revolutionary, school. Unfortunately, I can't remember his name. First and foremost, he and the other officers taught us shooting. We used ordinary Three Lines – frequently and at great length. By the end of our training our typical distance was 800 metres, while the maximum allowed was 1,100 metres. A shot of 200–300 metres was considered practically point-blank. Optical sights enlarged the target four-fold, later seven-fold; you could look at a man from a distance of 800 metres and it was as if he was right beside you – to say nothing of closer distances. We were also taught to shoot in the dark in instances where there was some source of light ahead – a torch or, say, an illuminated window – because devices for night-time shooting had not yet been invented.

In the morning we would leave the college, mount a hill which was about 150–200 metres high, and train in a specially constructed area. We were taught to estimate the distance to the target and the force and direction of the wind, and shown how to camouflage ourselves and recognise false signals. We were trained to develop powers of attention, the ability to measure by eye, and keenness of sight. We were worked to exhaustion. Then we went down again for dinner, followed by classroom sessions.

The rations were such that we were hungry all the time so the small amount of money we were given was spent on buying tomatoes, cucumbers and other food. Those who smoked bought tobacco as well; traders sold it right by the college entrance. It was not issued to cadets during training and we began to receive it only later, at the front. It was there that I started smoking.

The company was divided into three platoons of thirty men. Each platoon slept on three-layered bunks in its own room. All the cadets were split into sniper pairs. My partner throughout my training, and then for the whole of the war, was a Tatar named Nariman, but I've forgotten what his surname was . . .

At the beginning of October 1943, when our training came to an end, we were given ranks. I, for instance, became a junior sergeant. We were read a command sending us to the front. A few days later we were piled into railway wagons and set off in a westerly direction – to the Ukraine, as it turned out. We travelled quickly; in a few days we ended up to the south of Kyiv as part of the 28th Guards Motorised Rifle Brigade within the 8th Guards Tank Corps of the 19th Army. The operation to cross the Dnieper and liberate Kyiv was reaching its climax, so you could say that we made it in time for the ball.

Fierce battles raged; the Germans attempted to dislodge our forces from the Bukrin bridgehead on the Dnieper, but failed to do so. We lined up to the rumble of guns, and the commander of the 28th Brigade, Colonel G. R. Pivnyev, greeted us and began trying to clarify what sort of men he had been sent. On learning that there were snipers among the reinforcements, he gave orders for a sniper group of eight to be established under the sub-machine gun company. For the time being he decided to leave the newly arrived reinforcements on the east bank, so that we could help ferry stuff to the bridgehead. He realised that raw, inexperienced recruits were scarcely likely to achieve much and would just sacrifice their lives for nothing. Therefore, he merely responded to our objections with the words: 'You'll get your share of fighting later.'

On the east bank of the Dnieper we unloaded and set up full-scale plywood models of tanks and, a little further from the river bank, dummy aircraft. They were manufactured and then camouflaged in such a masterly way that the enemy reconnaissance failed to discover that they were fake. On 6 November Kyiv was liberated and on the 10th we crossed to the west bank and took part in the fighting; we attacked the enemy with sub-machine guns in our hands as part of a tank assault.

Our sniper group comprised only Russians, with the exception of my friend Nariman. The sub-machine gun company included Ukrainians, Belorussians and Uzbeks, but there were never any conflicts on the basis of nationality because the personnel were young – born between 1923 and 1925. There were almost no older soldiers.

At the end of the month our worn-out 8th Guards Tank Corps was taken to the rear for re-formation and this took place in the Darnitsa district of Kyiv on the east bank of the Dnieper. We handed over our small amount of surviving equipment to other units, so that only the personnel remained.

We had not even had time to relax properly before the alarm was sounded once again one night. An order came through for us to move out along the highway leading to the river and take up defensive positions. By that time there were only 150–200 men left in the brigade and the tank crews had no weapons but their pistols. What were we to fight with? But the Germans were hurtling into a gap and the command was to resist them. It was a fierce but brief battle; our reserves soon arrived and the enemy retreated. Finally, we got to enjoy the regularity of life in the rear. We received some brand-new sniper rifles and set about adjusting them.

I was wounded while the corps was still in the process of re-formation. It happened like this: on 29 February 1944, we were roused by the alarm; while moving through the Zhitomir forests the commander of the First Ukrainian Front, Army General N. F. Vatutin, and his guard had ended up in an ambush and fought back. The men of our company were sent to bail the general out. The enemy who attacked were well armed with machine guns, but quickly realised that they had fallen into a trap and began to surrender. However, we had been ordered not take prisoners and we finished them all off.

I was running through a gully in the footsteps of a sub-machine gunner, when a tall German appeared ahead and threw a grenade. The explosion knocked both of us to the ground. The main force of the explosion and the shrapnel struck the sub-machine gunner, and he was badly crippled. I was also wounded. I tried to stand up but couldn't. Soon two other soldiers from our company arrived and a nurse. I was suffering from contusion of the knee joints and shrapnel wounds in my calves. The two of us who were wounded were loaded onto a vehicle along with a couple who had been killed and driven off to the medical centre, while the battle continued. The lads told me later that they had killed up to 100 Fritzes in the forest.

My wounds turned out to be too severe for the medical centre and on 3 March I was taken to Kyiv and put in hospital. I lay in the area for rank-and-file soldiers and somewhere alongside, in the area for officers, was General Vatutin. He died on 15 April from the wounds he had received in that ambush.

Things were still not going very well for me after the first week of treatment. There was no improvement and I could not stand up. Then the doctor in charge handed me over to some of the walking wounded to help me to learn to walk again. Thus, little by little, with their assistance, I began to put one foot in front of the other and in a week or two everything was back to normal. On 21 March a vehicle arrived at the hospital from our brigade to collect us – seven men plus nurse Katya, who was looking after us.

We were well fed at the front, especially when we were being deployed for action. But sometimes we would have to make do with bread and water for two or three days. This usually occurred when the corps was on the offensive and the field kitchens just could not keep up with us or were simply unable to reach us on account of the fighting. We did most of our fighting in large population centres. Our tanks by-passed the small ones, so there were often situations where nobody could get through to us.

For this reason, we almost never had baths set up for us. It only happened once. Usually, it was just a case of a tank of water heated with firewood in a tent. We took off all our clothes and shook them out over the tank, then the tank was heated and the garments in it were rid of lice. We once had an emergency when someone's tunic was carelessly hung; it made contact with the red-hot side of the tank and was set alight. The fire spread to other things and all our clothing was burnt. It was tragic and comical at the same time. The *starshina* had to issue us with new tunics and trousers.

The corps also put out its own newspaper. We were very well informed about the situation on the various fronts, in the country as a whole and in the world political arena. When there was time, the company was given copies of the newspaper *Krasnaia Zvezda* ('Red Star'), which was at that time the principal organ of our army. Our political education officer read it to us and conducted political information sessions about the situation in the Soviet Union and the world at large. As chairman of the Komsomol branch for our company, I also organised political sessions on occasion.

Letters came from home and we answered them. Before the mail reached the addressee it was scrutinised by the censors and anything considered excessive detail was crossed out. The deputy political education officer warned us not to mention in our letters how many of us there were, where we were located, what sort of technology we had or where units were positioned. So, we mainly just tried to write that we were still alive and well, fighting, and missing home. That was all.

By the beginning of May our corps had completed re-formation and was sent to Belorussia, where it formed a grouping with the 2nd Tank Army of the First Belorussian Front. The army was under the command of Colonel-General Semyon Bogdanov and the front as a whole was under General Konstantin Rokossovsky. Under their leadership we were faced with the prospect of liberating sixteen towns and cities in Belorussia and Poland before reaching East Prussia.

We had barely come to ourselves upon arrival before action began. The corps was generally fighting its way in the direction of Lublin. Finally, we burst through and were ordered to capture the city in twenty-four hours. But that was not so easy. The front was forbidden to bomb and destroy Lublin with shells, so that whole burden of cleaning it out lay on us riflemen. Block by block and house by house we took it back from the Germans.

The Germans had turned almost every house into a fortress. Considerable forces had gathered here, including Banderites[3] and other such riff-raff. They all fought with the tenacity of condemned men.

Our sniper group was faced with the task of eliminating machine gunners. I killed a couple, while Nariman dealt with an officer and a sub-machine gunner.

At the end of the second day of street fighting, Army Commander Bogdanov came to see our brigade. He viewed the situation from an armoured carrier, but failed to consider that right in front of our forward line stood a huge Catholic church, where an enemy sniper in the bell tower was keeping watch. He seriously wounded the general in the shoulder. Bogdanov was swiftly bandaged up and taken away, while the company commander gave our pairing the order to wipe out the marksman.

We sought out a suitable multi-storey building in no-man's land and climbed up into its attic, made a hole in the tiled roof and began to keep watch – we had binoculars with us. A sniper's most important quality is patience. Sometimes we had to sit for two days in the same place and watch. My partner Nariman had one shortcoming – after twenty minutes of observation through binoculars his eyes began to water from tiredness. I could hold out longer than he could. We would change roles to allow for this quirk of his.

On this occasion Nariman turned out to be the more attentive; several minutes after a routine change, he showed me where our target was hiding. I caught him in my lens and fired, after which we instantly moved to another part of the attic.

It grew dark. We had a break, and a snack – we had something with us – and then suddenly we heard the cautious steps of someone climbing the stairs. We fell silent and soon saw against the attic window the shape of a man in German uniform with a sniper's rifle in his hands. I quietly nudged Nariman, he fired, and the enemy fell. We then sat there for a very long time, apprehensive that more Germans would come up but, as it happened, nobody appeared.

With first light we continued our observation and my partner managed to uncover another enemy sniper. At his prompting I quickly found him and eliminated him. Several minutes later yet another artillery barrage started, after which our T-34 tanks began rumbling along the paved road – our forces were on the move. We found the German Nariman had killed in the attic, then went into the church, where we discovered two more riflemen we had killed, collected all their weapons and documents, and set off back to our company. The thing was that our company commander demanded that, after completing a mission, we should bring him back the sniper's rifle as confirmation, or, in the case of machine gunners, some component from the enemy machine gun. And documents had to be retrieved at all costs. There were no cases in our group of mis-attributing other men's successes.

We got back from the church and reported to the company commander, backing up our words with material evidence. Beside him was the deputy political education officer, who was delighted and expressed his gratitude to us: 'That's what I call real stalking, a real prize. Well done!' As a result of the action undertaken by our corps Lublin was liberated on 24 June.

Readers may have formed the impression that the German snipers were 'weak', but that is not the case at all. They were better trained than us. Even though I knocked out half a dozen enemy snipers, I realised this only too well. They also came after us, inflicted losses on us and stalked our snipers, machine gunners and officers. After we had lost yet another of our comrades, we would convene a meeting, and discuss each case, so that we could avoid futile losses next time.

We did not use captured weapons in combat; we were more accustomed to operating with our own Mosins, and there were enough of them. There was even a reserve of them; when two lads from our group were wounded, their weapons remained in the company. Also at the disposal of our company commander was a solidly built American truck and all our weapons and cartridge stocks were kept on the back of it.

After the capture of Lublin our 28th Guards Motorised Rifle Brigade received orders to advance to the town of Praga on the outskirts of Warsaw. We broke through after a few brief engagements and by 11 September 1944, we were into the suburbs. The Germans had turned this population centre into one of their best-equipped strongpoints. This was facilitated by the large number of concrete buildings and other constructions there. Our forces took three days to capture it. There were numerous enemy machine-gun posts, which meant there would be plenty of work for us snipers.

Nariman and I were sent off to support the rifle battalion. The commander of the company to which we were attached gave us a detailed outline of the situation on the forward line. We set off there and selected a firing position for ourselves in the attic of a three-storey building. There, we removed several tiles from the roof and began to keep watch.

The first day of the assault on the city was coming to an end. By then I had already managed to wipe out one machine gunner, but my shot was picked up by a German sniper. The next time I stuck the barrel of my rifle through the hole in the roof, he fired . . . and the bullet hit the stock of my Three Line. I immediately crouched down. This was the first time an enemy marksman had spotted me.

I examined my rifle; it was still possible to continue firing with it. I moved over to the other half of the attic, found a crack in the roof and began to keep watch with binoculars. I discovered my adversary quite quickly, raised the rifle and fired without poking it outside. It soon got dark and Nariman and I went down and reported what we had done to the commander of the infantry company.

The next day our corps completely liberated Praga. I knocked out one more machine gunner and another sniper. A German had tracked one of our staff officers and killed him as he got out of a car. As a result, he became my special objective, which I successfully fulfilled. On 14 September the corps left the now liberated town of Praga behind and moved on further.

Another interesting incident occurred in the town of Nowe Miasto.[4] Our tanks and infantry burst into it in the early morning and fierce street battles ensued. The company commander called Nariman and me up and ordered us to wipe out an enemy machine gunner who was firing from the third floor of a building and preventing our sub-machine gunners from coming out from under cover.

We occupied a convenient position and began to keep watch. We worked out that our target was about 700 metres away. I prepared to fire and pressed the trigger as soon as the machine gun began its next round. The machine gun fell silent, but very quickly started up again. I fired a second time and he fell silent for ever. When our company had liberated this block, we entered the building from which our adversary had been firing, went up to the third floor and discovered two Germans; one lay dead and the other, mortally wounded in the chest, was barely breathing. We liberated Nowe Miasto towards evening on 17 January 1945.

We were well fitted out for winter combat; we were issued wadded trousers and jackets, overcoats and warm caps. We did not freeze, but at the end of 1944 I got frostbite in one ear; I had been lying in the snow in a frost for two hours before dark. We had been spotted and subjected to such bombardment that we couldn't move. I still feel the consequences of this today.

With regard to footwear, all we had were boots with foot wrappings; high boots were only issued after the war. We were not provided with camouflage clothing; we did our fighting mainly in the cities, so it was simply unnecessary.

We had a good reception from the local population in Poland. The Poles called us all brothers and comrades and often invited us to have a drink with them.

At the end of 1944 I got to meet Marshal Rokossovsky. We were still on Polish territory by the border with Germany and preparing for a new offensive. Seven of us were standing next to a staff vehicle and listening to the radio. At this point a whole column of traffic approached – armoured vehicles and automobiles – and from one of the cars emerged a senior military dignitary, who headed towards us. Our officer gave the command: 'Attention!' and reported to him that we were listening to the latest news from Moscow. It was Marshal Rokossovsky.

He shook hands with each of us and asked how we were feeling and how ready we were to thrash the Nazis in their own den. One of us said loudly: 'The Russians have always thrashed the Prussians!' Rokossovsky smiled and said: 'True, the Russians have always thrashed the Prussians. But what are the words of Suvorov that we should remember now?' There was a pause. Then the marshal prompted us: 'Every soldier must know his role.' He shook our hands again and wished us success in our combat on German territory.

By the time we moved into East Prussia, the majority of the local population had already fled. On the whole we were met by young people from the Soviet Union – Russians, Ukrainians and Belorussians who had been brought here to work. I did not encounter cases of the local population being subjected to violence from our soldiers and did not hear of anything like that occurring. We ran into captured Romanians, Hungarians and Czechs. They were glad that everything had turned out the way it did and called us '*Kamaraden*'; the majority of them had only fought because they were forced to.

I particularly remember the battle for Danzig [now Gdansk]. The advance units of the corps invaded the bounds of this port city on 27 March 1945. The tanks and sub-machine gunners stormed the first buildings, while we sat 'unemployed', waiting our turn. By evening we had begun to clear the streets. The sub-machine gunners knocked out the enemy anti-tank gunners. They were the most feared opponent for our tank crews. As a rule, they fired from the second or third floors of buildings. If they hit the engine, they would immediately put the tank out of action.

We came to the Kashubian canal, where our Lieutenant Ilyin was hit in the chest by a bullet while on a bridge. It was clearly a sniper. The company commander called up Nariman and me and ordered us to wipe him out. We took up a position in a fourteen-storey building. Observing through our optical sights for the rest of the day, we closely watched the houses beyond the canal, trying to guess where our opponent might be hiding. The observation continued from sunrise the next morning. And this is when fortune smiled upon us; in one of the blown-out window gaps we picked up the glint of glass; the sun was shining in his direction. The sniper had taken up a position behind the blinds on the top floor of a building in a neighbouring block across the canal. With more intensive observation we saw the blind move and the barrel of a rifle. This time our Three Lines fired simultaneously.

When the tanks and infantry of our corps finally crossed the canal and cleared the block occupied by the enemy, we entered this house under the cover of two sub-machine gunners and beheld the following scene: the door was open, by the window stood a small table and, on a chair next to it, sat the dead marksman with his sniper rifle in his hands. A second dead marksman, also with a sniper rifle, lay behind him on the floor. Apparently, the one sitting at the table was the spotter and the other one was doing the firing. Nariman's and my shots had killed them both. We of course were very glad; in fact, you could say we were delighted. We gathered up their rifles, documents and set off back to the company to report. It was a victory we had achieved from the greatest distance we had fired from in the entire war – around 800 metres. Usually, we fired from 350 to 500 metres, sometimes 700 metres. We did most of our fighting in city blocks.

After the taking of Danzig our 8th Guards Tank Corps was temporarily removed from the battle line and assembled close to the city. We had barely got ourselves in order again when a new command came – to make a forced march in the direction of Berlin and to concentrate 70 km from the enemy capital in the town of Prenzlau. Our units were following the forces of the Second Belorussian Front, so that we conducted no further military action up until the River Oder. We stopped in Prenzlau and began to wait for the order to move on to Berlin. Instead of this a message arrived in the evening of 2 May 1945 that Berlin had been taken.

The company commander ordered us to go there to obtain provisions and to try to get something to drink. We travelled in captured German trucks. There were only five of us, including a Belorussian lad who had a good knowledge of German. On entering the city, we were stopped by some German in civilian dress. Our Belorussian asked: 'Where are the storehouses?' The man agreed to show him.

We came to some storehouses. All the bottom storeys had been flooded and guards had been posted. We set off to find some others, but there were guards there too. We made an agreement with them that they would close their eyes to what we were doing for an hour and, with the local Germans, help us load up. We packed the truck up to the awning with food and drink; it would have been looted in any case.

We decided to call on this German to thank him for showing us where the stores were. It turned out that he was actually looking to see how he could get food for his family. We drove to his house on the outskirts of Berlin, left the vehicle under guard and called in. We were met by some women, no longer young, who began to ask us something. The Belorussian translated. It turned out that they were concerned that we were looking for young girls for our amusement. We had never even considered this and were surprised. We arranged a small feast in the home of this German. We sat down, drank a glass each and then went back to the unit. There we handed over everything we had obtained to the company commander and he distributed it among the platoons.

Another German soon appeared in our brigade. He told us that he knew the bank vaults in which valuables belonging to the Fund for the Defence of Germany were held. Senior Lieutenant Uvarov was summoned and ordered to put them under guard. We travelled out to the location and found the bank; the building had been destroyed. We had to clear the rubble to get through to the safes in the basement. I didn't see them myself – I was keeping watch – but Nariman told me later that they had found a few crowbars there and opened two safes. Then in the evening senior officers arrived in cars and trucks with the bank proprietor.

At midnight some personnel from the security forces descended on us and began to check things. It was only years later, after I had returned home, that I found out that our company commander had been arrested for stealing some valuables, sentenced to eight years and had all his decorations removed. A sergeant was taken away with him, but later released; he was a subordinate who had merely carried out the commands of his senior officer. Our Uvarov was lucky; if anything like this had occurred during military operations, he would simply have been shot.

After this our corps commander started jokingly referring to our company as the 'gold-diggers', implying that we were aiming to get our hands on some 30 million rubles.

We celebrated Victory Day in Prenzlau. We went to bed as usual, but then suddenly firing broke out from machine and flare guns. Everyone was shouting: 'Victory! Victory!' We were very glad; we had long awaited it, fought our way through 400 km of territory for the sake of it, losing friends and comrades along the way. Our losses were very significant. We acknowledged that and remembered the fallen.

On the day after, four of us who were friends from the same regiment took a walk round Prenzlau. It was approaching dinner time and we decided to have a snack. We found a bench, sat down, poured ourselves

100 grams each, toasted the victory and had a bite with it. Some local kids came up to us. From the very first day they had shown no fear of us and seemingly appreciated the kindly nature of the Russian soldier. At this point Nariman said that it would be good to give them some sweets. But our fellow serviceman Kolya replied to him: 'Yes, but what's the good of sweets? You can see the hunger in their eyes.' We called them over. To make sure they would not be too scared, we said the first few words in German: '*Kommen*'. They came up and we gave them all the food we had. They quickly gobbled it down without chewing; they were starving. Then they bowed, thanked us and went away happy.

We did not take any trophies in Germany. The only German object I have from the war is a silver spoon given to me by my partner Nariman – that and another one a bit smaller. But I gave it to my sister Tamara.

Right through my war years, 1943 to 1945, I fought as a sniper. I did not take part in reconnaissance and attacks. My basic objective was to wipe out snipers and machine gunners and I carried it out. If we saw a soldier on his own, we did not fire. There was no point in giving away our position for the sake of such 'small fry' and there was the immediate risk that an enemy sniper would spot us. After each shot, we tried to change positions.

I had twenty-nine confirmed kills, six of them against snipers. I saw all those I killed with my own eyes and produced evidence for each of them, so I can be sure of these twenty-nine Nazis. In other cases, of course, as a rule, we would fire and there would be no one there – or other Germans would take the body away with them, or we would miss.

Each of us was given a personal sniper record booklet. We got them back after the war when the commander of our company was arrested. Unfortunately, I no longer have mine. Right before demobilisation I was appointed head of the brigade's motorised company. I had an office where I kept a suitcase containing my things. One day we went out on a major training exercise and, in my absence, somebody stole my personal effects, including this booklet. I had to resurrect the list of my kills from expressions of appreciation on the part of commanders, six of which came from the supreme commander-in-chief, Stalin. They were sent to our unit, and then the commanders would decide who to give them to. The last one was for Königsberg, but it got lost in the post after I sent it home to my mother.

Military Career and Sniper Tally of A. N. Romanenko *(from the veteran soldier's personal recollections)*			
Russia			
No.	*Location*	*Victims*	*Class of Enemy*
1.	Smerdyn	1	Sub-machine gunner
2.	Torgovishche	1	Machine gunner
Poland			
3.	Lublin	2	Snipers
4.	Lublin	2	Machine gunners
5.	Minsk-Mazowiecki	1	Machine gunner
6.	Praga-Warsaw	2	Machine gunners
7.	Praga-Warsaw	2	Snipers
8.	Ciechanów	2	Sub-machine gunners
9.	Nowe Miasto	1	Machine gunner
10.	Działdowo[5]	1	Officer
East Prussia[6]			
11.	Deutsch-Eylau	2	Machine gunners
12.	Saalfeld	2	Machine gunners
13.	Mewe	1	Sub-machine gunner
14.	Starogard	3	Machine gunners
15.	Königsberg	4	Machine gunners
16.	Danzig	2	Snipers
	Total	29	

I was awarded the medal 'For Valour' for my part in the liberation of the Polish cities of Lublin, Minsk-Mazowiecki, Praga, Ciechanów, Nowe Miasto, and Działdowo. I was presented with the Order of the Red Star for the Prussian cities of Deutsch-Eylau, Saalfeld, Mewe, Starogard, Königsberg and Danzig. I had been recommended for another Red Star when we were near Berlin, but our brigade's staff car was blown up by a mine, and details of all our further decorations were burnt up with it. There were several cans of petrol in the car boot, so nothing survived.

In May 1945 our unit was redirected to Belorussia. The brigade commander and his chief of staff were immediately demobilised and a new command team appointed which had not served before and did not know us. We wrote to the decorations department in Moscow, but they replied that they could not help. In other words, we should seek out our old commanders and renew the document submission process. But where were we to start looking? With this everything came to an end.

I also have medals 'For the liberation of Belorussia', 'For the capture of Königsberg', and 'For victory over Germany', as well as the Order of the War for the Fatherland, 2nd Class. We invariably 'baptised' our decorations. When eight medals 'For Valour' were awarded to our entire sniper team, we put them in a pot, filled it to the top with vodka and circulated it around the group. Only when we had drunk it all did we retrieve the medals and attach them to our tunics – and without even bothering to check the numbers to see which ones belonged to whom. And so they remained, all mis-assigned.

Decorations were handed out in the intervals between battles. The company was assembled on parade and the certificates, orders, medals and attached documents were presented with due ceremony. Some staff officers came specially for the occasion.

Our losses in the sub-machine gun company were significant. There were not infrequent cases where we were bombed by our own planes. We were continuously on the offensive and from above it was difficult to gauge which troops were ours and which were the enemy's. The artillery would fire when necessary and extinguish every living thing in front of us. But sometimes the shells missed their target and landed in our lines. There were many such victims. By the end of the war only three out of the original eight remained in our sniper group, and they had all been wounded. Two of us were killed and three transferred to other units.

The dead were interred by a burial team, but sometimes we riflemen had to do it ourselves. We dug a grave to knee depth and wrapped the dead in their own waterproof capes, laid them down, filled in the grave and left a piece of plywood on a stick, on which it was inscribed who was buried here. Then the place and circumstances of death were reported to the brigade. Special teams followed us up and they took care of any further arrangements.

Nobody took the personal possessions of the dead as souvenirs; we collected only documents and decorations and that was just to hand them in or send them to relatives. We discarded identification medallions and did not even bother to fill in the form inside them.

Despite the heavy losses and fierce nature of the fighting I personally never encountered cases of treachery or desertion. We had volunteered for the army by adding a year to our age. Why would we bother to hide? We had no penal troops among us or blocking units and knew of their existence only from hearsay. We heard of course about Stalin's command no. 227 'Not a step back!' It emerged during the retreat towards my home town of Stalingrad. I believe it was the correct command. If only it had been in force from the beginning of the war! And when we began to advance, there was no need for it or for blocking detachments.

Our corps remained in Germany until 22 May 1945. Then we were put on trains and transferred to the city of Brest in Belorussia. From there we made our own way to some place in the forests about twenty kilometres from the city, constructed dugouts and lived there for a long time. We had a lot of equipment, nobody came to relieve us, and therefore there were never enough troops to man it.

We still had a year of our term to serve. Only at the end of 1946 were we transferred to a military township in Novogrudka, and then, in April 1947, to Pukhovichi,[7] another military township. In October I was put in charge of a motorised company and issued with a driving licence.

Here in Pukhovichi I gave up smoking, and I did so on account of a girl. I went off to a bank in town to collected the money due to us for our decorations – twenty-five rubles for the medal 'For Valour' and fifteen for the Order of the Red Star. I met her at the bank and we started going out together. But then we were both sent off for further study and, when I got back, it turned out that the girl had gone to work in Minsk and not left her address. With that our acquaintance came to an end.

I was only demobilised on 25 March 1950, having served twelve whole years in the army.

5 Klavdia Kalugina

I WAS FIFTEEN YEARS OLD WHEN THE WAR STARTED. In order to be able to feed myself I went to work at the 'Respirator' factory in Orekhovo-Zuyeva,[1] where you received 700 grams of bread per day – a real feast. While still working I joined the Komsomol and, as a member, I underwent military training and received a secondary education. Immediately upon finishing the course we were told that the Central Committee of the Komsomol had opened a sniper school. Many willingly put their names down for it and I was one of the volunteers.

We laid out the training area ourselves – dug trenches, knocked together the target boards. I was from an ordinary family; as a child I chopped firewood and fetched water, so I was accustomed to heavy physical work. I acquitted myself well when we were building the training ground. Those in charge noted my enthusiasm and I was even given a leave pass for home.

At the school we were taught shooting, tactics and the art of camouflage. And also ballistics – about the flight of a bullet. We fired from distances of 200, 300 and 400 metres; although the rifle could hit a target up to 2,000 metres away, the maximum distance for precision shooting was considered to be 800. Night-time shooting was organised for us, as well as firing with a cross-wind, and at moving targets. In the last-mentioned case, half the girls fired, while the others turned the handles to make the targets move. For those who moved the targets along there were special trenches, some nice and deep, others shallow.

God forbid that you should end up in a shallow trench – you would be lying flat in the snow all day and rip off your foot wrappings when you came in. All the girls suffered from sore feet after this.

While we were lining up and still in our civilian dress, I was assigned Marusya Chigvintseva as a partner. She was from the city of Izhevsk in Udmurtia[2] – snipers basically operated in pairs. Because we were standing side by side, they paired us up. We became friends – wild horses couldn't drag us apart. We trained together and went around together. A sniper platoon section comprised six pairs – twelve girls in total.

Shooting did not come easily to me at first – I messed up every time. Then the commander of our section, Zinayida Andreyevna Barantseva, took me in hand. Thanks to her, after nine months of instruction I graduated from the school with good marks. The better students were rewarded with American gifts received by Lend-Lease.

And so, thirty-six of us, girl snipers were dispatched on 2 March 1944 to the 344th Rifle Division in the 33rd Army of the Belorussian Front near Orsha. We travelled in railway wagons heated by stoves, but we did not go as far as the forward line. We were unloaded in a bare field in the middle of a snow storm and a truck was provided to take us to a reserve regiment. We ended up towing this truck practically the whole way – the snow was very deep.

I no longer recall how long it took to get to the front – a day, two days, three. At the reserve regiment headquarters we were issued camouflage suits and bandages to wrap around our rifles and disguise them. The initial plan was to send us all off to the 1,152nd Rifle Regiment, but then our three platoon sections were distributed among the division's regiments; twelve girls went to the 1,152nd, twelve to the 1,154th, and the rest, including Marusya and me, to the 1,156th.

We reached our regiment. In the early morning we were fed breakfast, given some sandwiches with American spam to take with us, and sent off to the trenches. Along with our rifles we were required to carry two grenades: one for the Nazis, the second for ourselves. The chances of a sniper surviving capture were zero, so we had no intention of being taken alive. Our rifles were well calibrated Three Lines furnished with optical sights. Every girl had to have a bayonet (in case we were required to join an attack), a spade, mess tin and pack of bandages.

On our first day on the forward line deep snow lay all around – a snow storm had raged for several days beforehand, and all the trenches were filled with snow. We were dreadfully afraid, but Nadya Loginova plucked up courage and crawled into no-man's land, which was mined. We called her back: 'Nadya, over here, over here!' She returned and we crawled into our trench. Each pairing had an assigned trench. They were about 500 metres in length and each was defended by something like fifty soldiers, ten of whom kept watch in turn at night.

The trench assigned to Marusya and me turned out to be snow-bound. It was the same for the Germans. We could see them brandishing their spades, digging themselves out. That day we could have knocked off a dozen of them, but we were still inexperienced and afraid of everything, and therefore we just watched. And besides, killing someone for the first time is a hard step to face, so that day we did not dare to press the trigger.

But another of our pairs, comprising Zina Gavrilova, a former partisan, and the secretary of the Komsomol branch Tanya Fedorova actually opened their tally. We felt very ashamed before them. All night we upbraided ourselves: 'What cowards we are! Why did we come to the front?' But the following day dawned and we saw an enemy machine-gun nest right in front of our trench. One of the crew was clearing the snow from the machine-gun tripod, and I shot him. The others dragged him away by the feet. So, this German became my first victim. The weather soon turned warmer and the snow melted.

In our sector of the front there was a lake on the enemy side. The Germans used to wash in it and run round in their underwear – until Zoya Gavrilova killed one of them.

We snipers were not subordinate to a regiment, but attached to the regimental commander's command post. We fired from various distances – from 200 metres and from 1,200 metres. But that came later – in Belorussia on defence the Germans were very close to us. I don't remember how many Germans I shot all in all. Only those we wiped out on defence were attributed to us; those killed when were on an attack did not count. We were not supposed to take part in any attacks, but we did.

If we managed to eliminate an enemy soldier while on defence, the command of the detachment in whose sector this had taken place would write a note for our commanders and we took it with us. Of course, the enemy could have survived our shot, merely be wounded, or even completely unharmed, but how could you tell? So, if he fell, he was registered as killed.

We went out stalking only in the daytime; at night we did not operate. We took up our position before it got light – usually in a trench dug by some advanced military outpost. We would fire just a single precise shot – that was all we were allowed, or else we would be discovered – and as soon as it got dark, we went back to our lines. Marusya was always with me – just an arm's length away.

We used our optical sights in preference to field glasses – they offered good vision, as far as two kilometres. We were in control of a forward line 800 metres in width. When I grew tired of observing, I would whisper to Marusya: 'I've had enough,' and she would take over, looking through the sights of her rifle. Our principal targets were the enemy command post, observers, snipers, signallers and machine-gun nests.

The front on our sector stopped moving before summer. Those around us kept advancing, but the enemy defence in front of us was so strong that at first the commanders had no wish to storm it. The Germans were cautious and rarely exposed themselves, so that our activity turned into a continuous long watch by the gun port; we kept watch during the day and soldiers took over at night.

It happened on 19 June, right before the offensive. My partner Marusya Chigvintseva and I had thrust a rifle into a gun port and we were taking turns at observing the enemy forward line through our optical sights. We swapped places because, if you watched for too long, your eyes got tired and your attention waned. Marusya said to me: 'Let me get up now.' While we were changing places, she accidentally moved a rifle. There was bright sun shining that day, a patch of light struck the sights and, as soon as Marusya got up from the gun port, a shot resounded and she fell.

I began to bawl out so loudly that I could be heard along the whole trench. The others calmed me down and said: 'Quiet, quiet, or else they'll open fire with mortars.' But how could I stay quiet if my friend had been killed? She had kind of sensed something that day; she did not want to go out to the forward line. She begged the commander to let her off, but he did not listen to her and she perished. I felt that I was now living for both of us – for myself and for her.

We duly buried Marusya and her grave was sprinkled all over with wild flowers. Apart from that loss, Nadya Loginova was wounded. Soon the offensive began, so there was no time to catch and deal with the enemy sniper who had shot Chigvintseva. I was given a new partner, another Marusya – Marusya Gulyakina. One day soon after, we heard the sound of artillery. Then the 'Katyushas'[3] opened fire. When they were in action, shivers ran down your spine. After the bombardment ceased, the infantry dashed forward in the assault, along paths through the German minefields that our sappers had secretly cleared at night.

In this battle we operated at first as medical orderlies – we dragged the wounded away from the forward line. I recall dragging one officer, who had a small suitcase. We had neither slept nor eaten since four in the morning and could barely walk, and he clung on to this suitcase. 'Take it with me,' he insisted. 'Leave it where it is,' we argued. Well, we took it. What could we do? Then, at a gathering of veterans after the war, we found out that he had a small violin in the case.

The day was declining towards evening, and still we could not drive the Germans out of their trenches, which changed hands several times. The commanders rounded up our entire sniper group, medical orderlies, horsemen and local residents, and we carried all the wounded we could to the rear. Then our platoon section came back and guarded the trenches while the surviving soldiers slept. Dreadful death cries could be heard from the German trenches, where the enemy were bayonetting those of our wounded who had remained behind there.

The area in front of us had been completely cleared of mines. Earlier, before the offensive, the barbed-wire barriers on no-man's land were hung with tin cans which jangled if anyone touched them. Now this was generally no longer the case; the enemy could counter-attack at any moment. I stood there, staring into the darkness – nothing was visible. By four o'clock I was dreadfully tired. I hadn't slept for 24 hours and all day I had been carrying our lads to the rear. The commander of one platoon – Lieutenant Menkulevyan – spent the whole night going from one girl to another, checking that they had not fallen asleep. But we were all ears.

In the morning reinforcements recruited from among the Belorussians were sent up. There was another artillery bombardment, and our forces moved ahead, ran up to the enemy trenches, only to find them empty. Evidently, the Germans had taken such a battering the previous day that they couldn't hold out and began to retreat. We were barely able to keep up with them and caught up with them only on 29 June next to the Dnieper.

On one side we were being attacked across a rye field, and on the other we were facing tanks. On one flank there was a hilltop, from which a sniper machine gunner opened fire. He made our riflemen go to ground and they couldn't raise their heads.

Lying near me was the regimental chief of staff, Aleksey Titaiev. He was wearing a cap with a brightly coloured peak, and he was almost mown down in the first volley. He turned blue and collapsed on the ground. Our regimental commander, Leonid Yerdyukov, shouted to us: 'Wipe them out!' We twelve girl snipers opened fire and of course knocked them all out – a whole enemy machine-gun squad.

During those engagements I hit the two most distant targets – a machine gunner and a sniper. They were sitting in a barn that was perhaps a kilometre away. I was able to hit targets up to two kilometres away.

Our soldiers rose from their positions and pursued the enemy across the Dnieper, while we began to carry the wounded away. I went up to one of them, begin to lift him, and his innards spilled out. I did not know what to do, said I would immediately call a medical orderly, and crawled on further. It was terribly hot that day and when I came back the wounded man had already turned black. Zina Gavrilova crawled up either to this soldier or to another one also wounded in the stomach. She told us later: 'He grabbed me by the arm and his hand went stiff. I thought I would never drag my arm away. But he had most likely decided that, if I didn't take him, nobody else would. And so, he died. I then crawled out with another soldier in tow, and he died too.'

We were the last to cross the Dnieper. The boat capsized and we fell head-first into the water. Then some lads came to the rescue and retrieved our rifles from the bottom of the river.

We crossed to the opposite bank and were greeted by the sight of our regimental commander hitting a young, beefy-looking German lad. We went up and asked why he was beating a German prisoner. His answer was that this was no German, but a neighbour of his and one of Vlasov's men.[4] In the end Yerdyukov killed him.

The offensive continued and the regiment bore heavy losses. Our sniper section also lost personnel. My partner Marusya Gulyakina (who had rejoined us after already being wounded) was wounded for the second time. Fedorova, Irina Grachyova and other girls whose names I no longer remember also suffered wounds. I was suffering from blast effects but was not taken to the rear. The medical centres had their hands full dealing with those who had lost arms and legs. And what had I suffered? Just a pea-sized hole in my tunic and near-deafness. What was the point of me going? So I stayed.

During that fighting our scout neighbours organised a dinner and managed to cover the whole table with treats. They had come across some German stores and brought back so much chocolate! We simply gorged ourselves on it.

In the meantime, the Third Belorussian Front was advancing further and further westward and soon our regiment set foot on Polish territory, where it got caught in a salient – when the enemy surrounds you on three sides like a horseshoe. Our regiment had to withdraw. We tied rags on all the metal objects which were liable to jangle: weapons, mess tins, spades. We made our way out of the salient and we were transferred to the Leningrad Front. I cannot at the moment say how many days it took to get there, but it was a long time. The Germans tried to bomb us and at one time there was even an aerial battle above us – shell splinters sprinkled from the sky.

We slept on the bare earth – we spread out our wadded coats and lay down. We practically froze to death. An accordion player would strike up a tune and shout out to us: 'Let's all dance to get warm,' and we would start dancing. It did help. One day we came across a completely empty house and crammed into it so densely that, however tiny I might have been (only 157 cm in height), I couldn't find a place to lie down. There was a small trough for cutting up cabbage, so I had the choice of sleeping in it or going outside. I decided to settle down in the trough. But it was uncomfortable – either an arm or a leg would slide out, and there was always somebody shoving and pushing. Although I felt sleepy, I could not get to sleep. Fortunately, somebody went out and I immediately took his place, so managed to get couple of hours of normal sleep before reveille.

In Leningrad Region we advanced after the snow had melted. The area was practically one big swamp. Water would accumulate in horses' hoofprints. We washed in this water and were sometimes forced to drink it.

Another advance and we were in the Baltic. I remember reaching the sea and seeing an enemy steamship on fire in the harbour. And a field next to the sea thickly strewn with the bodies of troops from penal units. We had pinned the enemy to the seashore and these units had been thrown into the attack first. And there they all fell in battle. The wind was blowing mainly from the sea and the stench of corpses made it difficult to breathe.

On 10 January 1945 the Germans counter-attacked in East Prussia, captured our trench, took some of the girls from our section prisoner, and then proceeded to kill them. That was how Klava Manakhova perished. Only one soldier survived from that trench. There was an abandoned dugout there, not even a dugout, but a hole in the ground covered with a waterproof cape, well camouflaged and covered with snow. He sat there all day and all night until we took the trench back.

Then came Königsberg, where our section was not involved in the fighting. A sniper was generally supposed to remain on defence and not go on the offensive, and so at the end of the war they stopped taking us into attacks. And the war finished soon after. I remember a stream of German prisoners being herded past us for several days. All we were doing then was eating and catching up on sleep, and they kept coming, and coming, and coming. Then the high command found some work for us; we had to get up in the morning and go out to clear pathways and make flower borders. They overloaded us so that the girls would not get up to mischief as a result of having nothing to do. Then we were all set free to go home.

6 Antonina Kotlyarova

I AM A MUSCOVITE, BORN IN 1923. By the time the war began, I had already completed Grade 8 at School No. 1 in Lenin District. It was situated next to the Tretyakov Gallery in Tomachey Lane. My classmates and I were actually strolling in the park at the Permanent Agricultural Exhibition when we heard the radio announcement that Foreign Minister Vyacheslav Molotov would be giving a speech. Everyone for some reason ran to Central Square. Molotov announced that Nazi Germany had perfidiously attacked our country.

I immediately went home. My parents and those of my future husband Kolya had been specifically instructed where they were to go in the event of war breaking out. Kolya's father set off for the headquarters of Moscow's Lenin District council; subsequently, as an officer in the reserve, he was involved in organising the Moscow home guard, fought at the front, and traversed the whole distance from Moscow to Berlin. My own father had no such status and went to the front as a rank-and-file soldier.

Lads our age were not yet being taken into the army, but Kolya managed to get himself called up. He fought as a tank-rider sub-machine gunner and occasionally came home from the front. I would ask him if it was scary out there, and he said no. His squad would hide behind the turret of a tank, go as far as the German ranks, fire at them, wait for the infantry to catch up and then advance further. In my stupidity I believed him, thinking it was really not scary, but when I ended up at the front myself, I found myself tormented by the question as to how such a beanpole – Kolya was just under two metres tall – could hide behind a tank turret. He was a sitting target.

I also requested a transfer to the front, but nothing came of it and I had to go to work as a turner at the Sergo Ordzhonikidze Lathe Manufacturing Plant. My daily ration was 800 grams of bread and I was constantly hungry. I would finish work, go to a bread shop on the Polyanka,[1] receive my bread ration, and split it in half. One portion I would eat, washing it down with water, leave the rest in my bedside drawer for the morning, and go to bed. But I could not sleep. I was still hungry and the bread was right next to me in the drawer. Unable to hold out, I would end up eating all of it and only then could I nod off. And the following day would be just the same.

When the air-raid alarm sounded, we were allowed to patrol the streets – we were wardens. Once, when we were standing next to a house, we looked up and saw that a window on the top floor was being systematically opened and shut. Clearly someone was sending a signal. Immediately afterwards a bomb hit the Maly Kamenny Bridge.[2] We reported this to our chief and he checked it out. It turned out there was some German woman living in the flat and she was signalling to her own side.

On 16 October there was a dreadful panic in Moscow. Apprehensive over the arrival of the Germans, many burned their copies of books by Lenin and Stalin. Although I too had their complete collected works, I did not burn or throw out a single volume. We went to the Kaluga exit from the city and chucked stones at the cars in which various senior officials were fleeing Moscow. The following day, or the day after that, I saw sackfuls of sugar and sweets being dragged away on sledges. People looted everything from the Red October confectionery factory.

By the beginning of 1942 the capital was empty; you rarely met anyone on the street. My factory was also evacuated, to Nizhny Tagil[3] but I didn't go. I had just been accepted as a member of the Komsomol and believed I should be fighting the Nazis. However, I was turned down again at the recruitment office and I had to find a new job. Situated by Kaluga Square (now October Square) back then was Trade College

No. 60 and I was given work there gathering up mortar bombs. Then I was employed stocking up firewood for the capital. After that I was sent to the Sasovo district of Ryazan Region.[4] On returning from there I managed nevertheless to achieve my objective, and I was taken into the anti-aircraft forces. My 50th AA Regiment was based at Bulatnikovo station.[5] At first, I served on a rangefinder. You had to spot the target through an eyepiece and the coordinates were passed on to the special device for controlling AA artillery fire and then on to the gun itself. I was only on the rangefinder for a short time and then transferred to the control equipment itself.

After the Germans had been driven back from Moscow, I learned that a Central Women's School for Sniper Training had been opened on Silikatnaia Street.[6] I left the AA and was accepted. At the school we all had our hair cut like boys, except for Marusya, who was sick that day and kept her long hair. I recall one day we were marching in formation from the dining hall, and one little girl called out: 'Mum, look at this gang of guys – and just one girl!' And there we were, all in trousers and, except for Marusya, all with short hair.

I graduated with distinction from the sniper school in November 1944 and, because my Kolya and both our fathers were fighting on the First Belorussian Front, I applied to go there. Apart from me and my partner Olya Vazhenina, about ten girls were sent to the same front. We ended up in the 143rd Rifle Division of the 47th Army. We first saw action in Praga, a district of Warsaw. Moreover, we fought as a single sniper squad – we asked not to be split up among different companies.

We operated in pairs. Olya and I would select a position and then occupy it before first light and begin observing. We tried to choose one in a spot that required no alteration to the natural setting. That was not easy because our position might turn out to be in a bare spot, while the Germans were always hidden in the forest or in bushes.

Here we learned through our own experience that practice differed markedly from the theory we were taught at the school. At the front everything was different. As it turned out, our service began not with a battle, but with a funeral. Through our inexperience on the first day a girl from Leningrad exposed herself to the enemy by looking through a gun port to see what the Germans were doing, and was killed. She stuck her head out and a bullet ricocheted off the wall and hit her just below the eye. This was the only loss our squad sustained during the entire war – except for Lena Medinskaia and Nina Mazyarova being wounded during an artillery attack, but they recuperated and rejoined our unit. We were all together right to the end.

However, we were not taught how to cope after killing someone for the first time in your life. I remember going back to my unit afterwards and being approached by a journalist asking questions and wanting an interview. I don't even recall how I answered him; I could not eat or drink either that day or the next, I was so upset. I knew that he was a Nazi, that he and they had killed, burnt and hanged Soviet people, but he was still a human being.

I still felt awful when I killed my second victim. Before firing I managed to get a good look at him through my sights. He was a young officer. He seemed to be looking straight at me and I shot him. But it was a human being! Then my feelings dulled and I went on killing the way we were supposed to.

Usually it happened like this: Olya and I would lie an arm's length from each other. Of necessity we spoke quietly because the Germans could be very close to us. The Fritzes tried to listen to us and their outposts were a bit better organised that ours. You strove not to move and, as a result, with time your whole body tended to grow numb, but it was impossible to stretch your muscles or move your rifle; it was locked into your shoulder, with your finger invariably on the trigger, and you were ready at any moment to press it. The range for a precision shot was up to 800 metres. Your sector of observation was right in front of you and your rifle was adjusted accordingly. You waited till a target appeared and, when it came into range, you fired.

If I saw a target, I would say: 'Olya, he's mine,' and she would know she did not have to fire; it was my turn. I would fire and then assist her to make observations. Or I might detect something and give her directions: 'There behind that house, there beyond the bush.' She would know where to look, then take aim and fire. We operated every day without a break; before first light we were out at our positions and we only left them when it got dark. The soldiers were very good to us, looked after us and didn't molest us; now and then they would toss us a bar of chocolate or some such thing.

But then came the siege of Warsaw.

Apart from rifles, we were issued with sub-machine guns, and we carried not two grenades as before, but five. When attacking a building a sniper's rifle is no use – you can be killed ten times over while taking aim. So we fought like sub-machine gunners. But there were times when your rifle came to the rescue. You would look through your sights and see there was more than a single German there, toss a grenade at them, and advance further. That was how we liberated Warsaw.

Then came the crossing of the Vistula. We women snipers plus 5–7 men were left holding a particular patch of high ground, while our unit advanced further. We were there for two days, defending it. The Germans did not know how many of us there were, or else they would have crushed us all of course. But as things were, they were afraid. At night they tried to grab a prisoner for interrogation, but that didn't work out. We didn't allow it.

While rebuffing enemy attacks I had occasion to fire both a medium machine gun and an anti-tank rifle that had a very strong kick. My sniper rifle was not the best weapon and I just used its sights for observation. We held the hill nevertheless and on the third day our own troops came by. From the entire group we lost only one lad. He appeared to sense that he would die soon: he just sat there, a sad figure, and did not go near the gun port or the machine gun. I did not see how he faced death.

Another time we snipers were sent along with some riflemen to comb a forest. It was right at the end of the war, there were few soldiers left, and therefore we went into the wood with sub-machine guns at the ready and our rifles on our backs. We ventured in from one side, while our scouts entered from the other. Thus, the two lines came together and captured those in between. I let one boy go – did not kill him or take him prisoner. He was such a runt, and I had a younger brother in Moscow of roughly the same age. Of course, I shouldn't have done this, but I let him be.

At the town of Deutsch-Krone in Poland[6] things were quite different. It is located in a forest. We had liberated it, taken many prisoners and gone on further, when we were told that the Germans had captured it again. It turned out that we had scattered them and they had hidden in the woods till we left and then gone back. We were so angry that we spared nobody. We killed a whole heap of them.

Our quartermaster always lagged behind during the offensive and we remained hungry. We would liberate a settlement, go into a house, and find the food on the kitchen range still warm. The girls would urge me: 'Go on, Tonya, try it,' and, like a fool, I did. It never entered my head that maybe it was poisoned. But I would sample it, the others would watch to check I didn't die on the spot and then tuck in.

For us the war ended on the Elbe. We were billeted in German houses and at rest when the alarm was sounded at 3 o'clock in the morning. There was shooting in the vicinity. We could not understand what was happening – surely it wasn't the Fritzes? It turned out that the end of the war had just been announced. We ran into the cellar, found some kind of swill, drank it with jam, and laughed and wept from joy.

We did not send parcels home, although that was permitted – we were soldiers, not some sort of looters. We merely changed our clothes at the Germans' expense; you would go into a house, open a cupboard and select some petticoat, trousers or underwear – nothing more than that. The girls completely stopped wearing foot wrappings and instead each put on five or six pairs of silk or cotton stockings.

I was caught out by all these changes of clothing. We had no packs with us, having long since left them with the quartermaster, and our gas masks too. We carried only our weapons, cartridges, grenades and the clothes on our backs. Just before the very end of the war I called at one house, where I found clean underwear tied with ribbons in a wardrobe. I did not pause to examine the quality, changed everything, and then it turned out that it was covered in darned patches. So I arrived back in Moscow in a darned petticoat.

 Victor Shcherbakov

I WAS BORN ON 26 OCTOBER 1926, in the village of Starosaratovsky, in the Novopokrovskaia district of Orenburg Region.[1] Although I was only little then, I remember the collective farm being formed – the way people began to smile and come together as a social group. With its establishment life became easier.

The population of our village comprised mainly Cossacks; every man served in the cavalry. My father too had a sabre, harness and saddle and a cavalry horse assigned to him. All the horses were kept in a collective farm stable, but the cavalry mounts were not allowed to be used as draught animals; they were only available for light work, for example, riding somewhere. We were fully familiar with these horses and we would feed them extra treats.

The 1933 famine affected Orenburg Region too. You could say the population of our whole village subsisted on grass. With other boys I would sneak through into the stable, where horse feed from the threshing floor lay in a heap. The surviving grains in it would fall to the very bottom and we would grab them along with the soil and take them home. Our mothers picked the grains out of this rubbish and added it to our food.

However, gradually life got better. The collective farm was issued a 1½-ton truck from the first batch produced by the Gorky automobile works and a wheeled tractor. But not everyone liked it and, when we had finished sowing, in which the tractor was very helpful, somebody set fire to it. The whole village wept. Another time someone burnt down the barn with our seed grain in it.

But in general, we did not live too badly before the war: everyone had a cow – there was always milk on the table – chickens and sheep. We could slaughter a ram for a special occasion. And the food at the collective farm's outstation was all right.

After I had completed seven classes at school, a year before the war, my parents sent me away to an industrial technical college in Orsk.[2] With the outbreak of war, we were transferred to a factory which had been evacuated to the city. Turners' lathes were set up in an abandoned church and we turned bodies for mortar bombs on them. About three days after the beginning of the war a recruiting office representative arrived in the village with a call-up summons for all reservists; they mounted their horses and off they went. Among them was my father.

He said goodbye to us and we never saw him again. Only one letter ever came, from an assembly point near Orenburg. I have never been able to find out where my father lost his life.

A friend of my father – the head of a collective farm work team – later returned from the front with one arm missing and said that my father was still alive at the time when he was wounded. This man had once caught his son and me stealing peas from a collective farm field when food was short. He thrashed us both with a horse whip, leaving bloody welts. My mother tried to talk to him, but he replied that there would be no indulgences for anyone; he was a man of principle.

I was called up on 15 October 1943, several days before my seventeenth birthday. I was in no hurry to get to the front, but I had no particular fear of it. Altogether there were six of us called up from the village and, without asking whether we wanted to go there or not, they sent us the village of Koltubanovka in the Buzuluk forest park[3] – site of the No. 12 Regional School of Sniper Training for Superior Marksmen. Standing in the forest were some big, long dugout barracks, about eighty metres in length and topped with logs. They were half sunk into the ground so that the bottom edge of the windows was at ground level. The log roof was covered with earth and camouflaged with moss and grass.

There were 250 men in each barrack block. The interior furnishings comprised bunks and four pot-bellied stoves. I spent almost six months in this school – I was retained afterwards to help train new arrivals. But the majority of the lads called up with me left earlier after quite a short period of training.

We were taught the art of sniping and the tactics involved in operating as a sniper. For instance, if the unit was on defence, you were supposed to go out to no-man's land at night and dig and camouflage a trench. And you could only occupy it and leave it under the darkness of night. We also studied the sniper rifle – a Three-Line with telescopic sights (I don't know what kind they were, or I don't remember). We were not told anything about the enemy snipers' tactics.

We spent a lot of time on shooting practice. I would struggle to remember how many shots I took during our period of training, but we were taken to the range at least twice a week. We began by firing at a target of a head from a distance of 100 metres, then went on to chest-level targets at 200–250 metres, followed by waist-level targets at 300–350 metres and, finally, full-length targets at 600–800 metres. The only thing we were not taught was night-time shooting, but we had no special devices for it. What we were taught was to keep a journal of our observations: what we saw, when and near what landmarks. Then you had to report it. If you didn't, you could expect to be told off and rostered to peel potatoes or something like that.

On duty in the kitchen, we were kept under constant watch because we were always hungry. Nobody would want to eat raw potatoes, but no one would give you boiled ones. I once spent three days in the guardhouse on account of potatoes. Next to the kitchen lay a storage pit which had been entirely picked over, but one of the cadets found out that there were still the remains of some tubers lying there under the snow. The two of us ventured out, cleared away the snow and dug out the potatoes. In the frost they seemed quite normal and firm, but when we put them in the stove, they disintegrated. We were both given three days for theft.

The teaching staff, officers and sergeants, had all been discharged from front-line service. They taught in a very disciplined fashion and did not spare us because they realised things would be much tougher at the front. For example, one day I had to sit from dawn to dusk up a tree in a sniper position. When I was taken down, my feet were numb. And we were shod in ordinary boots with foot wrappings rather than in felt boots, even though it was winter and the frosts were dreadfully harsh.

Generally speaking, we were very poorly clad – in uniforms which had been taken from those who had been killed or had died, and been laundered and darned, puttees 1.6 to 1.8 metres in length, and old leather boots with soles that kept coming off. Knee boots would have been better – puttees took a long time to put on when the alarm sounded. Besides, they were impossible to dry; there were a lot of people in the barracks, and only four stoves, so you couldn't get through to them.

Because we were poorly dressed, many cadets suffered from kidney problems owing to exposure to cold, resulting in incontinence or enuresis. They could not be accommodated on the top layers of bunks. But in time they practically all began to wet their pants and the question arose as to where they were to sleep.

Things were also pretty awful with regard to food. We were fed on dishwater with grain, of which there was so little that you could barely see it in the bowl. A bath tub of this hogwash was placed on each table and the monitor ladled it into bowls. Each tub contained two or three salted tomatoes which he divided up in the end between all those sitting at the table. Everyone was allotted 100 grams of bread to go with the soup, which did not quell your hunger. We couldn't wait to get to the front, mainly so we could eat our fill, and I was very upset when the lads departed and I was left behind to coach the newbies. By that time, I was shooting very poorly.

On graduating from the school, I was given the rank of corporal, issued a new uniform and designated a 'sniper-destroyer'. The thing is that snipers operated in pairs: one kept constant watch on the enemy, while the other, the sniper-destroyer, took it easy. As soon as a target of interest appeared, the observer informed the destroyer, who eliminated it. The snipers took up positions 5–6 metres apart. We could speak in a whisper and still hear each other very well.

Following graduation, representatives of front-line units came to the school, put me and other graduates on a train and took us off to the front. We had not been given any weapons at the school and travelled westward unarmed. Nobody told us where we were going and only after some time did a rumour go round that we were heading for Romania. This now June 1944 and our forces crossed the border shortly afterwards. It was also rumoured that we were to be enlisted in the naval infantry.

Finally came the long-awaited command to disembark. I don't know where they had brought us, but after a march of a month and a half we ended up in Poland at the Sandomierz bridgehead.[4] Along the way we were equipped and armed and I arrived in the forward area with a sniper rifle and a pack of 100 cartridges. And yes, I was able to eat properly at last. We were given nourishing food: soup, porridge, noodles or something similar and a piece of meat. We even had field kitchens with us on the march, so we did not go hungry.

In order to avoid bombing raids, we made our way to the Sandomierz bridgehead at night only. It was forbidden to light camp fires; the smoke could give us away during the daytime and the flame at night. From the flashes of artillery firing and flares hanging in the sky we realised that we were near the forward line. Our night-time marches were lengthy; we grew tired and often slept by the roadside during halts. Sometimes troops would roll into the gutter while asleep. They were duly stood up and brought round, and on we went.

In the end we reached our destination and then sat for a month on defence. The rains came. The soil on the forward line was clay, so there was mud everywhere and our overcoats were stiff with it. We lived in foxholes dug out from trench walls. In order to get warm, we would go to a small dugout where a fire was lit out of the Germans' sight. That was the only place where you could dry off.

There was another way of getting warm; each day 100 grams of 'regulation' spirit was issued, but back then I neither drank nor smoked. The senior soldiers, already grown men, who regarded my partner and me as children, would give us all their sugar in return for our tobacco and vodka.

On arrival I became a sniper subordinate to the battalion commander, although I was enlisted in a sub-machine gun platoon and messed with them. It was usually my task to observe and eliminate officers and those 'doing a runner'. By the latter term we did not mean deserters from our forces but rather Germans dashing from one trench to another. Most often they were signallers; ordinary soldiers would not behave like that. The sector requiring surveillance was given to me each day by the battalion commander personally. Apart from that, he advised me when and on what sector our scouts would be crossing the front-line, and so on. Apart from our pairing, with its battalion role, each company was supposed to have a couple of snipers assigned to it, but there were never enough to go round, so sometimes you saw them, sometimes not.

There were 400 metres between our trenches and the German ones. No-man's land and the enemy forward line were easily visible and that simplified my work. I hardly ever used any extra camouflaging, but just concealed my firing position with turf and shoved some grass under my helmet. I wore my helmet constantly; this was essential for a sniper.

We generally used the most ordinary ammunition. In addition, we took with us twenty armour-piercing cartridges just in case, but we rarely fired them.

I had the same partner right through from sniper school, so we called each other by our first names. He was armed with the usual Three Line, but always carried his eight-fold magnification binoculars.

We received our baptism of fire on 12 January 1945, near the village of Szydlow[5] right at the start of our offensive. I later found out that in front of it 250 artillery pieces were concentrated on our sector of the front. But we did not know about this and for us the artillery softening up was completely unexpected. It was the most frightening experience I endured in the entire war. When the cannonade began, I could not feel my cap on my head – my hair was standing up on end. You cannot imagine what it is like when such a conglomeration of artillery lets fly. But what would it have been like for the Germans? All the shells discharged by this armada were flying directly at them. Particularly terrifying were the Katyusha rockets. On the German side the earth seethed like water boiling in a cauldron.

Thanks to the bombardment we traversed the first 20 kilometres without meeting any resistance. The first, second and third lines of enemy trenches turned out to be empty; there were no Germans there, either living or dead. I noticed only two or three bodies; the other dead had been either churned up with the earth or taken away by the survivors. It is possible of course that the Germans fled immediately or had been led away earlier.

Our losses over these 20 kilometres were due only to slackness, where troops failed to follow the tank tracks, because the whole area around was densely mined. I particularly remember one Uzbek being blown up. All his fellow-tribesmen dashed over to him in a herd and began to set mines off too.

The tanks darted ahead. We could not keep up with them, and we had only the regimental artillery with us for support. We occupied a burnt village, beyond which there was a rise with a trench running across it. Here the Germans had set up a machine-gun ambush. Every 150–300 metres stood machine guns which opened fire murderously when our infantry drew close. The companies suffered big losses and went to ground.

All this time I was with the battalion staff and therefore remained a little behind the advancing lines. The battalion commander ordered my partner and me to wipe out some of the machine-gun nests.

Not far away stood a small single-storeyed house and we clambered up to its attic, removed the tiles from part of the sloping roof that faced the Germans and began to keep watch. Our companies went into the attack one more time, the machine guns opened fire, and we began to shoot at the machine gunners. Whether we killed them or not, I don't know, but we silenced the guns. Two of them remained lying on the parapet and our companies were able to cross the trench. I reported to the commander that his orders had been fulfilled.

I recall one other incident – in Germany. We had occupied half a village which was divided in two by a gravel road. The battalion commander ordered me to keep watch on the enemy half. I looked and saw an enemy officer appear from somewhere. I did not realise that it was a mannequin and drilled its head with lead. As a result, a German

A pair of cheerful Soviet snipers, perhaps counting recent successes. The soldier on the left has a standard Mosin Nagant 'Three Line' rifle fitted with a PEM sight.

Contributors to this book.

Top row, from left: Rem Altshuller (*Chapter 8*), Maria Bondarenko (*Chapter 13*), Petr Belyakov (*Chapter 9*);

Middle row: Anatoly Nevara (*Chapter 14*), Mikhail Budenkov (*Chapter 15*);

Bottom row: Klavdia Kalugina (*Chapter 5*), Fedor Dyachenko (*Chapter 3*), Victor Scherbakov (*Chapter 7*).

Snipers in training. A portrait of Hitler is prepared as a firing target while a group of students is practising in the background.

An instructor explains how to adjust the PEM sight.

Five high-scoring female snipers of Third Shock Army, pictured in 1943: (*left to right*) Aleksandra Shlyakova, Lidiya Vetrova, Nina Belobrova, Iya Golievskaya and Vera Artamonova. All recorded between 50 and 100 kills, emphasising the important role that these female combatants uniquely played in the Soviet forces.

Fedor Dyachenko (*Chapter 3*) adopts an action pose in a winter setting.

Nikolay Nadolko (*Chapter 10 – left*) in a studio image with an unidentified but well-decorated comrade.

Above: This watchful sniper has the Order of the Red Star.
Right: Antonina Kotlyarova (*Chapter 6*).

Above: A pair of snipers each wearing the Order of Lenin, one of the highest awards.

Left: Mamed Ali Abasov, who was a sniper with the 69th Marine Infantry Brigade (a Navy unit, not a Red Army one), is credited with 187 kills prior to a serious career-ending injury he sustained in December 1943.

Above: Vasiliy Korzanov (*Chapter 11*).

Left: Boris Godov, in later life (*Chapter 12*).

Left and below: Aleksandr Romanenko (*Chapter 3*) as a young soldier and later in life as a highly decorated veteran.

sniper spied my position behind a pile of firewood, from which I had removed some logs.

I sat there and continued keeping watch, and then I heard a bullet slam against a log. My position had been discovered and I had to change it urgently. I realised that an enemy sniper had worked out my location but I did not yet know that he was firing from a brick water tower. I withdrew into a trench. While I was making yet another dash, he fired again and fortunately the bullet flew past me. He was following me like my own shadow, the bastard.

I hid behind a house, but nothing was visible from there and I decided to seek out a new refuge. I made another five-metre dash and hid behind a tree which was only as thick as a man's arm. I remember it had netting wound around it so that rabbits would not gnaw the bark. A bullet landed right in its trunk and chips of wood sprayed me under my helmet. I jumped up, leapt over a fence and the enemy lost sight of me. Now it was my turn to track *him* down.

I kept watch for a long time, several hours, until I noticed an optical flash amidst the bricks of the water tower. I waited for the German sniper to expose himself to the maximum and fired. I don't know if I hit him or whether he just changed positions, but there was no more firing from that quarter.

I don't know how many victims there really were on my tally. I had a sniper's book for keeping count and recording what target I had hit and when. It had twenty-one entries, but I am only confident of five of them. One of these five was probably an officer; he emerged from a tank hatch and I definitely got him. In the other cases I am not sure; a man dropped, but what happened to him after that I have no idea.

I was wounded crossing the Oder. The crossing was organised as follows: the sappers strung a steel cable across the river, rafts were constructed from logs, and those on them crossed over holding on to this cable by means of special boards with holes in them. There were a number of these rafts and they moved 20–40 metres apart.

When my turn came to cross, a mortar attack began. The Oder at this point was not wide and at that time its banks were thickly covered with trees. The mortar bombs got caught in their crowns, which made them explode in the air, and we were showered with a hail of splinters from above. There was nowhere to hide, so many of our lads were killed on the rafts. Their bodies drifted down the river one after another and the river was red with blood.

We got off the rafts, but the barrage continued. I spotted a dead man lying there; I remember that he was a clean-shaven, middle-aged man of full figure. I crawled under him; he was already cold. On the one hand I was trembling with fear – he was a dead man after all and I was afraid to touch him – and, on the other, it was dangerous to get up from under him as the splinters were still flying all around. There was a pause in the German bombardment and I leapt out and hid behind a tree. And then it began again. Perhaps it had been unwise to come out from under the cover of that body; a shell splinter got me behind the tree; it ripped a hole in my boot, broke my ankle, and lodged in my foot. I grabbed it to pull it out and almost cried out; I had burnt my fingers. Then I wrapped my overcoat tails around it and gave it a tug. It was huge, twelve centimetres. I was lucky in that it had hit me at the end of its trajectory. Otherwise, it would have torn my foot off.

Afterwards I was taken back across the river on the same ferry and sent to a field hospital in the town of Czestochowa, site of the famous Polish Church of the Czestochowan Mother of God. The monastery was still standing on a hill and down below were various auxiliary buildings. That is where the hospital was.

I was put in plaster, which stretched up beyond the knee, and a sling was made to take the weight off my leg and stop it swelling. I lay for a couple of days on straw bedding, which served for a bed in the hospital, and then the lice descended on me. My leg under the plaster itched so much that I felt I was being eaten alive; I could hardly stand it. I recall that after that the front moved a long way forward and we were transferred to a now vacant barracks. If you asked for your leg to be raised a bit higher and thrust a stick under the plaster, the lice came spilling out – fat as anything, well fed on blood.

After twenty days, when the bone had knitted, the plaster was removed. The skin under it was covered with ulcers. They rubbed it with some kind of ointment and sent me back to the front.

This time I ended up in a team of twelve recuperating troops under the command of a *starshina* unknown to me who was following in the wake of some division. No transport was provided, so we went on foot. Sometimes we got a ride on a truck; sometimes we managed to procure bicycles. In Germany by that time the snow had already gone and the roads were clear, so we got as far as Dresden without any particular problems – until we were arrested, and not without cause. There were amongst us some who liked a drop or two and in one general's house we uncovered a cellar storing collectors' wines from the year 1812, which we drank with enormous pleasure. A patrol nabbed us and took us to the commandant, and from there we were taken back to our unit.

My military career ended in Czechoslovakia: I was a member of the force which liberated Lysá nad Labem, which is near Prague. Although the war officially ended on 9 May, we continued to fight the Vlasovites up until the 13th. These traitors were anxious to break through to the Americans, so they fought with real desperation.

# Rem Altshuller

I WAS BORN ON 11 SEPTEMBER 1926, in the town of Novo-Rzhev, Kalinin Region.[1] It is now part of Pskov Region. My father served in the border security services, while my mother worked as a teacher. My father had two brothers: Moisei was a sergeant in the naval infantry and Ilya was a lieutenant and commander of a mortar battery. He was at the Brest fortress when the war broke out and met his death there.

Father was constantly transferred from place to place and therefore our family lived in a variety of locations, even in the Far East. But after he was subjected to yet another transfer, this time to Uzbekistan, I was sent back to my grandmother in Kalinin Region; she lived close to Novo-Rzhev on a large housing estate called Bezhenitsy, where our entire family resided. My father was soon transferred to Leningrad and my parents rented two small rooms in Pulkovo[2] – at that time a large village on the turn-off to Pushkin[3] and I began to live with them.

It was my ambition as a child to gain the 'Young Voroshilov Marksman' badge. You couldn't buy one; it had to be earned. It meant achieving forty hits out of fifty with a small-bore rifle, but I could never manage it.

In the summer of 1940, I was on holiday in a Pioneer camp near Luga,[4] where we had some activities conducted by a military trainer getting on in years. One day he turned up with the news that some real military rifles – Mosins – had been delivered. He selected some of the stronger boys to undertake shooting tests with them, and I was included. We were issued special small cushions to place behind the rifle butt in order to reduce the force of the recoil. In order to gain a badge, you had to record 35 hits from 50 shots at a range of 50 metres. We fired several times and I finally managed to meet the standard, with 42 out of 50. To my profound disappointment the trainer turned out not to have any badges with him. I didn't give him a moment's peace and for over a year I went every two weeks to his home on Khalturin Street, until finally in the spring of 1941 he gave me the unfortunate badge. I have kept it to this day.

Before the outbreak of war, I had completed the seventh grade in Leningrad's No. 22 junior high school and my mother and I went for a holiday in Pskov Region, not far from my grandmother's place. I remember how I first heard the news of war; in the estate there was a powerful public address system with a home-made speaker. It was taken out of a building and placed on a window ledge, while a crowd gathered round.

I recall that several days later the Germans made an assault on the civil airport. The local lads dashed over there armed with hunting rifles and small-bore weapons. None of them ever came back. I remember, too, going to see Grandma and my mother imploring her, almost on her knees, to come back to Leningrad with us, but she absolutely refused. Back then people did not yet know how the Germans treated Jews. Consequently, my grandmother did not survive the war.

My mother and I set off home on the last train and travelled via Pskov, which was already ablaze. Somewhere in the region of Sushchyovo station two soldiers came into our compartment. They were very nice and told us they were travelling on a special mission. I remember very well that one of them had a medal 'For Military Service'. We spent an hour talking to them and then they got up and left. Practically every ten minutes thereafter NKVD security troops came running up – in their peaked caps with dark blue bands – and asking everyone whether they had seen two soldiers. When they asked my mother, she said that they had only just been sitting with us. At their request she gave a detailed description. It turned out that they were diversionists or saboteurs. I was stunned by the fluency of their Russian.

When we arrived in Leningrad, our apartment building was almost empty; some had left for the front, while others had been evacuated. We too soon gathered up our things and went to the Urals, where we settled in the village of Kusya-Aleksandrovskaia. Mother was taken on as a typist in some office and went to work at Uralzoloto, which mined diamonds needed for defence purposes. I worked first at a conveyor belt and then at the mining site; we transported the ore in trolleys along a narrow-gauge railway. There were not enough drivers, so I was soon sent on a course in Nizhny Tagil, returning when I had completed it.

When the Leningrad blockade was breached in 1943, an engineer from there joined us. He was looking for men for an organisation which delivered provisions to the city by water. I was keen to get to the front and had twice even tried to make a dash for it, but I was in a reserved occupation from which the authorities refused to release me. This engineer offered me an opportunity. I showed him my driving licence and he took me on. At my insistence he took my mother as well, although he did not particularly need her.

When we arrived in Leningrad, I was put in charge of a launch. Here too I tried to get rid of my reserved status, but my applications were either not accepted or simply torn up. This was until they began to issue vodka on our ration chits. I received my bottle, a friend gave me his, and I stuffed them under my shirt and headed off in the direction of Byeloostrov, towards the front. A military patrol would not let me through and turned me back. The soldiers refused to see things from my viewpoint as someone who was dying to fight. But then one of them noticed that I was concealing something in my clothing. He asked what it was and I told him. At first the troops didn't believe me and demanded to see it. Then I was asked to drink some of it, just in case it was poisoned. Although I had never tasted spirits before, I did as I was told. Then they took the bottles and pointed to a wood, where newly called-up troops were assembled and so-called 'shoppers' from various military units were recruiting.

It was there that I first saw the deputy of my future battalion commander, Junior Military Engineer Zalman Lvovich Kaminsky. From my grandmother I had picked up Yiddish, which is very similar to German, and I told him that I had a good knowledge of German. They set me a short exam and took me on with the words: 'Both speaks and understands German. Take him; he will come in useful.' In this way I became a rank-and-file soldier of the 129th Leningrad Guards Rifle Regiment, within the 45th Guards Order of Lenin, Red Banner Krasnoselsky Rifle Division and the 30th Leningrad Guards Rifle Corps.

First, I was enrolled in the 1st Company of the 1st Battalion and issued a uniform, boots and foot wrappings, a leather belt, helmet, and Shpagin sub-machine gun with a spare magazine. I was given a Red Army record booklet and even once taken to a shooting range. But then about a week later an officer arrived and we were lined up and asked who wanted to go on a sniper course. Of course, I instantly stepped forward.

It turned out to be a short-term course. I was issued a Three Line rifle, but with German Zeiss sights, and training began. If you calibrated it well, the Three Line was an excellent rifle, dependable and very simply constructed. The sight protruded quite a long way towards the stock and therefore the bolt handle on my rifle was bent over closer to the stock's forend, so that it wouldn't catch. The sight itself was better only in one respect – it had a rubber eye-shade. Our own model was a little longer and had no eye-shade and consequently the lads were apprehensive about the rifle's recoil, in case they damaged their eyes. As a result, accuracy tended to suffer. In other respects Soviet optics were just as good as the German.

Theoretical exercises alternated with practical ones. We began shooting from a distance of 100 metres, then worked up to 200 and then 400. Changing the distance required preliminary adjustment of the sight. The targets were at both waist and standing height. Apart from firing at them during the day we were taught night-time shooting. Special forked stands were made for this purpose. They were fixed in position after a shot had been taken. If a torch-beam appeared at night in the same place, the rifle was laid on the fork and a shot fired. The Germans had a lot of torches, so this kind of shooting could come in handy.

We were taught camouflaging, moving undetected from place to place, preparing basic and reserve firing positions, and operating in pairs. As a partner I was assigned Sonya Parfyonova, a Siberian from Tomsk. She was three years older than me and significantly larger – I was quite puny as a youth. I remember when we first met, she gave me a pitiful look. Only many years later did it become clear that she was feeling sorry for me – I was her third partner and she had lost the previous two. The main responsibility for the actual sniping lay on me; Sonya was supposed to cover my withdrawal in case of necessity.

After the course was over, I returned to the 1st Company, but now with a sniper rifle. Although it wasn't a new model, the previous owner had calibrated it superbly. If you aimed well and didn't breathe out at the wrong time, you were bound to hit the target. We used the most ordinary cartridges but we were taught to grease them very carefully before going out stalking, and then to wipe them dry. In winter we kept them close to our chest because, if you fired a frozen cartridge from a pouch, there would be a significant deviation, especially over long distances.

In summer we were not given camouflage gear and fought in ordinary infantry dress. In winter we were issued very warm underwear, a coat, wadded trousers, felt boots, and a camouflage suit with a hood, though not every rifleman was so well equipped. Your rifle was covered with a white cap and the sight had gauze wound around it. The same applied to the eyepiece because it could flash when you moved and give you away to an enemy marksman. We would take the cap off once we had got to our positions.

At that time our division was trying to penetrate the enemy defences and losses in the company were very high. So there were no sniper groups among us and we too were driven into each attack. On the course we were told that a sniper should advance slightly behind the other troops in order to cover them with his fire. But what talk could there be of 'behind' if your section commander was Vanya Budarin. He didn't care less whether you were a sniper or not; you had to advance or he would shoot you as a coward.

June 10th, 1944, saw the beginning of the offensive on the Karelian isthmus. We occupied the boundary the night before and, in the morning, a combined artillery softening-up attack began to thunder, after which we dashed across the River Sestra[5] on pontoons. There was no response from the Finns. Apparently, their high command realised that in a direct clash their formations had no chance. Therefore, they chose semi-partisan tactics: their mobile ranks prepared ambushes for us on the roads, in the forest, and on the former Mannerheim Line. Their soldiers were well trained and had a superb knowledge of the locality; true, they were not as well fed as the Germans. We bore significant losses from their activities and mines. There were a lot of booby-traps: you would walk into an abandoned house and there would be a mine under the floorboards. However, the Finns could not hold back our advance and within ten days we had liberated Vyborg. Our regiment did not enter the city, but went round it and camped on the site of the present-day settlement of Gvardeiskoye.

The Mannerheim Line had been destroyed by our forces back in 1940 and, with their meagre resources, the Finns were, of course, unable to restore it. However, they set up firing points within its ruins. What weapons didn't they possess! British, French, Swedish and German guns. We did not encounter any of the Finnish 'cuckoos', however.[6] That was understandable – climbing up a tree meant certain death; one shot and you would be spotted.

The company commanders did not like snipers and there is a simple explanation for this. Imagine the situation where a battalion is on the defensive and has adopted a relaxed, regular lifestyle. There were situations in which there might be only a single well for the whole neighbourhood, and both we and the enemy would use it in turn. And then a sniper like me comes along and kills some German or Finn and, in response, the other side begin to let off all their guns and mortars. Goodbye, peaceful existence! For that reason, snipers were particularly unwelcome, and in no small degree.

About twenty years after the war, I met a former colleague who was also a sniper. He wore two Orders of Glory on his chest. We got talking. I asked how many Germans he had killed. He gave me an intense look, laughed and said: 'Not a single one.' His deputy battalion commander had told him not to disturb the peace with the battalion; they would do for him what was necessary, and he would have notches on his rifle butt and decorations on his chest. Maybe this sniper was lying, but maybe not – there's no way of telling now. But this of course was an exceptional case. In the main our snipers were *real* snipers.

Following the capture of Vyborg, military action ceased and negotiations began. There were leaflets hung up along our lines warning troops to be vigilant and watch out for '*lahtars*',[7] that is, Finnish soldiers. But I still got wounded. A shell splinter grazed me and cut the skin. I was sent not to a hospital but to a regimental dressing station. After I had recovered, I was returned to my company in accordance with Stalin's order that wounded Guards should be sent back to their units upon recovery. From the outskirts of Vyborg, we were taken to the railway station, which is now called Kirillovskaia, but I can't for the life of me recall what it was called then. The carriages rolled up but there was nothing in them. Then we began to make do-it-yourself bunks from doors and window frames stripped from the station. The stationmaster ran up and down, shouting that he would not allow us to leave, that we had looted his entire station for the sake of bunks, but why should we care? Let him hold us up as long as he liked!

We arrived in Pskov Region and settled in not far from Lake Pskov. Reinforcements began to arrive. Those with experience were allocated platoon by platoon, but I remained in Vanya Budarin's. Given that conventional wisdom proclaimed that a platoon commander lasted one and a half attacks, Budarin was a survivor. In the new location he began to put us through the mill. He would get us up in the middle of the night, illuminating his map by torchlight, and set us a certain point to be reached by a particular time, and the platoon would make a forced march with full kit. We would be running at pace, but he would run beside us with a loaded pistol and demand that we go faster. We would get back to base, go to sleep again, and then it would all be repeated. Only after we had crossed Lake Pskov did we realise that Vanya was preparing us for an offensive.

Back then I was curious and attracted by anything mechanical, and Budarin entrusted me with mastering a 50-millimetre mortar. For me it turned out to be a simple enough matter. This weapon was small, light and very simple: a round baseplate, a barrel, a sight and a small stand;

it did not even have to be dismantled. The bombs were small, weighing only 900 grams. Beneath the barrel was a swivel washer which acted like a tap. If you turned it firmly, the ignition gases would enhance the shot, and the bomb would cover its maximum range. But if you released it, some of the gases would escape and the bomb would not travel so far.

On one occasion, however, I thoroughly disgraced myself with the mortar. On 18 September 1944, we were firing under light rain, and the soil got damp enough to become muddy. The lads were using their sub-machine guns and I had my sniper rifle, when up drove the corps commander, Lieutenant-General Nikolay Pavlovich Simonyak with the divisional commanders and other senior figures. Up until then I had never seen generals in my life, and especially in such numbers.

Budarin showed how well his detachment could shoot, but then he went and said that we had a mortar as a back-up. In other words, he pointed at me and said that I had mastered the art of mortar firing. 'Show us,' said the general, and Budarin shouted: 'Mortar over here!'

In my fright I completely released the washer. The platoon commander blew his whistle twice and those sitting in the trenches and raising the targets posted them and then withdrew as far as they could. Then he gave me the order to fire. I dropped the bomb down the barrel, the percussion cap clicked, and the bomb flew lazy as you like (since the ignition gases had all escaped) and plopped down just a few metres away from us. Our generals were battle-hardened, immediately sized up what was what and, without thinking too long, threw themselves to the ground, into the mud. Budarin and the entire platoon also took cover, while I alone remained resting on one knee by the mortar cannon. The bomb exploded, fortunately not injuring anyone with its splinters and the generals got up, covered me and the platoon commander with obscene abuse, and departed. Vanya subsequently had a few strong words with me too, but that was as far as the unpleasantries went.

With the start of the offensive, we crossed Lake Pskov on motor boats and fishing vessels and landed in Estonia, in the neighbourhood of the town of Kallaste. We then proceeded to the north of Tartu, until we came across a concentration camp. I shall never forget what happened there.

We saw six piles which the Germans had not had time to ignite. On a bed of logs soaked in diesel fuel lay a layer of human beings who had been shot through the back of the head and, on top of them, more logs and more people, and so on for three or four layers. My friend Sasha went up to a shed and opened the door. For the only time in my life, I saw someone instantaneously turn into an old man. No, he did not go grey. At the age of 22 or 23, which he was, he began to stoop.

I went up to him, as did the other lads, and the picture we beheld was horrific: children's shoes in rows and women's hair. Beside them worn children's clothing was packed in neat piles.

In the camp we took over thirty SS troops prisoner, mainly Estonians. After viewing what was being kept in the shed, our platoon commander Vanya Budarin turned to them, and I have never seen a more frightening facial expression. Not far away stood some large wooden latrines, each with around twenty holes in the seats. Vanya turned to me. 'Get some crowbars and spades,' he said. 'Tell the Germans to rip out the boards around these holes.' We went over to the Germans, explained what needed doing and showed them how. They did it.

Budarin then measured out a length of wire and ordered us to cut it up into as many identical strands as there were prisoners. Next, he ordered the SS men to put their hands behind their backs and us to tie them. We carried out the order. 'And now,' said the platoon commander, 'take them over there and drown them in the shit.' The lads obliged, about five of them, and the prisoners were all . . . Of course, they all screamed and struggled at meeting their death. It was just as well that we had tied them up beforehand.

At this point a second assault group arrived and Major Kondratyenko came running up, shouting' 'Where are the prisoners?' When we captured the camp, we had reported that there were some. Budarin pointed to the latrines, which had already been set alight: 'Over there.' When the major began to shout in fury: 'Who did that?', I stepped forward. Kondratyenko began to tear his pistol out of its holster, but at this point the platoon commander intervened, said that he had ordered it, asked the major to come and have a look at what was in the shed. When Kondratyenko came back, he asked what my surname was and said that, if he ever saw a recommendation for decorations with my name on it, he would tear it up personally.

Further on we fought our way across the River Emaigi (in Estonian its name translates as 'mother-river') and went on ahead. At first the weather was good, but then it turned sour, and this marked the beginning of what was for me the most arduous physical test of the entire war. I now understood why Budarin had driven us so mercilessly during battle training. We advanced under constant rain, day and night, at a rapid forced march, and this with full kit – weapons, ammunition and grenades. We would cover 40–45 km in a night. Transport for the entire battalion consisted of just one horse, which belonged to the battalion commander. He gave it to the radio operator, who carried our only radio transmitter, because communication was the most important thing. Machine guns, mortars, mortar bombs, shells – all that we carried on our own backs.

On one occasion a forced march of several kilometres under a downpour exhausted the soldiers. Finally, we were given a break and we dropped down in our overcoats on the side of the road, right in the mud. To our left was a large potato field.

Returning from reconnaissance, Vanya Baranov's scouts informed us that a hundred metres ahead was a huge barn full of straw. They had checked that there were no mines there. The battalion commander begged, literally implored the men to go there, but nobody even moved, that's how tired we were. It was not surprising: three days without sleep is no joke.

On seeing the state of things, the battalion commander commandeered several horses and carts from the Estonians and we loaded them with our machine guns, mortars, mortar bombs and some of the other baggage. Those who were particularly exhausted walked holding on to the carts. But there were cases of such men going to sleep on the move and falling down. They would be helped to their feet, given a shake and put back into position. One day we met a huge band of young women whom the Germans had herded on to some construction site. They realised that their own forces were approaching and ran to meet us. They hugged and kissed us, and we cursed and swore because they were not Germans; if fighting had broken out, we would at least have been able to lie down on the ground legitimately and have a rest. But, as it was, we had to keep going.

We reached the little town of Jõgeva and burst into the enemy trenches on its boundary. Three hundred metres to the right a German machine gun started firing from a window of the only house there still standing. 'What are you messing about for?' yelled Budarin. 'Take him out!' I turned round, fired several times and the machine gun fell silent.

At this time some of our assault aircraft flew over and we fired off flares in the direction of the Germans to show them the way. However, they quickly realised what was up and began to launch flares in response, but in our direction. As a result, the Ilyushins pounded us rather than the Germans with their cannon and rockets. They made two sorties. Right in front of me one of the medical orderlies had his cheek torn out, but he was smiling with the other one; he now had full rights to be evacuated to the rear.

The Germans and SS troops counter-attacked. They clearly outnumbered us, with ranks of 200 men. They advanced at full height, firing their sub-machine guns from the hip. It came down to hand-to-hand fighting. I was really skinny, weighing just forty-eight kilos, so there was no sense in me being involved. Budarin yelled at me to go to ground at the side and, if I saw him being taken prisoner, to kill him along with the Germans. He also gave me his Sudayev PPS sub-machine gun and retained just his Tokarev pistol.

Altogether in forty minutes of fighting there were seven enemy counter-attacks and, during two of them, the SS troops managed to get as far as our trenches. This led to hand-to-hand fighting involving bayonets and sapper spades. On one occasion, when the main German forces had drawn back, a German officer stayed behind. He went to ground behind a mound and began crawling towards our machine gun with the intention of pelting it with grenades. Budarin shouted at me to grab my rifle, or else that bastard would blow everything to kingdom come. I ran a little way forward and went to ground but, in my excitement, I was unable to take proper aim. First shot – missed, second shot – missed. The German was only forty metres away from the machine gun when I got him with what I think was my fourth shot. He half-rose from the pain, but then the machine gunners finished him off.

I was spotted by enemy mortarmen and the German machine gun at which I had been firing earlier started up on the flank. The company commander yelled at me to knock it out again. I hit it with the second shot, leaving the machine gunner hanging out of the window, while the gun fell to the ground. But this was what I was told later; I did not see it myself. A mortar bomb exploded beside me and I lost consciousness.

My partner Sonya noticed and shouted for an orderly to take me away, while she covered him. The orderly crawled towards me, but at this moment some Germans leapt out of the house and opened a hail of fire on us. But Sonya saved both of us and shot them down. True, she was hit by a bullet in the collar bone, after which she lost the use of her left arm and remained a life-long invalid. After the war she gave birth to three boys and a girl. She wrote to me in humorous vein that I must realise that as a non-believer, I could not be a godfather to her children, but was welcome to come and see them anyway.

The mortar explosion had merely knocked me out rather than wounded me, and within an hour and a half I came to – just as we were going into an attack. Volodya Klushin chased after an enemy officer, but the rounds in his magazine were exhausted. He unclipped the drum, which turned out to be an unfortunate step, and threw it at the German, who turned round and fired his pistol; the bullet hit Volodya in the left side of his chest, below the nipple. We gathered up his documents, and sent a death certificate to his home address ... and then fifteen years after the war I met him in Moscow. It turned out that the bullet had passed within a couple of millimetres of his heart just at the moment when the organ was contracting. That is what saved Volodya. That engagement cost us many, many men, but we managed to beat off the attack.

The offensive continued beyond Jõgeva and we soon broke out into a large grain field with stooks piled head-high. They stood in groups of a few stooks each, resting on one another like lean-to shelters. Our platoon dispersed and went ahead, and Budarin and I remained together. After the mortar explosion my rifle was clogged with soil and, in order to fire it, I needed to clean it, but there was no time. Then we saw a dead Fritz lying there with a carbine. The platoon commander told me to grab it, while he took the German's cartridges and gave them to me. The carbine turned out to be Belgian.

I shoved a cartridge into the chamber. 'Keep still,' said Vanya, as he took a magazine for his PPS, stuffed it with cartridges and once again told me to keep still. He finished what he was doing, installed the curved magazine and clicked the bolt. 'And now,' he said, 'you can fire.' I turned round and there were two hefty SS men crawling out of a stook 'lean-to' about eight to ten metres directly behind us.

I had never seen live Germans so close at hand. At first, I was struck dumb, but I still managed to fire at the nearer of the two. The bullet hit him in the cheek bone and came out through the back of his head. He turned to one side somehow and collapsed face first. Budarin in turn mowed down the second soldier.

Vanya went up to the Fritz I had killed, sat on his hips, took a razor out of his knapsack and asked: 'Do you shave?' I was unable to say a word; I froze. He threw away the razor along with something else and then took out a small orange box of the kind Germans used to keep margarine in. He unscrewed the lid, scraped out the remaining margarine with his finger, shoved it in his mouth, wiped his finger on the German's shoulder – the one that wasn't covered in blood – poured into it some tobacco from a pack, and stuck it in his pocket. 'Let's go,' he said. He had been at the front since 1942 and, in contrast to me, had been witness to all sorts, so this situation was just commonplace for him.

We caught up with our platoon on the march, while it was passing through some Estonian settlement. The local residents set up tables along the street and put out bowls with piles of rissoles, salted gherkins, basins of sour cream and bread. The kitchens could not keep pace with us, so that by the time Budarin and I got to the tables, the rissoles and sour cream had already all gone, However, we filled a helmet with gherkins and bread and ate our fill of them at our leisure. And some of the children gave us a rissole each.

We went on further. Here I was overcome by a strong urge for what I would apologetically term 'number twos'; seemingly, the recently consumed gherkins were making their presence felt. I turned off the road and squatted down under a bush – only to see a German officer in a similar pose right beside me. I dashed back to the road, just as I was, with my trousers down, shouting that there was a German there. Vanka Baranov and his scouts rushed over there, came back about 10–15 minutes later and gave me a Luger Parabellum, an expensive fountain pen and some boots from the dead man.

The boots were a luxurious pair, with inflexible shafts. I quickly removed my old rags and tried on the new trophy; they fitted me perfectly. The deputy battalion commander, Captain Ivanov, who was driving past at the time, began to pester me to exchange them for his specially sewn artificial rubber boots – which were not a bad pair either, but not as flash. He would not give up till I agreed, even though the lads tried to persuade me not to.

At night I felt nauseous and thought it was the result of what had happened during the day. Then someone was going about all night, shouting out our names: 'Altshuller, Kurunov, Gavrilov!' The lads concluded it was Captain Ivanov. We guessed the German boots must have shrunk on him overnight; so he couldn't walk in them and he was looking for me to get back his old rubber pair. In the morning it became clear that the reason was much more tragic than that. It turned out that the rissoles which we had been treated to were toxic. Those who ate them suffered from extreme food poisoning, and some of the lads went blind. Budarin and I were saved by the fact that we had eaten a great many gherkins and the liquid from them dissolved the poison. The two women responsible for this were later caught. One of them turned out to be a school teacher.

From the impact of all these experiences I forgot my captured Belgian carbine in a stook, when my sniper rifle had been lost, so I ended up with no weapon at all. But my friend Sasha did not panic and pinched one from a cart driver, who was bound to find another one; there were so many of our lads lying dead, with their weapons.

On the same day I was awarded the medal 'For Valour'. Our platoon dispersed around a field and ran into an assault. I caught sight of a rod underfoot about half a metre in length and enclosed in a case with a clasp, and bent over to see what it was. While I was sorting this out, the lads charged ahead and occupied a huge shed standing on a hill in the middle of the field. It turned out that what I had found was of absolutely no use to me, a spare barrel for a German machine gun, but there was no time to get upset about it; shots could be heard right beside me. I fell to the ground and crawled on my elbows in their direction.

It turned out that the fire was coming from a trench, where an enemy officer in a rubber-coated cape and peaked cap was standing with his back to me and pumping bullets from an automatic rifle into the shed where our company had taken refuge. It emerged later that the Germans had been storing their schnapps there and our lads had of course made a bee-line for it. I froze on the spot; for me it was too much – to see a live Fritz close up for the second time in a day.

The German soon used up the cartridges in his magazine and he turned side-on towards me in order to get another one from a canvas bag hanging on his belt. I was overcome by the idea that he was looking at me and in fright I gave him a burst in his left side, shoulder, neck . . . and again . . . and again, but he was still standing. My magazine was empty and he still hadn't fallen.

I ran round the trench and dashed towards the shed, where, it turned out, the German had managed to wound six lads from our company. They were still being bandaged up amidst a lot of noise, shouting and general uproar. Also there was our battalion commander, Major Sirotkin, who was cursing everyone, but to no avail; the company were all drunk. I reported that there was a Fritz in a trench firing at the shed. We went there, Sirotkin jumped into the trench, but the German was still standing. The major pushed him in the left shoulder and he fell down. It turned out that I had shattered his whole chest.

Found on the officer's body was a satchel containing a map showing all the enemy firing points. Sirotkin immediately summoned a radio operator and ordered him to convey that the 131st, 134th and our 129th Regiments must urgently suspend the offensive. Then he began to report the coordinates of the enemy firing points to make sure they were checked out. We sat there for forty minutes receiving reconnaissance results which indicated that these were valid firing points.

Then suddenly an armoured car stopped by the shed, followed by several jeeps. The corps commander, General Simonyak, whom I had quite recently forced to lie in the mud with my mortar, had arrived in person. He asked what the matter was, why the division was not advancing. Sirotkin reported what had happened. 'Have you got proof?' asked the general. 'We have,' and he was shown the body of the German I had killed. He asked who had fired and I was brought to his attention.

Without pausing to think too long, he turned to his adjutant and asked for a medal. The other handed him a medal 'For Valour' and he presented me with it himself on the spot. True, it was without the relevant documents, but they were later back-dated for me.

While all this was happening, our company inconspicuously stole back to the shed, and the schnapps. But in the meantime, some border troops in green peaked caps arrived and they riddled the whole lot with bullets. Our lads were adequately refuelled already, though.

After these engagements we stopped in a small place called Iru for relaxation and reinforcements; by that time our platoon alone had lost six or eight men. We were accommodated in a two-storeyed house. The owners had two or three cows and there was enough milk to bathe in. The detachments were assigned zones and the troops took turns at patrolling them. The front had gone a long way ahead, so we just rested and restored our strength.

At the very beginning of the offensive, when the platoon was just crossing Lake Pskov, machine gunner Igolkin had been wounded. It was all very inept. We were securing a road, when an Opel Blitz truck appeared suddenly from round a bend. Somebody threw a grenade, but it bounced off the vehicle and rebounded into our trench. Everyone leapt out, but Igolkin did not make it. We knocked out the truck; it plunged over a bridge into a river, and all the Fritzes were killed.

I went up to Igolkin. His fingers were hanging by shreds of muscle and skin. 'Come here and take out your knife,' he said. It was a dreadful spectacle: blood, flesh, mud – all mixed together. I was about to take my knife out, but then thought better of it and shouted to the lads to take him to the regimental medical centre.

Two months went by and our platoon had a visit from the *starshina*, Vanya Filimonenko, a hefty Ukrainian, swarthy of complexion, with fists like big rocks. 'Bring me Altshuller!' he yelled. Everyone was puzzled. What had happened? Vanya walked away, and behind him stood Igolkin holding a huge bottle of moonshine in his hands, which had all their fingers complete. It turned out they had treated him, sewed his fingers back and helped him to get them functioning, and when he had recovered, he came back to us, in accordance with Stalin's order that all Guards should be returned to their units. We all got drunk. Igolkin told us he would make us drink until we could only crawl on all fours. Thanks be to God, he survived the war and went back home to Siberia.

But now reinforcements had arrived and Vanya Budarin began to put us through our paces again; the war was not yet over. After a short break we went back to the front. It was October 1944. We were transported in heated railway wagons but the food along the way was very poor.

Smirnov, our company captain, really wanted a drink. One day he began to play the Jewish song 'Give me change for 40 million'[8] on his guitar. Although I am a Jew, I did not know the words but Misha, one of our two Odessa Jews, did know them. He sang along with the captain, then asked him to play some more, but Smirnov would not play on an empty stomach. Then Misha gathered up the snow-white fur jackets and felt boots belonging to Smirnov and four other officers. He told me and my friend Sasha to put on our red patrol arm-bands and take our submachine guns, and all three of us set off for the local Lithuanian market. There Misha exchanged the garb for a few kitbags of smoked meat, fatback pork, moonshine and bread. We went in after him and got all the stuff back, saying: 'There's a war on and you are depriving the army of clothing! Do you want to take a stroll with us to the commandant's office?' We then lugged it all back to the train, each of us carrying three kit-bags of food. And so, we had a snack and went on our way, not yet realising that many of us would soon perish.

In Lithuania our battalion was practically decimated. We disembarked at a station and then undertook a forced march to the forward line. Twice we assaulted the enemy trenches across the snow and twice we were repelled. Finally, we managed to occupy these trenches and drove the enemy out.

Major Sirotkin was no longer with us. He had been sent off on some course before the offensive. There was a different battalion commander and it so happened that I ended up not far away from him while he was talking with his superiors on the telephone. He was asking for tank or self-propelled gun support, but he was told he should go round the enemy via a forest to the right. Four scouts were sent out in that direction, but they came across an enemy self-propelled gun and only two of them returned, one with his hand shot through. The battalion commander rang the high command again, but they just yelled at him and he began to look around.

The lads who were with me were more experienced and quicker on the uptake; they realised that someone was going to be sent out to blow up this vehicle. But I failed to put two and two together and remained standing where I was. So the battalion commander called me up. He ordered me to take another six men with me, arm each of them with two anti-tank grenades and a Molotov cocktail and go out to blow up this self-propelled gun. Among the six was a lieutenant who had been reduced to the ranks for cowardice. The battalion commander had promised to give him back his epaulettes if the mission was successful.

While we were crawling across the snow towards this vehicle, which turned out to be a 'Ferdinand' tank destroyer, this former lieutenant and two other soldiers took cover. I went to ground in a shell hole two metres from the cutting through the forest, while they lay by a tree almost at the edge of it. I kind of felt that something was not quite right and waved to them to crawl back a little further, but they failed either to understand me or to obey me, and stayed where they were. Meanwhile the Ferdinand was coming down the cutting. If it completed this manoeuvre, it would emerge on the flank facing the considerably thinned ranks of our battalion and simply wipe it out.

The Germans in the Ferdinand seemed to be in no particular hurry and stopped about thirty metres away from us. Two of them got out and stood facing me by one of the tank tracks while they examined a map. It struck me that this was a huge opportunity – to knock off the entire crew without blowing up the vehicle. Unfortunately, I did not realise that these two were not the entire crew.

I switched my sub-machine gun over from single-shot to rapid-fire mode but, in my excitement, I leapt up and thereby gave myself away. I managed to fell one German, and he dropped near the track, but the other one managed to dive into a hatch. Meanwhile the Ferdinand pointed its gun and fired. The shell hit the tree beneath which the three soldiers were concealed and they were killed on the spot. One splinter penetrated my helmet near the temple and lodged in my head, and, as a result of this wound, I lost an eye many years later. A second splinter hit me on the left side and penetrated my belly. Besides that, I was tossed into the shell hole, having felt the full force of the blast, but did not lose consciousness.

When I came to, the Ferdinand was already three metres away from me; I can still picture the snowflakes melting on its side. I raised myself a little and threw the Molotov cocktail. By that time the bottles were filled with the KS mixture,[9] which did not require igniting; it was sufficient if the bottle broke and the mixture made contact with air. As soon as the vehicle caught fire, I dashed into the forest without even taking my sub-machine gun with me.

Instead of running towards the battalion I took an adjacent dirt road; I was just not thinking straight. Besides that, I was probably bawling because I remember there were tears flowing, snot running and blood gurgling in one boot. I looked around and saw two SS tank-crew members running after me. I accelerated, and so did they ... I would stop, and they would too. I stopped to grab my pistol from under my waterproof cape or one of the grenades hanging from my belt. But during the fighting the belt had become unclipped and slid down my leg under the cape; there was no way of retrieving it quickly.

I managed nevertheless to retrieve one grenade from my clothing and jumped out onto the road, squeezing it in my hand – only to behold our own Dodge trucks towing 76-millimetre guns travelling past. The column halted and a lieutenant-colonel leapt out of the jeep at its head and bent over me. It was the commander of the artillery regiment. I pointed back were I had come from and said there was a tank there.

The lieutenant-colonel gave a command and immediately his subordinates set off in that direction taking a couple of guns. About twenty minutes later the gunners returned and reported that they had killed one of the tankmen who was chasing me and brought the other one back as a prisoner.

The lieutenant-colonel bent over me and asked: 'Did you blow up the Ferdinand?' But I was not concerned about the Ferdinand; I thought I was dying. Then the adjutant took my Red Army record booklet out of my pocket, and they wrote something in it and put it back. Then they put a bandage pack over my stomach, gave me a carbine, so I would not remain completely unarmed, got into their vehicles and took off.

I was left sitting by the roadside, feeling worse and worse. Everything was swimming before my eyes. I saw a Fritz coming up to me, pointed my carbine at him, fired, and got a stream of Russian obscenity in response. It turned out to be our sergeant-major, Filimonenko.

Our battalion had eventually been given some self-propelled guns, and burst through the enemy defences. Everyone moved forward. The *starshina* had followed in their footsteps and found the burning enemy Ferdinand and my three dead comrades, and then found me. He tossed me over his shoulder and carried me to the medical centre. There, they gave me an injection, removed the shell splinter, covered the wound with a dressing and sent me off to Leningrad by hospital train.

For knocking out the Ferdinand, I was subsequently awarded the Order of Glory, Third Class – but only after I had ended up in hospital again, following a second wound, until after the war was over. Along with it I was presented with a certificate signed by Stalin himself.

My treatment for the first wound lasted all winter and I was only discharged in March 1945 – and immediately seconded to the naval infantry. We were assembled at the Base Sailors' Club, where reinforcement companies were formed from men who had recovered from their wounds. When our company was ready, some transports drove up to the gates facing the Potseluyev Bridge and we were taken off to the railway station. After a short journey we ended up in the Lithuanian town of Pagegiai. It is situated only a few kilometres from the River Neman, and across the river from it was Tilsit, where a separate battalion of naval infantry was being assembled.

Preparations were under way for an offensive on East Prussia and a command from General Chernyakhovsky was read out: 'No house-to-house fighting!' The local population had earlier been warned to vacate the battle zone. If a machine gun or artillery weapon began firing at us from any building, an ISU tank would follow up and turn the building into a pile of brick rubble, after which we went on further.

I remember that, after breaking through, we ended up tired and worn out on some road. The naval infantry were barely moving – until our deputy political education officer, Senior Lieutenant Yamoshpolsky, mentioned that this road was called the 'Berliner' because it led to Berlin. I don't know where everyone got their strength from.

After the fighting was over one day, I was summoned to the staff headquarters on account of my knowledge of German. I was to accompany eight scouts beyond the front line to grab a prisoner for interrogation on the eve of the next offensive. The battalion commander promised that, if his order was fulfilled within twenty-four hours, we would all be decorated. He did not subsequently keep his word, but let that be on his conscience. We went.

At night we crossed no-man's land successfully and penetrated eight or nine kilometres into the German lines. All around were sand dunes, but there were no Germans visible. We sat considering what to do. At this point one of our lookouts crawled up and said: 'There's a German coming!' We looked and indeed there was a German striding along the path – an *Obergefreiter*,[10] whistling something. We nabbed him; he didn't have time to let out a squeak. I began trying to interrogate him, but he couldn't speak – his teeth were chattering from fear. But it turned out all right; he calmed down and began talking.

He turned out to be a somewhat elderly captive – fifty-two years old and employed as a boilerman at a sanatorium not far away, a rest and relaxation home for pilots. He was the last kind of informant we needed and it was going to be difficult to take him along with us as we continued our patrol. The German realised all this, asked for a sheet of paper and wrote his home address and a note to his family. He explained that he lived in Bremen, had three children, and asked us, if we survived, to pass this message on to them. His note said that he was seriously wounded and hardly likely to come home.

According to all the rules we should have killed him, but the lads just sat there – it was hard to do with an unarmed man. At this point the prisoner said that nearby was a military road running parallel to the front and I translated this to the scouts. The commander of the group – the deputy commander of the reconnaissance section and a senior lieutenant by rank – left a man to guard the prisoner with orders to finish him off if a firefight eventuated.

One of the scouts, a senior sergeant, had brought with him a German officer's cape, peaked cap and a metal tag of the type the German military police wore around their necks. He put all this on and went out to the roadside, while we lay down in the bushes on both sides of the highway. We were barely in position before a car appeared, an Opel-Kapitän. Our stooge went out into the middle of the road and raised his baton; the vehicle stopped. We immediately jumped out and made a dash for the car doors.

Inside sat two enemy officers. One of them had managed to pull his pistol out of its holster and shoot himself at the very sight of us. The other was just sitting there, trembling and pressing some sort of briefcase to his body. It turned out later that he was a 'big catch', deputy head of a divisional or corps operational section. The chauffeur managed to leap out and run for it, but someone cut him down with a shot in the back.

The scouts quickly ransacked the car; in the boot were two baskets of vintage French wine. As true navy men, we could not of course leave this prize behind. We had abandoned the car and started running back to our first German captive and the sentry who had been left with him – or else, hearing the sound of gunfire, he might follow his orders and kill the prisoner. We ran up to find the sentry peacefully asleep, even snoring, and the terrified prisoner sitting there, bound head and foot, with a gag in his mouth.

We returned safe and sound to our unit at night, handed over the German officer at staff headquarters and wrote a note to say that we had procured him thanks to information from the *Obergefreiter*. We gave this sheet of paper to the second German and sent him off to make his own way without a guard to the POW assembly point.

The most frightening battles were at Königsberg. We burst through the Lithuanian Rampart not far from the River Pregolya. To our right lay a cemetery and over a bridge across a ditch stood an ancient brick fort with statues of knights on its roof. It was here that we sustained the biggest losses. As I realised later, our reconnaissance had not operated well. It often happened that we would move forward, and then suddenly the enemy would turn up in our rear, and they were also sailors – removed from German ships. They were practised and well-prepared.

I particularly remember one incident from those engagements. We had broken into a two- or three-storey building. Further on the entire street was exposed to enemy fire and we were waiting for the rest of our lads to catch up. Inside the building was a museum, with glass cases containing coins and medals. At this point a rifle detachment headed by a captain burst in. He saw the coins, grabbed a kitbag from one of the soldiers and cleaned out three or four cases.

With us was a senior lieutenant, also a naval infantryman. He saw what had happened, pointed his Tokarev TT pistol at him and said: 'Put it back. It doesn't belong to you. It belongs to all of us.' And he ordered the captain's subordinates to leave the building. The captain shouted out an order for them to defend him. Then the senior lieutenant told us to point our sub-machine guns at the soldiers and force them to leave. But that turned out to be unnecessary; they left of their own accord. The senior lieutenant led the captain to the stairs and gave him such a shove that he tumbled head over heels downstairs. He shouted and threatened from below that he would return, but of course he didn't.

At Preussisch Eylau, now called Bagrationovsk,[11] we charged in without firing a single shot; the Germans had abandoned it. I remember us waiting there for some reason and smoking when a motorbike came along, and on it a German general, riding straight into our hands. He started shouting, but I did not know German well enough to understand what precisely. But with him was an interpreter with a black beard. It turned out the Fritz was indignant at our being there. A German unit was supposed to be located in the same spot.

I twice took part in tank assaults, when we were seated on the armour plating of a T-34. The tank crews told us to kill any Germans who had grenade launchers as soon as we saw them, or else it would be curtains for everyone.

When we burst into the town of Pillau, which is now called Baltiysk,[12] the fighting was no longer as fierce. We quickly dashed through it and onto the Vistula Spit, where we ran across 400-500 men, who turned out to be Vlasovites. They were greater in number than our battalion but, after we had surrounded them, they surrendered and the question arose of what to do with them. The battalion commander thought about it and decided. The battalion would move on further and one platoon remain behind. Twenty of the prisoners would be separated out and the remainder would be shot. The twenty would then drag the bodies away and toss them in the sea. I don't think our battalion commander had any other option because, if he had left these hundreds of prisoners in our rear, they would have presented a danger to the badly thinned ranks of our battalion. If these Vlasovites had stabbed us in the back, they would have completely wiped us out.

I do not remember how we made it from Pillau to Danzig. On the outskirts of one city, maybe Danzig, I recall some Germans settling into one of the buildings. They set up their machine guns in the cellar and left the Polish civilian residents on the ground floor. Then, on the second floor their riflemen were firing through gun-ports in bricked-up windows. The third floor remained with its civilian residents, while there was a machine gun in the attic. This had to be destroyed, first and foremost because it covered every approach to the building.

To start with, three lads were seconded for the job, but they were all killed. Then I was sent along with Petty Officer Danilin, who was from Belorussia. When the Germans had captured his village and seen a photograph of Danilin in his naval uniform on the wall, they had hanged his wife and two children at the door to the house. When Belorussia was liberated in 1944, he received a letter in which the neighbours outlined the fate of his family. Danilin stopped taking prisoners after that. If the lads brought any in, he asked for them to be taken aside, and there he dispatched them.

We cased the building for a long time and crawled through something resembling a sewage pipe, except that it was dry. Danilin had noticed that on one corner of the building there was a bit where we could climb up. I went up first and we made it onto the roof, where there was a hatch to the attic. We got our grenades ready, opened the door, threw them in and stepped to either side. And then Danilin stepped on a mine which included a tank containing petrol. He turned into a burning torch and there was no way of helping him. I dived towards him, nevertheless . . . and plunged into darkness.

When I woke up, I was in hospital. They had extracted some shell splinters from me and given me a blood transfusion. Soon after I was put on a train and sent back to Leningrad to the same hospital which had put me back on my feet just a couple of months back. With this my war ended.

9 Petr Belyakov

I WAS BORN ON THE LEFT BANK OF THE MEDVEDITSA, a tributary of the Don, in the town of Archedinskaia. We lived quite well – until the war began.

In the summer of 1942, the Germans were hurtling towards Voronezh and Stalingrad and aircraft with crosses on them were flying over our town more and more frequently. By that time, I was just finishing the tenth grade at school and my classmates and I were preparing for graduation exams. But we were less interested in the exam subjects than we were in our initial training for war. These sessions were run by Sergeant (reserve) Aleksandr Pavlovich Stavropoltsev.

Our military trainer was quite young – only twenty-five. He had taken part in the Finnish War and been seriously wounded. His platoon had been given an order to find a covert route through to the enemy rear. At first it appeared that the enemy had not noticed them, but unexpectedly a shot rang out and the platoon commander fell dead – killed by a Finnish sniper. The soldiers went to ground in the snow. One of them soon lost patience, raised his head, and also copped a bullet.

Stavropoltsev was a deputy platoon commander, so it was up to him to take command. He got his soldiers up to attack, but soon fell himself with a bullet in the chest. The platoon nevertheless managed to fulfil the objective, but suffered big losses. The senior sergeant once unbuttoned his tunic and showed us his lilac-coloured scar. This was how I first heard the word 'sniper'.

A notification to appear at the recruiting office was delivered to me on 22 August. Marched off in infantry formation, we recruits reached Kamyshin, and from there we made it by train or on foot to Baskunchak station. Both these population centres had been intensively bombed by the Germans. We travelled further to the south on open coal wagons and, as a result, within an hour we were covered with coal dust and looked as though we were Black. This was how we arrived in Astrakhan,[1] where we were enrolled in the 159th Independent Rifle Brigade of the 28th Army of the Stalingrad Front, which was protecting the Astrakhan zone from the enemy. The brigade commander was Lieutenant-Colonel Aleksandr Ivanovich Bulgakov.

We new arrivals were issued uniforms and weapons and I was designated a rank-and-file rifleman. Our 2nd Battalion was stationed in the small village of Staraya Kocherganovka, from where we went into the steppe every morning. Here we were taught how to dig in, make an attack, throw grenades and crawl on our elbows. We returned half-dead to barracks in the evening, and in the morning it all began again.

One day I was called up by our company commander, Iosif Kalinovich Tuz. He had already been involved in the fighting and the Germans had knocked out almost all his teeth in the course of a hand-to-hand tussle. Because of this he wore dentures and, consequently, when he was giving orders, he sometimes enunciated the letter 'R' three times instead of just once, which made his commands sound a lot more authoritative and intelligible. On this occasion he ordered me and one other private soldier, Volodya Spesivtsev, to go to sniper school. We were selected because, prior to call-up, we had succeeded in gaining the honoured title 'Voroshilov Marksman' for our shooting.

The school was in Astrakhan and the man in charge was Lieutenant Vasiliy Shtanov. He had already earned the medal 'For Valour' in battle and had badges for top-class shooting. We were taught using ordinary Three Lines to which optical sights had been attached. There was no actual firing during the first few days; instead we learned how to aim precisely. It was only on the tenth day that we did some real shooting. The lieutenant fired first and all five of his shots fell within the black circle and three of them hit the bullseye. We cadets did not shoot as well, but acquitted ourselves not too badly. Only in the case of a man called Moroz did all his bullets miss the target. Shtanov was encouraging: 'Don't hurry. More haste, more waste. Patience leads to prowess.' These words served as a guide to me for the whole of the rest of my life.

A lot of time was devoted not just to handling a rifle, but also to the art of camouflage. Shtanov instructed us that nothing must be allowed to give away a sniper's position. If there were thick clumps of overgrown vegetation in your military sector, it was best not to settle down there, because they would be the first thing the enemy took a note of. They would be bound to keep an eye on such a spot and occasionally riddle it with fire.

He explained to us the meaning of the actual word 'sniper'. It entered the Russian language from the English word 'to snipe', which means 'to fire from under cover'. But there is another version – that it comes from the name of a bird called a snipe. Only a very well trained, professional marksman can hunt this small, easily startled bird. The lieutenant talked about the first employment of snipers in the Russian Army. Suvorov, for example, used them at the siege of Izmail[2] – they dislodged Turkish marksmen from its walls – and whole teams of snipers were formed during World War I on the orders of General Brusilov.

In the evening the sniper rifles were brought in. Their wooden parts were covered with varnish and polished, while the metal bits were carefully greased; the sights had covers and the eye-pieces had leather caps on. Brigade Commissar Maxim Nikiforovich Mikheyev came for the presentation of these rifles to us. He shook each of us by the hand and wished us well.

Daily firing sessions commenced. The shooting range was poorly equipped, so that after every five rounds or so we had to run up to the target and see what we had hit. The new rifles were accurate. Their barrels had apparently been carefully selected and they had been adjusted at the factory range. In our own unofficial 'dead-eye' contest the leaders were Spesivtsev and myself.

On our way back to barracks one day we noticed an empty tin can which someone had hung on the branch of a pussy willow growing on the banks of a dam. The lieutenant stopped and proposed a competition to see who could hit it with a single shot. I was called up first. I laid the rifle on the shoulder of Volodya Spesivtsev and took aim. A gentle breeze began to make the can sway, but I still managed to get it. One shot and the can dropped.

The sound of the shot attracted a jeep carrying Brigade Commander Bulgakov and Commissar Mikheyev. They began asking about the shooting and wanted to tear a strip off our lieutenant. But when they found out that it was a competition staged within the context of sniper training and the results so far were quite excellent, their anger gave way to indulgence. The brigade commander ordered that the best marksmen be rewarded and a shooting test held for the whole school within three days.

On the orders of Lieutenant-Colonel Bulgakov the shooting range was finally put to rights: head-high plywood targets were made and a newly arrived group of soldiers dug out the trenches from which the targets were supposed to appear. Lieutenant Shtanov took us off into the steppe, where we learned how to make speedy ('lightning' speed, he termed it) adjustments to allow for the wind. This required complex mental calculations prior to adjusting the lateral movement flywheel on the sight. He also taught us how to reload and aim quickly and how to fire at moving targets. In this case you needed to be able to evaluate both the speed of the wind and the speed of the moving target and to act rapidly, precisely and faultlessly.

After all his explanations the lieutenant fixed a copper coin to a stick. In this contest whoever dislodged it with his first shot would shoot first in the final competitions. The lieutenant's idea appealed to us.

First to try was Moroz; he missed. Next shooter – missed. I raised my hand and Shtanov allowed me to shoot third. I lay down on the ground, pressed my cheek close to the stock, took aim at the target and remembered the lieutenant's words: 'Make sure your heart is behind every bullet... Believe in your shot. And don't hurry when you have the opportunity to take good aim.' There was no limit on time, but that can even be a drawback – your eyes may begin to water from the lengthy preparation, your arms grow tired ... I smoothly pressed the trigger. The shot resounded ... and there was a whoop of joy from Volodya

Spesivtsev: 'Bullseye!' Our pairing was set down to shoot first in the final competitions.

While we were returning to the city, we were met by a column from a battalion of the 34th Guards Rifle Division, whose advance units had already fought at the front. The soldiers wore blue tabs – the division consisted mainly of assault troops. In the first row marched a strapping Guardsman with a sniper rifle over his shoulder. He gave us – his colleagues – a friendly wave and wished us success. I did not know at the time that before me was a man who was to become one of the best-known snipers of the Southern and Stalingrad Fronts, a man whom fate would bring me up against several more times.

The day set down for the final competition was cloudy and windy. Brigade Commander Bulgakov arrived at the shooting range. He did not bother to listen to Shtanov's report, waved it away and ordered the shooting to begin at once. Spesivtsev and I occupied the prepared shallow trenches. We had agreed that I would fire first and he would follow. A bugle announced the start. A moving target was supposed to appear first, followed by a chest-level target either to the left or to the right. But there was no sign of them. Five minutes went by, ten minutes, and nothing. The captain responsible for the range reported to Bulgakov that there had been a communications failure. Finally, a new bugle call. But still no targets. This time the trolley ropes had got tangled up in the bushes. The brigade commander was beginning to get agitated and my eyes were starting to water from the head wind. A treacherous thought was boring through my head: 'Surely, I'm not going to miss.' But then the black figures began moving 500 metres away. It was all on! I pressed close to the stock and began to take aim at the first target. One shot, two, three . . .

Several minutes later the three targets I had hit were laid at the feet of the brigade commander. Bulgakov noted that some excellent shots had been made and voiced his gratitude to Sniper Belyakov, that is, to me – for the first time in my military career.

After the shooting was over, the school graduated its first batch of snipers in the history of the brigade. By evening we were all back with our companies. Lieutenant Tuz, still roaring out his multiple 'Rs', enrolled Volodya Spesivtsev and me in the company administration cell, which also included the *starshina*, his liaison officer and his orderly.

At midday on 19 November there was a meeting at which we were informed that Red Army forces had broken through the enemy defences and launched a decisive offensive near Stalingrad. On the following day our 28th Army moved ahead under the command of Lieutenant-General Vasiliy Filipovich Gerasimenko. Its advance units inflicted a crushing blow on the enemy in the neighbourhood of the Kalmyk[3] settlement of Khalkhuta. Now our own brigade was also heading there.

We got there on foot, marching for three days over snow-covered steppe which disappeared into the horizon. The weather here in winter is capricious: sometimes a biting wind blows in your face, lashing it with fine crumbs of ice; sometimes the sun is shining and snow flakes fall from above, while down below you squelch through muddy slush.

From the company's political education officer, Selyutin, we found out that we would be fighting the enemy's 16th Motorised Division, which bore the nick-name 'Brown Bear'. Our comrades-in-arms, snipers from other detachments, had already had a good taste of them. The political education officer brought us newspaper cuttings about their activities. Sniper Boris Viktorovich Milashchus from the 152nd Brigade had killed twenty Fritzes in a single engagement and six of them were officers. I later had the chance to meet this sniper and hear how he wiped out one of them.

The enemy were advancing and our troops had launched a counter-attack which Boris was covering with his rifle. He saw a German officer point his sub-machine gun at our company commander. Without giving the matter further thought, Milashchus fired and the dead enemy dropped his gun, took two or three steps from momentum and fell down.

Another sniper, Dmitry Iosifovich Chechikov wiped out sixty-eight enemies in the fighting near Khalkhuta. A member of the 34th Guards Division, he was the one who waved to us that time when we were returning from shooting practice and wished us luck. As a hereditary Siberian hunter, he needed no training to hit the target dead-on. I also had the opportunity to meet him at a 26th Army sniper rally, which took place shortly after. He told me about one of his successful ventures at Khalkhuta. With the permission of his commander Chechikov dug in one night in no-man's land. For a whole day nobody left the German dugouts. Only towards evening did an enemy soldier decide to shake his blanket out before going to sleep. It was the final act of his life.

Another time, while supporting an offensive by his own company, Chechikov knocked out an enemy machine-gun squad whose fire was impeding access to a hill. He was also a masterly machine gunner. On one occasion a man in charge of a Maxim had to give up. Dmitry took his place and repelled a German attack, killing up to forty enemy soldiers.

Another sniper, Nikolay Nosov, wiped out seventy-five Fritzes. His hunt for 'Brown Bears' often featured in the newspapers. It was against people like these that we young snipers at Khalkhuta measured ourselves.

By that time nothing of the settlement remained except the name; on retreating the Germans reduced it to ashes. The steppe country around it was hilly and marked by the tracks of enemy tanks, pitted by bomb craters and shell holes and criss-crossed by trenches. Strewn everywhere were crates from mortar bombs, bags of gunpowder, German cartridges, helmets and enemy corpses.

We occupied our defence sector in the evening but had still not had time to dig out our trenches fully before we found out that enemy tanks were advancing against us. Our 159th Brigade was in the second line of defence, so other advance units would take the initial blow. A counter-attack against the Germans was mounted by the 6th Guards Tank Brigade and the Rifle Division. The earth hummed and trembled with the explosions. Through binoculars we could observe the tank battle unfolding in front of us.

Meanwhile we hurriedly started digging and finished the work in about an hour, raising an exceptional sweat. Towards evening the frost descended and, if we were hot earlier, we were shivering now. Lieutenant Tuz ordered that 100 grams of vodka be issued to each soldier.

I had never drunk spirits up until then. And, on top of that, Pavlik Dronov gave me his ration out of the kindness of his heart. After a while it began to appear to my drunken eyes that the glass in my lenses had gone cloudy, and I was gripped by real panic. Thank goodness, the company commander understood my situation and sent me off to the dugout to sleep. In the morning I discovered that fortunately the enemy attack had been beaten off without my participation. I was extremely ashamed and resolved that I would not drink another gram of spirits, so as not to lose my ability to function as a top-class marksman.

So-called personal tallies were recorded for the snipers in our brigade. Each of us kept an individual count of enemy casualties. On the sheet for personal tallies were printed the words of Colonel-General Andrei Ivanovich Yeryomenko, commander of the Stalingrad Front: 'Every soldier must regard it as a matter of pride and honour to destroy as many Nazis as possible through rifle and machine-gun fire. If you kill 10, that's good; if you kill 15, that's excellent; if you kill 20, you're a hero, and snipers should double this norm.'

For a while, my personal tally remained at zero, but I eventually had the opportunity to put that right. At the beginning of December 1942, the 159th Brigade was transferred to the front line. We were set the objective of breaking through south of Elista[4] towards the settlement of Lola. This involved exhausting marches in savage frosts and bone-chilling steppe winds, your face buffeted by a mixture of snow, sand and dust. Lieutenant Tuz used me as an observer; from a position at the head of the company I surveyed the surroundings through the optical sights on my rifle and reported back to the company commander.

On 31 December our battalion reached the boundaries of Elista, which was in flames. Without entering the city, we began to make our way around it in order to block the path of the retreating enemy. At night our forces completely liberated it and on the following day our front was renamed the Southern Front. Now we were faced with advancing on Rostov[5] in order to cut off and encircle the enemy's Caucasus group.

First, we had to cross the River Manych and liberate Divnoye station. The brigade's advance battalions went into the attack as a thick fog enfolded the steppe, while we remained in the second line. Finally, the news came that they had broken through and the battalion moved forward. We crossed the broad, slimy river, which was unfrozen in parts and smelled of hydrogen sulphide, and spread out in a chain. Now we were advancing in the front line.

When we got close to Divnoye, a snow storm came up. We headed immediately in the direction of the railway station, where we were exposed to shrapnel fire. Lieutenant Tuz gave the order to disperse and for me to climb onto the roof of a nearby barn to see what lay ahead.

The picture that emerged from up there was of the Germans hurriedly abandoning the station; their transport had already set off back westward. We hurried towards the station and soon reached the snow-covered adjacent streets. Divnoye was the first population centre which the enemy had failed to destroy before we got there.

In the evening of 28 January we drew near to the small village of Karalnichek, where, according to our reconnaissance, some Germans had based themselves. The companies spread out in a line. The enemy machine gunners had roosted in the attic of one of the houses, but the squad was wiped out by Syoma Marchuk's Maxim. However, there was another machine gun rattling away and sowing death from the attic of a building on the edge of the village. Lieutenant Tuz gave me the order: 'Objective – the far house on the left. Machine gun to be eliminated!'

I plonked myself on a stack of mouldy hay. One shot, two shots ... and the machine gun fell silent. To make sure, I sent another three shots into the attic doorway. That was that; we could move on. The company commander gave the order, and the line charged forward. Set alight by the Germans, the village of Kalnichek was burning.

Next morning, when the company was getting ready to move on further, we discovered the lacerated bodies of some Red Army soldiers next to an incinerated wattle fence. One had had his head cut off with some blunt instrument and his eyes had been put out – seemingly by the heel of a boot while he was lying on the ground. The second showed the marks of torture on his body and a stake from the fence had been stuck through his stomach. This filled us with a thirst for vengeance and it was with this that we set off in pursuit of our retreating savage foe.

Next came the village of Bezvodny, where our battalion was attacked by German tanks – eleven of them at once. The column emerged from a gorge and spread out along the front. Behind these 'crates', which had been painted white for winter, ranks of enemy infantry were advancing.

Captain Ibragim Magomedovich Kulakaiev galloped up on a dashing steed. 'Not one step back!' he admonished us. But before he could get back to the command post both he and the horse were felled by a burst of machine-gun fire.

Our guns opened up with direct fire. The one beside us only managed to fire a single shot before the squad comprising lads of my own age from the village of Yeterevskaia[6] was swept away. We fired back in response and the enemy infantry went to ground. Only the tanks broke through to the village. They were already drawing close to the trenches of a reconnaissance platoon which had dug in up ahead. One of the scouts threw a grenade under the tracks of one armour-plated machine, but it failed to stop it. This tank was then blown up with a Molotov cocktail by Victor Shtrekker, who was instantly cut down by a machine-gun round.

I fired into the tank's vision slits in an effort to blind the crew but I didn't see Political Education Officer Chernoivannikov from the reconnaissance platoon leap on one of the vehicles at the same time and use his rifle butt to knock out the machine gun firing at us. Other troops also began to clamber onto the enemy tanks.

One of the tanks turned towards me and Pavlik Dronov. There was an explosion beside me and for some time I lost my hearing, except for a humming noise in my head. I ran my hands over my body; I didn't seem to be wounded. I saw the company political education officer, Timofey Selyutin, crawling across to a tank with a grenade in his hand . . . but he did not have time to do anything with it before he was blown up by a shell falling beside him.

Pavlik was wounded. As I crawled over to him, I noticed that a tank was moving directly towards me. I managed to roll to the side at the last moment, and the armoured vehicle crawled on further into the depths of our defences. The tank attack was stopped by the 3rd Battalion, which was on defence behind us. We had sustained big losses near the village of Bezvodny. Later we found up that we had been confronted not only by the 'Brown Bears' from the 16th Motorised Division, but also by the SS troops from the SS *Viking* Division and the 23rd Tank Division.

On 5 February the 159th Rifle Brigade approached Bataysk. This city is located on the southern bank of the Don and immediately downstream on the other side of the river lies Rostov; it was not far away at all. Preparations began for the assault. On the night of 7 February our reconnaissance broke through into the enemy rear. It turned out that the Germans had taken refuge from the frosts that night and retreated into dugouts, leaving only sentries in the forward line. We attacked suddenly at night and broke through into the streets of Bataysk.

At 2:00 on the following morning formations of the 28th Army took up their starting positions for an assault on Rostov. The 159th Brigade was aiming for the city railway station. If this was successful, our 2nd Battalion would continue the offensive further along Engels Street towards Budyonny Avenue.

The reconnaissance crept ahead. They succeeded in noiselessly removing the enemy patrols and we crossed the frozen Don without a single shot being fired. The troops charged towards the railway station and captured it almost without a struggle and further on our 4th Company turned into Engels Street. Speeding towards us along the icy paving was a motorbike, which was shot down almost point-blank. In one of the buildings, we captured a prisoner, and Lieutenant Tuz, who knew German well, interrogated him. The Fritz turned out to be a 'Brown Bear' from our old acquaintances, the 16th Motorised Division. We moved on further.

A van showed up. Volodya Spesivtsev took aim through his optical sights and killed the driver. An officer who managed to jump out of the cab was cut down by a burst of sub-machine gun fire from the company commander. Enemy soldiers poured out from the back of the van, but not one of them survived.

On we went. Next thing we caught the rumble of tank engines. Lieutenant Tuz ordered Spesivtsev to get up onto the roof of one of the buildings and report on the situation. It emerged that four armoured vehicles were bearing down on us and, behind them, trucks carrying motorised infantry. They soon approached the building from which Volodya was conducting his observations. He ended up blocked inside, while we had to withdraw to Dolomanov Lane.

We occupied a corner building in which some of our troops had already established themselves. Standing out among them was a stocky, broad-shouldered officer in a white fur jacket, with a holstered pistol and two grenades on his belt. The lieutenant told us that this was our new battalion commander, Senior Lieutenant Aleksey Maximovich Oreshkin. In total there were up to fifty of us packed into the building and, apart from us, another group of soldiers from the 248th Division burst in, headed by Senior Lieutenant Veniamin Grigoryevich Manotskov. Soon the Germans surrounded our building. In the meantime, the brigade's main forces were fighting in the vicinity of the railway station.

The battalion commander organised the defence on a circular basis. I occupied a position near a corner window and concealed myself behind the first object that came to hand – a Vienna dining chair. It turned out to be an excellent viewpoint; through the eyepiece of my optical lens, I could see both streets far into the distance, a house on a hill and the railway line. Then the first guests arrived; a group of Fritzes ran towards us from some railway carriages, led by a man in a peaked cap with binoculars – an officer. I caught him in the eyepiece of my lens, allowed for the deflection and fired. The officer dropped his pistol and fell to the ground. I waited for his subordinates to attempt to carry the body away; they would surely make an attempt. And they did. The first one crept up and, bang! He was dead.

Slightly to the right someone was running along clad in a shawl. Was it some local woman in trouble? I took a closer look and saw a sub-machine gun peep out from under the shawl. Either it was a looter or a Fritz who was too clever for his own good. One shot, and he was tumbling head over heels on the ground.

Behind my back I heard the battalion commander's voice: 'Well done, but look for some more important targets.'

After the losses they had suffered the German soldiers became more cautious; they would not take risks or poke their heads out from under cover any more than they had to. Their officers tried to get them up in attack, but it was not easy now. So one of the enemy officers thrust his head out from behind a concrete wall and shouted: 'We surrender!' but why were his subordinates not dropping their weapons? Apparently, it was a ruse. The Germans could not understand whence they were being fired at, and wanted to clarify it in this way.

The battalion commander was the first to realise this and shouted to me: 'Fire! Fire!' I trained my sights on the cunning enemy officer, squeezed the trigger, and he fell silent for ever.

The battle lasted for several hours. All my cartridges were used up. I reported this to Lieutenant Tuz. Barely thinking about it, he called over machine gunner Zavalishin: 'You've got ten cartridges left in your magazine. Give them to the sniper.' The gunner resisted: 'Take what you like – my overcoat, my boots – but I'm not giving up my ammunition.' But he had to all the same because with these ten rounds I would knock out more enemies than the machine gunner would, and everyone realised that, including Zavalishin himself. He unclipped the drum from his Degtyarev gun and handed the bullets over one by one, parting with them like a hungry man parting with his last crusts of bread. We counted out eleven 'crusts'. That was not very many, but all there was. I went back to my position.

A Fritz was hiding about fifteen paces behind a water pipe. He was not very well concealed and I could see his legs shod in boots with short shafts. It was cold in a Rostov winter in footwear like that; he needed Russian felt boots. The man was freezing, knocking his heels together in an apparent effort to get warm. If I had had more cartridges, I would definitely have shot him, but I couldn't; I had to wait for bigger fish. Although, if the Germans launched an attack, we would have to expend our ammunition on rank-and-file soldiers.

Suddenly, there was an explosion. A shell from an enemy tank flew into the building from the direction of the German rear. One of the solders had his belly ripped open by a splinter and the battalion commander carefully covered him with his fur jacket. By this time the attic of the house was already alight. Lieutenant Tuz settled down by a hole in the wall, opened up with his sub-machine gun, but then stopped and called out to me: 'Finish the bastard off . . . The gun's jammed!'

It turned out that one Fritz had concealed himself behind a woman and, pushing her in front of him, attempted to move along the street. The company commander managed to wound him, and now the German was crawling towards the nearest cellar in the last stage of exhaustion, in an effort to hide in it. I deprived him of that opportunity.

In the meantime, the enemy ring around our building was closing tighter and tighter. The Germans had worked out that we did not have many cartridges and gradually became bolder. Round the corner from Engels Street came a tank with a large white *Balkenkreuz* on the turret. Some Fritzes ran up to it, banged their rifle butts on the armour plating and indicated the way to our building. I went cold all over – one or two shots and we would be lying under heaps of brick rubble.

The tank really was turning its turret so that the gun barrel pointed in our direction. But then the hatch opened and its commander emerged down to the waist. 'Wipe him out!' the battalion commander whispered. All eyes were fixed on me and I duly took aim. One shot and he was hanging out of the hatch. After this, to our surprise, the tank turned a sharp 180 degrees and departed. The infantry gave up on their siege of the building. Fighting had erupted with new force at the railway station.

At night our commanders organised a military council in the yard of the building. Ideally, we needed to make our way back to the main brigade forces at the station, but the Germans had assembled significant forces in front of it, and we had no ammunition left. The battalion commander took the decision to get through to the River Don as soon as the moon clouded over and further on to Bataysk on the other side. The strike group was headed by Senior Lieutenant Manotskov.

We began to move out at four o'clock in the morning. In the reconnaissance group at the head were Lieutenant Lushchenkov, who was from Rostov, Sergeants Pavlyukov and Koshevarov and myself. Lushchenkov's own house was 400 metres away from us. In this district of the city, it was easy to find your way around, even when it was pitch dark, and we silently made our way through dark alleys and patches of waste ground to the spot where the Don was once crossed by a railway bridge. The nearer we got to it, the more cautious we had to be; there would undoubtedly be Germans on the river bank. We crawled the last few hundred metres on our elbows.

Finally, the whole group came together again. We tried to hear what was happening. A sharp call of 'Halt!' came from the right. With the command 'Follow me!' Oreshkin leapt from the cliff under the bridge. The rest of us went after him.

By the river bank I plunged into the wormwood. Resting my rifle on the ice I scrambled up. An enemy machine gun was rattling away from the bank. I grabbed my last grenade, tore the ring out with my teeth and threw it. It exploded, but the machine gun kept going. Maybe it was a different one, but there was no time to sort that out. I ran across to the opposite bank and dived into the wormwood again. As I got up once more, I noticed that Lieutenant Tuz had fired a final round at the enemy from his sub-machine gun. Now all his cartridges were gone.

We had made it to the opposite bank but there were still barbed wire barriers in our way. I tried to get over them, got stuck in the steel barbs, and cried out for help. Bullets whistled by beside me and there were flares hanging in the sky. Lieutenant Tuz ran up, laid his fur jacket on the wire, crawled across the barrier, grabbed me by my overcoat collar, and pulled, and I rolled onto the ground. Leaping up, we ran to the railway embankment, crossed over it and hid in the undergrowth.

On the south bank I found our baggage train and lay down to sleep. I was wakened by the sound of the drivers bringing me gifts, having learned that a single sniper in one engagement had wiped out sixteen Fritzes. I got a camouflage suit, a cigarette lighter, some fatback, bread and a pouch of tobacco. I did not smoke but accepted the present with gratitude.

After breakfast a brigade staff officer came into our room and told me that I, Sniper Belyakov, had been selected for the brigade commander's guard. Along with the reconnaissance group he wanted personally to break through into the burning city of Rostov and there, on the spot, sort out the situation and the position of Captain Gukas Karapetovich Madoyan's group. Madoyan was in charge of the 3rd Battalion and had been given the task of holding the railway station and the buildings to the north of it. In the course of the day the commanders of both the 1st and 4th Battalions were wounded and Madoyan had taken command of all the brigade detachments operating in the vicinity of the station.

In the twilight our small group of twenty men ventured out onto the frozen surface of the Don. We went to ground and crawled on our elbows towards the tall north bank and, to our surprise, Brigade Commander Bulgakov was crawling with us. We crossed the river without a single shot being fired. On one street we bumped into one of our patrols. It turned out that the general staff of the 248th Division was located close by. There we were told that during the day the Germans had managed to force our battalions out of the station, but Madoyan had been able to make a stand in the workshop of the locomotive repair factory, which he was still holding on to at that moment. The scouts from our group immediately crawled away in that direction. They soon returned and confirmed that the battalions blocked by the Germans were holding on, but the captain was requesting ammunition and reinforcements.

We crossed the Don again without misadventure. The brigade commander left me and three scouts on the bank and set off himself for the staff headquarters. Before he went, he ordered me to wipe out the enemy manpower on that bank and the scouts to report on the situation. It soon became quite light.

I occupied a position by an electricity transformer box on which someone had painted a skull and crossbones. I looked around and at that moment an explosive bullet hit the box. There was no time to work out whether it was a stray shell or if I had I been discovered; I immediately took up a new position about fifty metres from the previous one and began to keep watch.

The Germans were not concealing themselves at all. Although there were little more than 400 metres between us, they were walking around on the bank at full height, both in groups and on their own. Another Fritz came along. Holding my breath, I took aim, smoothly pressed the trigger, and the enemy soldier found himself on the ground. Soon after, his hand went up; he was wounded.

Medical orderlies ran out of a building with a stretcher. I hesitated. Should I fire or not. I could easily wipe out both of them. The Nazis bombed our medical trains, hospitals and medical centres without hesitation, but I was not a Nazi; I was a Soviet sniper. While I was pondering, the orderlies with the stretcher disappeared. But I could not waste time on regrets. A tank had appeared over a nearby rise with white stripes on its armour plating, and attached to its engine section was some kind of box. Beside it were some men in black uniforms – maybe tank crew, maybe SS troops, maybe SS tank crew. That was not important; in any case I took aim with special care. In my crosshairs I could see one man on the edge of the group gesticulating. I fired and, throwing his arms out as if he had slipped on the ice, he fell on his back. The others took cover where they could.

The artillery observers situated not far away spotted a tank. The artillery opened fire from a pebbled stretch behind our backs and the shells went whistling over our heads. To the left the heavy howitzer batteries started up. This was the artillery softening-up process intended to precede an assault by the 4th Guards Kuban Cossack Cavalry Corps. The Germans on the river bank began to flap around. Some opened fire in a rather disorderly fashion; some ran for it. I got one of them in the back; he fell to the ground face first and lay still.

We finally liberated Rostov on 14 February, but the detachments did not stick around in the city. I caught up with my own 2nd Battalion as it was marching to the village of Chaltyr. By that time Lieutenant Tuz was in command; Oreshkin had been wounded. I found out from the company that my friend, sniper Volodya Spesivtsev, had been seriously wounded in Rostov. He had been rescued by local residents, who had risked their own lives to do so. There was no time to dwell too long on his loss; the brigade was liberating Matveyev Kurgan[7] and drawing close to the ill-omened Mius front,[8] which had given rise to a lot of talk among the soldiers.

Our army was ordered to take up a defensive position along the bank of the River Mius to the right of Matveyev Kurgan. The enemy-held west bank dominated over the east and was occupied by our old acquaintances, the 'Brown Bears' from the 16th Motorised Division. In their positions the Germans had earlier constructed several lines of full trenches, communication saps, and firing points, erected barbed-wire obstacles, sowed minefields, and built pillboxes and other firing positions.

Along with another sniper of my age, Pasha Khromov, I was called up by my former company commander, Senior Lieutenant Tuz, who was now battalion commander. He set us the task, starting from the following day, of maintaining constant watch on the enemy facing us and not allowing them to raise their heads.

We had a good night's sleep and prepared for the 'hunt' before it got light. The morning was exceptionally quiet; not a shot could be heard. I removed the cover from the eyepiece of my lenses, loaded five cartridges into my rifle magazine and pressed my cheek against the stock.

Ahead lay my first target: quite close by a damp enemy helmet was sparkling in the morning mist. I smoothly pressed the trigger and, following the shot, the figure of a German stiffened up in an unnatural way and collapsed onto his left side. There were sounds of commotion in the enemy trench. Several minutes later another shot followed, and an ammunition bearer threw up his hands and fell down for the very last time on Rostov earth. That was my partner Pasha Khromov opening his account for the day.

Not realising that there were snipers operating on their sector, the Germans walked around at full height for several hours afterwards and only towards midday did they become more cautious. And quite right too! They had no business striding around our land as if they were at home.

Here on the Mius, in March of the same year, I fought a sniper duel, which almost cost me my life. By that time the ice on the rivers had melted, the steppe was clear of snow, and the meadows were green. The trenches were filled with water and it took a big effort to stay dry. Each of us built himself a little island of earth to sit on – like a hare caught out by a flood.

It was boring in the trench and I got into the habit of visiting the machine gunners, who were commanded by my old friend Semyon Marchukov. His squad, which was attached to the 4th Company, occupied a position on a bend of the river. Marchukov's subordinates were not particularly pleased to see me, because each time Semyon would allow me to fire one of the machine guns, after which they had to load the ammunition belts with new cartridges.

One day, when I asked again to use the machine gun, Marchukov said that it was dangerous; their position lay within the sights of an enemy sniper. Besides, the 'bastard' was only firing when the squad fired. The enemy marksman was trying to fire into the observation slit in the machine gun shield but, so far, he had been unable to achieve this; the bullets merely struck sparks off the armour plating. But why tempt fate?

I kept begging him to allow me to let off a couple of rounds and Semyon surrendered his place at the machine gun to me. I grasped the back-plate and pressed the lever. The steady rattle of the precisely functioning death machine was interspersed by loud clicks against the shield. I stopped shooting and carefully examined it. Only two centimetres from the observation slit were the traces of an enemy bullet. The sight made me feel all churned up inside; I had just been within two centimetres of death.

Leaving the machine gunners, I went straight to the company commander, reported what had happened and made a vow to track down and eliminate the enemy marksman at all costs. By that time the company was commanded not by Tuz, but by Senior Lieutenant Nikolay Petrovich Pokhiton. He gave me permission to take up a position in no-man's land, of which I notified our lookouts.

For the first time I made a mistake. I began to move out while it was still light. I was crawling through the rough grass, warmed by the March sun, and became hot. I was just about to untie the laces on my fur cap, when I felt a blow to the head and heard a shot at the same time. I turned over in an instant and rolled down to the river. I took off my cap and examined the hole in it. The bullet had passed within millimetres of my head. Just a little closer, and the duel would have concluded, and not in my favour. Feverishly I began to think; where was the firing coming from? Judging by everything, the enemy marksman was not shooting from a trench; he had clearly gone to ground much closer to our positions.

I crawled towards the scouts under the command of another friend, Vanya Gurov. When he heard about the sniper, he exploded in a fit of cursing. It turned out that this German had long deprived his platoon of the ability to observe the enemy trenches as usual and he had even wounded one scout. He indicated where he thought the 'bastard' was firing from. Vanya's view completely coincided with my own.

Having selected a suitable spot at night and reliably camouflaged it, I began to keep watch the following morning. There were thirteen bushes on the slope of a rise. By one of them the soil had been dug up and an empty food can lay nearby. No sniper would take up such a conspicuous position. But maybe the sniper was trying to outwit us and had in fact gone to ground there. I kept watching.

An enemy mortar attack started up. A mortar bomb exploded in our lines, then a second, and a third. Between the explosions three sharp dry shots rang out. It emerged later that one of them had wounded a Kazakh rank-and-file soldier named Dzhaldaspekov, who had only recently joined the company along with reinforcements. I noticed that in a low-lying area one of the bushes had turned dark, as if someone had cast a shadow over the space below it from within. I recalled Lieutenant Shtanov's admonition: pay special attention to any shady bush; there could be a sniper hiding behind it. Now all my attention was concentrated on this sector. The bush really was suspicious. There was a short trench leading away from it. Where was it leading to? Apparently to a latrine. The German took up his position before daylight, but went off to answer nature's call in full comfort at a specially constructed toilet. My assumptions were soon confirmed: the glass in the optical sights of the enemy sniper rifle glittered in the light of the morning sun.

I inconspicuously crawled away from my position and hurried towards the machine gunners. I arranged with Semyon that in half an hour he would begin to strafe the enemy trenches. I was soon back lying in my camouflaged position and waiting, but barely restraining my impatience. The seconds and minutes ticked agonisingly by. What were they waiting for? Maybe something had happened.

Then finally the Maxim began to despatch round after round in the enemy's direction. All my attention was concentrated on the ill-omened bush. Barely noticeably it stirred and moved to the left. Near it the figure of a Fritz in spotted camouflage garb came to light, plain as day. We fired almost simultaneously. But I got him!

I almost ran back to the company commander to report that I had eliminated the enemy marksman. At my prompting he looked through binoculars and picked up the enemy sniper rifle lying on the parapet.

Soon after, our mortars descended on the position. The wave of explosions forced the rifle out from under the bush and it lay on view for everyone, unneeded by anyone and completely harmless. As a reward I was accepted as a candidate member of the Party in the evening of the same day. For me it was a great honour.

Several days later the snipers of the 28th Army assembled for their next army rally. As was the case in winter following the fighting at Khalkhuta, Dmitry Chechikov was presented to us as an example to follow. By this time, he had raised his tally from 68 to 148 dead enemy. For his feats in battle, he was awarded the Order of the Red Banner.

The rally gave further impetus to the sniper recruitment campaign in the army. Within the battalion Senior Lieutenant Tuz entrusted me with setting up a group for which the top sharpshooters would be selected and trained to become snipers. The following day Corporals Pavel Khromov, Aleksey Adrov and Yegor Bazhanov and six privates became my trainees.

In the mornings I took them out into the woods, where I shared the knowledge I had myself gained from Lieutenant Shtanov only a few months earlier. I talked about the principles of camouflaging and ways of uncovering enemy marksmen, and I revealed the secrets of precision shooting. Special attention was given to developing the virtues of caution and patience. The theory was then immediately reinforced in practice. For instance, one soldier would set up a camouflaged position and the others had to uncover it. Whoever found it first earned the right to prepare a new hidden firing point.

Following Shtanov's example I organised improvised shooting competitions with a five-kopeck piece or a rifle shell as the target. I often repeated to my pupils his saying: 'Patience leads to prowess.'

I also kept up with items in our army newspaper. It was from there that I picked up the method of 'nomadic' firing points developed by Chechikov. It meant that a sniper had to set up not just one firing position, but several. Migrating from one to another, he would create the impression that there was not just a single sniper operating in a particular sector, but a whole group of them. Spotting and eliminating a sniper like that was very difficult.

The best marksman in our group was Alyosha Adrov. Almost all his shots hit the bullseye and he was the first to be allowed to go out stalking on his own. Soon after, the other marksmen I trained also went out to apply their knowledge in practice.

Not everything ran smoothly straight away. At a Komsomol meeting one day there was a spontaneous debriefing of sniper operations. Snipers Bazhanov and Khromov criticised their colleague Klimenko for his lack of care. Forgetting about precautionary measures, he had arrogantly taken up a position in a tree in the open and nearly collected a bullet. Another rifleman, Onishchenko, took poor care of his weapon and failed to grease it on schedule. The reproofs that followed had a sobering effect on the culprits; they subsequently operated more circumspectly and, in time, showed themselves to be excellent snipers in combat.

At the same meeting Sniper Mamyedov talked about a blunder he had made himself. The German he was stalking realised that his trench was in the sniper's crosshairs and played a dangerous game. He would peep out like a gopher and then hide down below. Mamyedov fired in haste and, as was to be expected, missed. Scoffing at the unsuccessful marksman, the German waved his sapper spade above his trench, as if to say: 'Hey, Russky, you missed.' But he did this to his own cost. Mamyedov stalked his mocker for several days at mortal risk to himself and in the end shot him.

As my group became more active, the enemy on our sector became more cautious; it was no longer as simple to raise one's combat tally. We worked out a cunning tactic to lure the enemy out: one of us would fire from a parapet and then expose himself by raising a cloud of dust; then he would replace himself with an earlier prepared dummy wearing a helmet. Following this Mamyedov would make the dummy move, while Khromov, Adrov and Petrishev kept watch on the enemy, establishing where their fire was coming from. If it was necessary to provoke the enemy again, the marksmen turned to Mamyedov, and he would make the dummy move again.

After that I would dispatch a precise shot at the exposed gunport. If there was no more firing from that quarter, the Germans had most likely been put out of commission.

One night our brigade was transferred to a sector opposite Matveyev Kurgan, to the left of positions which we had occupied earlier – in an area which had been occupied by the 5th Company and one platoon of the 4th Company. Our trenches ran along the western bank of the Mius. This whole section of the bank was pitted by deep gullies, while, opposite, on the eastern bank, there was a small green forest which verged on shrubberies and orchards. Here the 159th Battalion concealed their transport vehicles and rear services. Here, too, the battalion staff headquarters was located.

The group set about closely examining the enemy foreground. Within three days we had a good knowledge of where the Germans had set up their firing points and where their observers were located. No changes escaped our attention, whether it was a new foxhole dug overnight, or a trench, or the glass of a trench periscope glinting in the sun in a new place, or a new food can thrown out onto a parapet.

One day we noticed we noticed a suspicious-looking mound with a hole in its side and covered with dry grass, which had sprung up overnight in no-man's land, closer to enemy trenches than to ours. When we took a good look, we discovered that leading towards it was a communication trench covered by a camouflage netting. It was most likely a firing point which the enemy were planning to put into use at some critical combat moment. We informed the artillery about it and within an hour they had flattened it.

Senior Lieutenant Tuz convened us practically every night at his command post and listened to reports on the operations of the sniper group and the situation on the forward line. At one such meeting we reported that in the neighbourhood of the village of Shaposhnikovo the enemy had constructed pillboxes armed with large-calibre machine guns which were impossible to subdue. The battalion commander decided to involve the anti-tank artillery in the solution of this problem.

At first light the following day the commander of the anti-tank guns, Sergeant Aleksandr Lugovoi, and I set off for the forward line. He marked on a map all the enemy pillboxes I pointed out and looked for a convenient position. The objective was to roll out a gun at first light the following day for direct fire from what was for it point-blank range and put the enemy crews out of action before they could open fire. There was a risk of failure, but Lugovoi was full of confidence that it would all work out. We had one advantage – the high ground on which the enemy firing points were situated became clear of mist more quickly than the low ground from which the artillery would be firing. It was the role of us snipers and machine gunners to provide covering fire.

At night the infantry helped the anti-tank troops to construct an emplacement for their gun and at first light our operation began. Lugovoi's squad put the first two pillboxes out of action in the very first minute. The gunners planted one armour-piercing and one general-purpose shell in every gunport. The third pillbox took a bit more trouble and required four shells, but it was smashed in the end.

Destruction of further pillboxes followed and, all in all, five were accounted for; in addition, they managed to 'work over' the enemy trenches. When the enemy responded with artillery fire, the ordnance was immediately wheeled under cover.

On 10 May 1943, our 159th Brigade was combined with the 156th, giving birth to the 130th Rifle Division. It was then that I was presented with the Red Star.

Several days later, and with the permission of our company commander, Snipers Aleksey Adrov, Pavel Khromov and I set off into no-man's land. Located there were the ruins of a solid barn which we wanted to use as a firing point. Tagging along with us was Sergeant-Major Gerkushenko from the medical corps. Taking him was contrary to every unspoken sniper rule. But he was a man of some merit and had seen service in the early days of the war on the border, where he was wounded. And he was so insistent and so keen to 'go after the Fritzes' that I could not turn him down.

We made it as far as the barn safe and sound. It turned out to be made of limestone, which was capable of withstanding rifle fire, but scarcely offered protection against mortars and shells. However, it stood close to the enemy forward line and therefore the enemy were hardly likely to be able to bombard it with artillery. True, there was a risk that the infantry would attack it with a sudden charge. In this case our machine gunners should be able to come to our aid with flanking fire.

We knocked holes in the walls and opened up an excellent firing view of two pillboxes situated a mere 200 metres away from us. The sun was shining in through their gunports, which was to our advantage; it meant that, if they grew dark, there was an enemy soldier lurking there and we needed to fire.

First to shoot was Adrov, and we were instantly spotted. A real duel began. We fired at the enemy gunports and they responded with fire directed at the gaps in our walls. One time I leant over to one side to reload my rifle, and that saved me; a bullet flew in through my gunport and smashed against the opposite wall. Khromov fired back in response.

There was a flash of helmets in the enemy trench, as if they were attending to a wounded man. Gerkushenko asked for a sniper rifle, but never managed a shot – an enemy bullet struck the stone edge of a gunport and the sharp, solid splinters sprayed into his eyes. Grasping his face, he fell to the ground, wailing in Ukrainian: 'Oh, my eyes! They've knocked out my eyes! I can't see anything!' We rendered first aid, bathed his eyes with water and soon established that his alarm was in vain. The foreign body in the sergeant-major's eye was a speck of stone and it had not damaged his vision. Several minutes later he grabbed his rifle again and this time he did manage to open fire.

The pillboxes appeared to be paralysed by our fire; nobody inside risked coming close to the gunports. But the neighbouring pillboxes managed to set fire to the dry shingles of the barn roof with incendiary bullets. We couldn't stay; we were on fire and had to run for it. Helmets were being waved back in our trenches, indicating that they would cover us.

Gerkushenko was the first to make a dash. He had almost reached our lines when he grabbed his left arm with his right hand and tumbled into the trench. It was not clear if he was wounded or dead. We ran after him. I fell from the parapet into the arms of my comrades and Adrov plumped on top of me, followed by Khromov. We got up, shook ourselves off and took a look around. In the heat of battle, it was easy to miss a wound. But no, everyone was intact, except for Gerkushenko, who was groaning and being bandaged by some soldier. It turned out that a bullet had hit him in the place where he was wounded two years earlier. 'Bastards!' he was moaning. 'Hit me in the same spot! Is there a magnet there, or something?' In other words, we got off lightly.

Almost a month later we were operating from a position set up on the northern side of Demidovka. I took out a German who was carrying two full mess tins along a path. There was nothing remarkable about it except for one thing – up to quite recently the Germans had been afraid to walk there during the day. This signified only one thing: we were facing a new enemy formation which had most likely been ordered to knock out the bridgehead which we were occupying on the west bank of the Mius. The other snipers – Adrov, Bazhanov, Khromov – came to similar conclusions. We conveyed our thoughts to the company commander.

At night the scouts captured a prisoner for interrogation. It turned out that the trenches in front of us were occupied by infantry of the 17th Grenadier Division, transferred from France. Our commanders failed to take any particular measures. Soon after, a powerful enemy artillery attack resulted in an offensive and we had to leave the high ground in the hands of the 1st and 2nd Battalions of our 528th Rifle Regiment.

We went to ground in a gully and fired at the enemy, who were dashing all over our former positions, finishing off the wounded. I saw one Fritz pull the boots off one of our dead soldiers. One shot and he was stretched out beside the corpse. I also killed a German officer. But then the Germans launched another artillery attack. I was tossed up in the air by an explosion and I went deaf for a time. Fortunately, I survived.

Our own artillery responded with a bombardment. The command came through for a counter-attack. Our initial attempts were unsuccessful, but then a volley of Katyushas secured dominance. The grenadiers faltered and we regained our former positions. The Germans would not rest; again, they went into the attack. This was when our real work as snipers began. Adrov wiped out sixteen Germans in the course of that engagement and Bazhanov thirteen. The others also substantially increased their tallies.

After sustaining big losses, the grenadiers eased off and life on the Mius front returned to its former relatively calm routine. My snipers continued stalking, frequently changing their firing positions.

One day we were sitting, relaxing, in the cellar of a house, when the deputy battalion commander, Senior Lieutenant Rybalko, dropped in with the words: 'Here you are just sitting and the Fritzes are playing football under our noses.' It emerged that, according to reconnaissance reports, the Germans were enjoying some civilised recreation with a ball by an oak grove in a gully. We set off for the northern side of Demidovka.

The field where the Germans were playing was visible in full only from the eastern bank, and then only from a tall spreading oak tree, the crown of which was periodically sprayed by enemy machine gunners. Climbing it was a risk and firing from there was a double risk, but we were so keen to punish the invaders for their arrogance. I climbed up first and Adrov followed. Khromov remained below to cover us. From the top of the tree, I took a look through the eyepiece of my sights and, indeed, they were running after the ball as if they had not a care in the world.

Adrov noted with some regret that they were 800 metres away. This distance was practically the maximum possible for precise shooting from our weapons. I ordered him to set his sights, load the rifle with heavy, armour-piercing bullets and get ready to fire. We agreed that we would take two shots each and get straight down again.

We started firing. The Germans began dashing around: some rushed up to those who had been killed; others began to take cover. We too needed to seek cover. We leapt down branch by branch like squirrels and ran to the side. Almost immediately the enemy machine gunners opened fire on the oak. Lyosha Adrov remarked with some *Schadenfreude*: 'Game over. Score: four–nil to us!'

When he found out about our escapade, the battalion commander frowned and commented that we had acted too riskily; it would have been safer to strike the 'footballers' with an artillery round. But then he ordered a certificate of appreciation to be drawn up for us.

We also sustained losses. On one particularly tragic day for us Sniper Klimenko was seriously wounded before dinner and towards evening Pasha Khromov was mortally wounded. He was still alive when we found him lying on a stretcher by the medical centre. The bullet had passed through his left shoulder and lodged in his chest. He livened up when he saw us, said his goodbyes and urged us to strike the enemy without mercy.

A few days later Lyosha Adrov was conducting observations from that same oak tree and discovered a place where food was distributed to the Germans. Clad in camouflaged waterproof capes, we perched in trees at night. After some agonising hours of waiting, we heard rumbling wheels of the field kitchen in the pre-dawn mist. We waited for the Germans to crowd around it and opened fire. We fired quickly, without considering that there was simply no time left for it. Having exhausted our magazines, we almost tumbled down again and hid amidst some young oaks. The Germans finally came to their senses and directed a hail of fire at the tree tops, but we were already safe.

In the evening the scouts brought in a newly captured prisoner for interrogation. He confirmed that their unit was suffering big losses from sniper fire, which was what the regimental deputy political education officer told us. And on 7 July the Soviet Information Bureau included us in its broadcast to the whole country: 'Over a month and a half, 37 snipers from X unit have eliminated 472 German soldiers and officers. Sniper Petr Belyakov wiped out 101 Nazis, Aleksey Adrov – 66, and Pavel Khromov – 65.' We had to pay in blood for these successes. The following day Alyosha Adrov was seriously wounded.

In the first days of August the battalion took up positions opposite a wood near Saposhnikovo. There were not enough officers and, even though I was only a sergeant, the company commander ordered me to take charge of the platoon formerly led by Junior Lieutenant Valery Mirgorodsky, who was now wounded.

My detachment's position was not very advantageous; the Germans had established themselves on a hill, and we were 80–90 metres away from them on its slope. The trenches we inherited were not dug to full depth, so we had to move along them on all fours, even crawling in some spots. We were separated from the 1st Platoon by a deep gorge, and there was no trench connection with the 3rd Platoon. The ground in front of us was not mined and therefore we expected an attack at any moment. It seemed as if the Germans were in the same situation and, at night, they continually illuminated the forward line with blinding flares, which, owing to the short distance between the trench lines, fell in our rear.

Sometimes the enemy conducted harassing fire and once they even tried to carpet our trenches with heavy artillery fire, but they were not very successful. One shell exploded behind us, collapsing part of a communication sap, a second hit a trench, but a German one rather than ours, and a third dropped in no-man's land. After this the enemy stopped firing, apparently realising that they risked inflicting damage on themselves as much as us. Thereafter the enemy only bombarded us from hand-held grenade launchers.

One afternoon three of my observers lost their lives, one after another, all three from bullets in the head and under their helmets. It was clear that another enemy sniper had appeared on our sector. I reported this to my company commander and he gave orders for the enemy marksman to be eliminated. Moreover, he forbade me to leave my platoon's location, insisting that the mission be entrusted to someone else.

I defied his order, having decided to exact vengeance personally from the over-stimulated Fritz. Up until now I had fulfilled the obligations of a platoon commander with a sub-machine gun in my hands. Now it was the turn of my sniper rifle. I retrieved it from the recess where it was awaiting its hour, carefully covered with a waterproof cape, and set off to select a firing position.

In no-man's land stood the ruins of a building which had been either some kind of holiday home before the war or a storehouse for vegetables. I decided to set myself up there. There was of course a risk that it was mined or an ambush awaited me inside, but you couldn't avoid risk on the forward line. I left my assistant, Sergeant Pekker, in charge of the platoon. Before going out I explained to the platoon machine-gun squad how to cover my departure and withdrawal.

I got to the building without misadventure, and there were no mines, or ambushes there. I removed a brick from the wall and stuck my sniper rifle through the aperture. The enemy trenches were 70–80 metres away, which is point-blank for a rifle with optical sights. From that distance I could easily hit a five-kopeck coin, to say nothing of a human figure.

In the enemy defensive sector stood a pillbox. My target was probably directing his fire from a gunport there. The question was which one. I did not take my eyes off the pillbox. In the meantime, Sergeant Pekker had, by previous agreement with me, begun to shout out words from a propaganda broadcast in German, holding a shining tin-plated megaphone next to his mouth. Something moved in one of the gunports, a sniper rifle appeared, but I did not give the marksman time to take a shot. To the right of the pillbox an enemy soldier looked out from a trench and seemingly guessed where the shooting was coming from. Bang! It was the last guess he ever attempted.

My position had been revealed but I was in no hurry to leave. I chose my targets and fired one shot after another, until the magazine was completely empty. Now I could go back. Mortars were exploding near the ruins and machine-gun rounds were hitting them, but I was safe, in my trench. Pekker was still shouting something, whether suggesting that the Germans surrender or poking fun at them, but I was struggling to get my breath back.

I was called over by the telephone operator; Lieutenant Pokhiton was on the line and asking what the shooting was about. I explained. He flared up; I had been forbidden to leave the platoon. But the ruins were on my sector, so I had not formally left the sector and there was no point in him going on about it. The lieutenant's anger gave way to approval and he voiced his gratitude.

The next day I was wounded myself; a rifle grenade exploded beside me. I was lacerated by splinters, but not to a dangerous extent, so our doctor, Yekaterina Ivanovna Lavrova, allowed me to remain at the divisional medical centre. In a week I was back in action again.

The morning of 18 August, when the mist was still hanging over the Mius water meadows, saw the start of our artillery softening-up. Ground-attack aircraft were circling over the burial mound of Vorony Kamen, which was occupied by the enemy, ploughing its surface with bombs and shells. Our battalion had moved up to the enemy positions beforehand. Anti-tank guns were firing directly at the earlier reconnoitred targets and battalion mortars were crushing the German firing positions. Finally, a red flare soared over the trenches. Lieutenant

Pokhiton sprang onto the parapet and the company charged. Unable to withstand our onslaught, which quickly turned into hand-to-hand fighting, the Germans abandoned their first line of trenches.

Coming to themselves again, they attempted to counter-attack. We practically mowed down the first ranks with machine-gun and rifle fire. The same story was repeated a second time, and a third. In the end our foes were exhausted and we went on the offensive again.

On 30 August the forces of our Southern Front liberated Taganrog.[9] To the west of Mariupol, by the village of Melekino, the sailors of the Azov military flotilla undertook a seaborne assault and we were given the objective of linking up with them. In extended file our battalion moved forward until it came under fire from enemy machine guns. Some of them hit us practically in the back. We had ended up in a ring of fire.

Several soldiers were killed, the company commander was seriously wounded, and the situation became critical. A lieutenant unknown to me took command. He divided the troops in our company into two groups. One was led by me, and it was supposed to wipe out the Germans who had ended up in our rear. Sending me on my way, he cheered me up with the news that the enemy there had no more than a platoon and he advised me to take a sub-machine gun; it was handy for a commander to have one in combat.

I took heed of his view, handed my sniper rifle to some soldier whom I had never seen in my life and, taking a Shpagin PPS, I led my soldiers into the attack. I soon regretted this decision. When an enemy machine gun started up ahead of us, I uncovered it straight away and could have easily wiped out the enemy squad with my rifle, but the soldier carrying it had disappeared. Then I led my group in an attack for a second time and the Germans fled. There were indeed not very many of them and we took four of them prisoner.

All was quiet, too, from the direction in which the lieutenant had led his group. I hurried over there. From the dead soldiers I realised that the second half of our company had also had to attack an active machine-gun position. If there had been an experienced sniper covering it, extra casualties could have been avoided. Soon I caught sight of the lieutenant.

He was motionless on the ground, holding the forend of a sub-machine gun with a dead man's grip. One of the soldiers took the documents out of his breast pocket; his name was Barantsev, Nikolay, from Gorky Region. Some human figures showed up ahead. I put the binoculars to my eyes. They were sailors. We had carried out our orders nevertheless.

There were further battles – on the River Molochnaia, in Melitopol, for the Nikopolsky bridgehead on the Dnieper. On 20 November 1943, I was wounded again, this time seriously. After my recovery I ended up in the 10th Guards Army, with which I remained until victory, which found us in Prague. I had no further occasion to fight as a sniper.

10
Nikolay Nadolko

I WAS BORN ON 16 JANUARY 1926, in the village of Seyatel, in the Alsheyev district of the Bashkir Autonomous Soviet Republic.¹ By nationality I am Ukrainian. However, my family were not the victims of exile; it was just that, at the beginning of the last century, there was no spare land left in the Ukraine and people spread out in various directions in search of a better life. So, my grandfather and grandmother left home and settled in Bashkiria, where there was plenty of spare land at the time.

We lived harmoniously and contributed our labour to the collective farm. If you worked a day, you would be credited with one or two labour days and, in return, receive grain, honey, water melons and everything else the collective farm produced. On top of that, everyone had their own private plots of 70 hundredths.² Before the war I worked on a two-horse cart, carrying grain from the combine harvesters to the threshing floor. Then I got a job in the stable, which was a bit more complicated – I had to feed the horses, look after them, clean the place out and sometimes assist at foaling time.

After the war began, train-loads of evacuees came to us – mainly from Moscow. They were accommodated among the villages. Those hosted by our village were mainly Jews, who for some reason tried to pass themselves off as Ukrainians. But that was their business. We were good to them and, although they were from the city and unaccustomed to agricultural labour, they soon got used to it; they ploughed, harrowed and sowed just like us.

They began to call reservists up into the army and my father soon left. Then in 1942 I travelled to Ufa[3] and entered the Bashkir Medical College. With the outbreak of the war food became scarce in the city. A student's bread ration was 400 grams per day and you couldn't string that out for very long. But I came home every holiday and collected a full rucksack of food, so that made life tolerable.

I was called up in my second year in the autumn of 1943, when I was about four months short of my eighteenth birthday. I was sent to the settlement of Kovtubanovka in West Kazakhstan Region, where the 14th District Sniper School was located.

The school was a hungry place – the food was meagre. You got up in the morning wondering what you would eat. We would dash out to the market to buy seeds for 40 rubles a beaker. We lived hand to mouth – in large, semi-exposed, dark, windowless dugouts, each of them accommodating a whole company. Heating was provided by two smoking pot-belly stoves. Instead of a light in the middle of the barrack there was just a wick lamp on the NCO's desk, and kerosene was replaced by some alkali solution for cleaning table tops. The soot from it was so bad that, in the morning after a night's sleep, the only glow on our faces was from our eyes and teeth.

Lice were rife from the congestion. If you shook your tunic over the stove, they would sizzle on the red-hot metal. At the front it was not so bad: there were occasional sanitary inspections and our uniforms were baked through, but in the rear nobody bothered.

We lived right in the forest, but had to walk up to ten kilometres for firewood. Why, I have no idea. They got us up at five in the morning for this. At first, we each hauled back a large log: a hundred men resulted in a hundred logs. Then we got cunning; we would take two small logs and drop one on the way. This was soon discovered and we got a strip torn off us. No trucks, carts or other transport was made available to make our lot easier.

There were three sniper schools operating in the same place; ours was No. 14 and the others were Nos. 12 and 13. Most of the training was in shooting. We went on foot to the firing range and back. Teaching sessions continued through the winter, and it was a snowy winter –

snow up to your waist, so you were already tired before you got there. And from time to time the officer in charge would call out commands: 'Aircraft! Air strike!' On hearing these words, we were supposed to scatter in various directions along the road, and there the snow was not just up to your waist, but up to your chest. And then further orders would come: 'Tanks to the right!' 'Tanks to the left!' By the end you would be so worn out that life didn't seem worth living.

Our officers had no front-line experience and that is why they drove us like Pharaoh's slaves; they wanted to gain favour with their superiors, so they would not end up at the front themselves. But they knew their job well.

We fired from various distances. At first the targets – both chest-high and head-high – were not too far away. Then the exercises became more difficult. The hardest of all was shooting at a head in a gunport 300–400 metres away. But there was one tragic incident with the targets. Nothing was automated and the targets were raised on request by a soldier, who sat in a trench right on the firing range. The officer in charge kept delaying the call. The soldier lost patience and looked out to see what was happening. A sniper fired, and his brains went everywhere – he was killed. The officer in command was immediately sent off to the front.

We were not issued with camouflage gear at the school, but we were instructed in the art of camouflaging – how to blend in with the snow, how to use turf to conceal your position. As well as basic tactics, we were taught how to hold out without coughing, moving in short dashes, crawling and digging in.

Apart from these disciplines we also had parade-ground drill and bayonet practice; these exercises were the most exhausting. Our rifles would have bayonets affixed and the orders would follow: 'Long thrust', 'short thrust', 'parry to the right', 'parry to the left', 'parry from below to the right' ... First your partner would attack you and you would fend him off, then you would attack him.

Everyone there – cadets, officers, sergeants – was roughly about the same age, but there was no bullying or intimidation on the part of the sergeants or even the officers. On the contrary, the sergeants willingly shared their experience with us, for example, in putting on foot wrappings or sewing on under-collars.

Every cadet was assigned his own personal rifle and everyone tried to adjust the optical sights to suit himself. My sights were the simplest imaginable, but I knew what marking to set them on for a particular distance in order to be sure to hit the target. And also what vertical correction to make and what adjustment for movement. My rifle was likewise of the simplest kind – a Mosin. But it stood up to everything and did not jam if it encountered sand or dust.

We were trained as individuals and only put into pairs at the front. Usually, 'greenhorns' were assigned to experienced snipers, so they would learn some common sense.

The training lasted nine months – from November 1943 to August 1944 – and then we were loaded onto *teplushki* (heated railway wagons) and sent to the front along with ordinary line units. We were not given any particular title and so went to war as ordinary privates. We had been dressed in new uniforms just before departure. Along the way, in Kuibyshev[4] I think, we ran into wounded from our school's previous drafts. They were in a good mood; they were heading deep into the rear.

We were taken to a small town near Rovno (now known as Rivne) in the western Ukraine; the train went no further, as the tracks had been wrecked. We were then marched to the formation point, under the trees in a forest, where I was enrolled in the 585th Regiment of the recently formed 213th New-Ukrainian Rifle Division. Here we were under officers with combat experience. While the detachments were being cobbled together and coordinated, they told us and showed us the best ways of proceeding in various situations. It was here, deep in the army rear, that my brief fighting career began.

I ended up in a company where I became a sniper subordinate to the company as a whole. I was partnered with an experienced rifleman whose first name I remember precisely – Volodya – and his surname was something like Churikov or Chumnikov. The principal weapon of our company was the rifle, but the battalion also had a company of medium machine guns.

We marched on foot from near Rovno to the front line but, because it was already in Poland by then, it turned out to be a long trek. We usually moved by night and, the closer the front came, the more they tried to keep us out of view.

The whole of the western Ukraine at that time was thickly covered with farms. Apart from solid houses their owners had large barns with no walls which were used for drying grain. That is where we usually stopped during the day. On the march at night, we were often shelled by the Banderites. One soldier called at a house to ask for a drink without the permission of his section commander; the company moved on and he never returned – maybe he deserted or perhaps he was killed for his rifle.

On we went through Polesia,[5] surrounded by pine forests, on roads that were mainly of sand. Because the sand had been ploughed up by thousands of feet, wheels and tracks, it was very tough going. One day I was exhausted and looked around; there seemed to be no sign of the company commander and I went over to the side of the road for a breather. But, as if to spite me, the battalion commander was surveying the battalion on his mare. He spotted me, showed his anger and ordered me to carry the wheeled undercarriage of a Maxim medium machine gun. I didn't so much carry it as drag it after myself, but it was difficult to say what was easier on the sand – it seemed as if I was pulling the whole weight of the world behind me. I had to do this for an hour and I couldn't wait for this hour to come to an end. After that I didn't dare take a break on the roadside. We got so tired even without an extra load that, when a halt was called, we paid no attention to any mud below, slumped down and slept – until they got us up again.

Personally, my pack was not too heavy: a rifle, mess tin, flask, a small infantry spade on my belt, underwear, toilet items, a mug and a spoon. True, I often carried my spoon in my foot wrappings, so as not to lose it in combat. It was impossible to carry it in a *kirza* boot because it jingled around. We had to take a gas-mask with us – we were forbidden to pile it on the cart and forced to take it with us. Cartridges and grenades were not supposed to be carried on marches; they had to be issued on the forward line. In the event of an attack by the Banderites, only the patrols at the head of the column and along the flanks had ammunition.

We marched like this for about three weeks, finally reached the River Vistula and crossed at the Sandomierz bridgehead in south-east Poland. The unit which had been defending this sector of the front before us moved to the side and we occupied their trenches and dugouts. It was now the end of September and beginning of October.

Although we had taken over a ready-made line of defence, we were still constantly digging new trenches, constructing dugouts and setting up extra firing positions. Work ceased only at bedtime or in the event of a German artillery strike.

There were no enemy attacks and therefore our main activity was combatting German machine gunners. One of them got into the habit of spraying our company lines. He had several reserve firing positions which he constantly changed. You had the feeling that this was an enemy with experience – he would not allow you to raise your head.

Our company commander called me up and said: 'We've got to get the better of him.' One day before first light my partner and I advanced along our communication saps and further into no-man's land, but keeping close to our trenches. We set up firing positions 15–20 metres apart and began to keep watch. This observation period lasted only till the sun came up, so our flashing optics would not give us away. When we had finally worked out the pattern of this 'rambling' machine gunner's firing positions, we began stalking.

As a rule, Volodya kept watch while I tried to provoke the enemy: whether by raising a helmet or moving the optics on my rifle in the sun. The machine gunner opened fire several times at my position, and in the end my partner caught him – and he appeared no more. We were officially commended for this.

Another time, when a sniper appeared on our sector, I provoked him in the same way and Volodya shot him. We stalked a sniper and a machine gunner until we eliminated them, and then went out stalking every day. We usually fired from 300–500 metres – that was the most effective distance. We fired until we began to feel that our position had been spotted. Then we swiftly changed it.

I don't know how many Germans I wiped out, but somewhere near fifteen. We had no sniper record booklets, so this figure is not accurate. No confirmation of our successes was required of us – our superiors took us at our word. After I had killed my first enemy, I felt upset for a good while; after all, I had killed a man, and maybe he was not at the front of his own choice? But then I got used to it; I grew relaxed about killing, but still felt no pleasure from the other's misfortune.

One night I was resting in the dugout prior to our offensive, when I was called up by the company commander. I went to his dugout, where I found lads from various platoons assembled. He questioned each of us about our education, disposition and health, and then sent us to the battalion command post. From there we were sent on to the regimental command post, and from there to the divisional headquarters. There, after facing a commission, we were informed that we were being sent to the rear to train at an infantry college. Nobody asked us whether we wanted to go or not.

The lads with me turned out to be a cunning lot. They would rub a block of TNT with soap and pass it off as real soap to the village girls who traded all sorts – in exchange for moonshine or bread. Later they even sold their uniforms. I travelled with them to the Red Banner Odessa Infantry College, which had been evacuated to the city of Uralsk[6] in Western Kazakhstan Region. This is where my front-line saga concluded.

# Vasiliy Korzanov

MY NAME IS VASILIY AFANASYEVICH KORZANOV. I was born on 9 May 1926, in the village of Semtsy, Pochep District.[1] During my childhood it was part of Bryansk rather than Oryol Region. My mother was called Aleksandra Martynovna and my father Afanasy Demyanovich. He was born back in 1899 and took part in the Civil War, fighting on the Denikin Front.[2] I remember how, during the period of repression around 1937–8, I came home from school once and carried out the teachers' instructions – pasted over the portraits of Marshals Aleksandr Yegorov and Mikhail Tukhachevsky in our text book; they had been declared 'enemies of the people'. My father saw this and became indignant: how could they be enemies of the people if they fought for Soviet power? Tukhachevsky had been his regimental commander and Yegorov his divisional commander.

After the Civil War my father was demobilised, came back to our village of Semtsy, and went farming. In 1929 collectivisation began and he joined the collective farm. At that time, we all lived together in one house – along with my grandfather and an uncle. It was only later, when they all began to earn a bit, that they moved to houses of their own.

My father had a good knowledge of farming and was appointed deputy chairman of the collective farm. He remained in this position until the beginning of the Finnish campaign,[3] for which he was mobilised as a reservist. True, he did not actually make it to the front; he and other reservists were kept back in the rear – and then the war ended. But in World War II he *did* have to fight and he ended up as a prisoner of war.

I spent my childhood in the country. Life there was basic – today's younger generation would struggle to imagine how it was possible to go barefoot through a forest. But we did it all the time. We gathered mushrooms and berries – wild strawberries were particularly numerous around there. We could drink the water collected in hoof marks and not fall ill. The harsh peasant life toughened me up and prepared me for future ordeals.

Not far from our house was a large collective farm enclosure. As you entered, you came to a community hall and, further on, a cowshed, grain elevator, sheep pen and stable. In the middle was a well from which the stock were given water and, beside it, a conglomeration of carts and wagons. In a building close by was a storeroom in which various agricultural tools were kept.

Beside it stood a small caretaker's lodge with a clay stove and a cauldron in which potatoes and other foodstuffs were boiled up for stock food. There was a small room there of sixteen square metres, where the local men liked to gather and tell stories – about their war experiences or those of their fathers or grandfathers, their visits to other countries and the way of life in distant lands.

They also touched on the intimate details of a soldier's life and they were liable to drop in the odd coarse word during their narratives, so the presence of young folk like me was not welcomed. But nevertheless, I still found my way in there, climbed onto the stove and listened with bated breath. But because up there was the warmest place, a multitude of bed bugs crawled up there with me. We did not have them at home for some reason, but in the caretaker's lodge they bred prolifically and, as a 'reward' for listening to those stories, I often took them home. There I was begrudgingly cleansed of them. The most interesting thing was that the man with most war experience, my father, did not go to the lodge, so that, on the whole, its regular patrons talked not about their own experiences, but those of their parents or grandparents.

On Sunday 22 June 1941, many of our village residents went in to the market in Pochep; it was not far to town – only seven kilometres. People from the entire district would gather there during non-working days and exchange items of news. But that day I remember them coming back from Pochep with the news that war had broken out. Then Molotov's famous speech was broadcast by radio loudspeaker.

Mobilisation of reservists began in the village on 16 August. Because the Germans were already actively bombing neighbouring districts by then, recruitment posts were set up in the nearby forest rather than in Pochep itself. Because they had rounded up all the men on the collective farm, it was up to me, a sixteen-year-old lad, to help them on their way. I hitched up a horse, they piled their packs onto the cart with rusks and other goods, and we set off for the district centre, whence they departed for the front, and I brought the horse and cart home.

While we were passing through the forest on that occasion, my father told me a story and I have remembered it ever since. In 1914, when he was fifteen years old, he had likewise escorted the local villagers who had been called up for the First World War. They took the same road and along the way the men argued as to when the war would finish. Some claimed that they would not even be in time for it – no sooner would they have reached their destination than the war would be over. Others said it would go a bit longer. And one man nodded in my father's direction and said that there would still be time for him to take part in this war. My father remembered this very well because this man's words turned out to be prophetic. This experience was repeated in my own case.

For us the war was inconspicuous at first; however, there was one occasion when an aircraft fell right before my eyes into a small field planted with buckwheat. We boys called two men over, went up to the plane, shone torches into the fuselage and saw the bodies of two Soviet airmen. I could not sleep for two nights after this, such was the impact made on me by the sight and smell of death. But then the front moved right up to our village and the sight of death became commonplace.

Located not far from us was a poultry farm. With the Germans approaching, the civilian population, mainly women, were assembled there and began to dig an anti-tank ditch. The Germans dropped leaflets on them reading:

> Girls, don't dig these ditches in vain.
> Our tanks will cross them again and again!

When the retreating Soviet forces were passing through Semtsy, a group of scouts stayed at our place. My mother listened to what they were saying and told me that the Germans were already between our village and Pochep. We soon saw this for ourselves. In the evening shells began to burst above us; the scouts called them shrapnel. I remember the shells shrieking like a pig when they flew over.

We fled to hide in the forest beyond the village of Krasnaya Gryada, which was a kilometre and a half away, and the rear of our units was still located there. The battle for our village went on all night and all day, after which the Germans occupied it.

The forward line ran through our village fields for two weeks. Our forces even managed to drive the Germans out of Semtsy for a time, and the front moved seven or eight kilometres away from us. It was then that I first experienced the terror of bombing and hid in a covered trench which we had dug for ourselves. I managed to count thirty-six enemy bombers in the sky. As a result, the collective farm threshing floor, where we processed rye and wheat, burnt down. Many stacks of harvested grain were destroyed. Then some fields were crossed by tanks, which crushed the remaining grain crops into the ground.

Within a month and a half, the situation had changed again; the Germans took our village once more and the occupation began. I have many memories of that time. For instance, of a good-looking girl walking alongside a German column, when Soviet aircraft swooped down to bomb it. She was killed.

There were almost no men left in the village and therefore the main burden lay on the shoulders of the teenagers – those of my age. We gathered in the grain that had not been burnt and milled it. During the occupation the land was divided among families according to the number of people in them. I got a section which was sown with oats. We did not have time to reap it and it shed its grain, which sprouted in the spring. When it was ripe, we gathered it in, milled it and then exchanged it for something – I don't recall what.

Life was far from tranquil; the arrival of the Germans was followed by killings. My first teacher, Raisa Lvovna, for instance, was shot merely for being a Jew. She and other Jews were driven into the poultry farm in winter. I was told by those living close by what happened. For example, one woman with a child in her arms was shot by a German, who had smashed the infant's head in with his rifle butt, and they both fell into an anti-tank ditch.

With the arrival of the Germans, those fellow-villagers who had been called up into the army but ended up in encirclement began to return home. They first came back to their families and then dispersed. Such was the case with Lieutenant Koshelyov, for instance. He came back, looked around, changed into civilian dress, and off he went to join the partisans. He was later appointed commander of a brigade and he gave the Germans what for. They offered a reward for his head – a horse, money and other things besides, but he was never caught. He met his end just before the Red Army returned, when there was fighting in our area.

Unlike most of the other buildings in the village, our house survived by some miracle. But we did not live in it; we were forced out by the Germans and migrated from cellar to cellar. Then my grandfather and I dismantled a collective farm shed which we had spotted in the forest when we were hiding in the autumn of 1941. We transported it to the village and assembled it in a new site. My grandfather lived there while he was waiting for me to come back from the front, but he did not live to see it; he went to sleep and did not wake up. But up until then he managed to send me a number of letters at the front.

Because of the hardships of life under occupation my brother, who was ten years younger than me, died before the return of our forces in the middle of 1943. He caught pneumonia from the damp in the cellar and neither doctors nor medicines were available.

Our village was liberated on 22 September 1943. Before we knew what was happening, the district council was operating again and the recruiting office opened in the same building as before the war – it had survived by some miracle. I was called up ahead of time on 9 October of the same year. Interestingly enough, I was demobilised exactly two years later to the day – on 9 October 1945.

At first, they wanted to send me to a military college, but, seemingly because I had been under occupation, they changed their minds and I ended up with a cadet machine-gun battalion in Bryansk. In actual fact we spent very little time on machine guns and mainly studied their mechanics, or else spent the time clearing snow from the neighbouring airfield, where our planes flew in at night. The Germans also sometimes bombed it at night.

One day at the end of November 1943, however, the alarm sounded. We were lined up and sent to a station in the Bezhitsa district of Bryansk. A train arrived in the morning, we crammed into it like sardines in a can and were taken east through Moscow and over the Volga to the city of Melekess,[4] Ulyanovsk Region.

The city turned out to be half empty – war is war. We were led, several thousand of us in civilian dress, through the city in file. Our only stop was outside the city in some wood. As I recall it now, there was a small hill there and a road. On one side of the road stood a building and on the other, a bath house, which had been set up in the former house of the forest warden. Some front-line captain emerged and began to pull out the recruits one after another from the line-up. When my turn came, he asked about my education and my eyesight. My seven grades of education and good vision satisfied him. 'Fall out,' he said.

In this way this captain, who represented some military unit (men like him were known as 'shoppers'), assembled 250 men. We were lined up and led further into the forest. We were taken to a dugout in which five men were sitting. They started letting each of us into it in turn. A sergeant recorded everyone's name, after which we were drawn up again. We were divided into platoons and then it was announced that we were now soldiers in a sniper company.

Most of us were born in the year 1926. The company commander was Captain Sakharov. There were also three junior lieutenants, who were in charge of the platoons, and nine sergeants, who commanded the platoon sections.

The training commenced. In actual fact the commanding officers knew nothing about sniping and therefore in the beginning we merely studied the weaponry – the old Three Line Mosin rifle of 1891. It could be said that these studies were completely useless because in all that time we did not take a single shot or use a single cartridge. The tactical exercises comprised nothing more than constant traipsing around the forest. Nobody taught us real sniper tactics and we had no optical sights.

The food was very poor – worse than anywhere else during my period of service. When fish was served, it was fish only in name – just soup with fish bones floating in it. We were served potatoes that had been frozen at a temperature of minus 40 degrees. I remember that, because of the hard frosts in Ulyanovsk Region, we often came across the frozen bodies of birds. We were each allowed 650 grams of bread, but it was often issued half-baked and, by the time it had dried, you were lucky if half its weight remained.

We were so weary of the hunger and the pointless exercises that we couldn't wait to get to the front. In this 'unhealthy' situation I turned out to be the most 'learned', with experience in writing official letters, and I wrote a statement on my own behalf and that of several of my mates requesting a transfer to fighting units. But in the army such reports are only supposed to be directed in the first instance to one's direct superior and only via him to a higher-ranking officer. Thus, the document should have gone first to the section commander, then to the platoon commander and, only after that, to the company commander, and we had written directly to the boss.

I was summoned, asked why I thought I was smarter than my commanding officers, and put under arrest for three days. In the guardhouse the food was even worse; we barely ate at all. I was saved only by what my mates brought me. Those of us under arrest were driven several kilometres into the forest to haul firewood.

In the spring of 1944, our training finally came to an end. One morning we were put on a train and taken westward. We travelled for a while and then suddenly stopped. There was no population centre visible – just some small forest. We were led through it to a military township where dugouts and benches were set out. A while later we were taken for a meal and, for the first time in my whole period in the army, we were fed normally – in accordance with ration standard no. 9 rather than starvation standard no. 3.

A farewell was arranged for us on departure for the front. The deputy political education officer made a speech. I was stunned at the time by what he said: 'Esteemed comrades. We are farewelling our comrades who are leaving for the front. Many of them will give their lives for their motherland and never again see their native land.' He was giving us an early burial. A concert followed.

But the following day we did not leave; apparently there were no spare carriages. Another farewell evening was organised, the deputy political education officer spoke again, and once again he repeated: 'Many of them will give their lives.' We witnessed such farewells three or four times, and every time it was the same procedure. Finally, the carriages turned up and we set off; we slept practically the whole distance of a very long journey.

A while later I ended up in the 380th Rifle Regiment under the 171st Rifle Division. In effect our company arrived at the front untrained. We were saved only by the fact that the deputy divisional commander, Lieutenant-Colonel Bakeyev, organised sniper courses for us right at the front. They were directed by Captain Pirogov, who later became commander of our battalion. To this day I still offer prayers to Bakeyev; but for him I would have been killed during my first days on the forward line.

In general, he actively promoted training within the division and ran various classes. Those for snipers were immediately followed by sessions for junior officers. They were most often conducted when there was a lull at the front – although of course lull could be termed a relative concept; stray shells could still fly through to our lines now and then.

For the purposes of our training, snipers were assembled from the whole division, both those who were active and those who no longer went out to the forward line. They shared their combat experience with us and talked about the ways of German snipers, while we listened with huge attention, because our lives depended on what we picked up from what we heard. It was possible to meet and talk to each of our tutors, including the best-known sniper in the division, Captain Ivasik.

I did not get to take part in the fighting near Staraya Russa. My first military ventures were at Idritsa, Sebezh and Pustoshka.[5] I remember that, when I had only just arrived at the front, I had some tracer bullets foisted on me and I was very fearful of them, thinking: 'What if they're not suitable?' But they turned out all right. I used them to provoke the Germans into combat on my first sortie.

I had noticed them near a small copse, which consisted literally of several trees. The Germans were striding round quite blatantly and attending to their own chores. I fired a shot and they scattered. The following day their snipers embarked on a real hunt for me in this sector. Their fire kept me pinned to the ground only halfway towards the spot where I had been the previous day. The gunners came to my aid and told me I should crawl along their trench, which happened to be not too far away. They showed me where the enemy marksman was and gave me a mirror. I raised it up on a stick and the German sniper smashed it with a single shot.

Then began the day-to-day life of a sniper. We were directly under the company commander and operated against both moving and stationary targets. We tried to fire as soon as the target appeared, so that in our inexperience we often forgot to make allowance for the wind.

We were issued sniper booklets in which we made various notes, but mine has not survived. Those who confirmed the death of a German victim would sign the booklet. Apart from sniper rifles we also had binoculars. We fired from distances up to 800 metres; beyond that it was difficult to see the target.

We did not use any particular camouflage in summer – we fought in ordinary tunics, and I did not have the opportunity to serve as a sniper in winter conditions. Furthermore, when I returned to the division after being wounded, I did not see a single sniper or a single sniper rifle.

We also operated at night if there was a chance of sighting a target and annihilating it. The best-known sniper in our division was Captain Ivasik, and he always went 'stalking' (as he put it) in the evening. In his tally were over 300 dead Germans. When I reached the front, he was serving mainly as a battalion commander – he used his sniper rifle only in his spare time.

He and I got to meet, but not often. I remember in the Madona district of Latvia our battalion was encircled and only a few men escaped. We ran in some direction for a long time and met up with the remains of our own battalion, who were following that of the very same Captain Ivasik.

I ran up to him and reported that our 2nd Battalion was done for. He gave the command: 'Battalion, into battle!' and led it forward to close a breach which had opened up. Then Ivasik himself was killed. He was posthumously awarded the title Hero of the Soviet Union. Apparently, a street in the Baltic town of Madona has been named in his honour.

The first really serious engagement in which I got to take part in occurred in the vicinity of the River Velikaia.[6] It was a thickly wooded area and we were moving through it. Suddenly, a command came: 'German tanks on the right! Get out of the forest!' I thought at the time that it would not be a bad thing to shoot whoever gave orders like that. It would have made more sense to seek refuge behind the trees and, if the tanks plunged into the forest, we still had our grenades.

But some still obeyed this command and left the forest. There, for some reason, our soldiers fell under the command of some penal battalion members (troops with no epaulettes or stars) fighting there. They kept shouting: 'Forward, forward.' One of them made an unsuccessful attempt to throw a grenade, but he killed both himself and another soldier. I don't remember how but we actually repelled this tank attack.

Further on was the River Velikaia, beyond which lay a rise we dubbed Bald Hill. It changed hands several times. Once more the penal battalion troops attacked, and this time captured it, and we finally dug in there.

We then went on to fight in the Baltic, in Latvia. We had no problems with the local population but it was unpleasant dealing with the local Russian Old-Believers.[7] In the area of Tutini[8] we were attached, just a few of us, to the artillery. They were my age, all born in 1926, and we were accommodated in the same building, where I ended up arguing about religion with a Latvian who spoke Russian. At this point a gunner ran in, shouting for me to give him a grenade; he was going to throw it into the house next door, where apparently there were Nazis living. It turned out he had wanted to take a hot coal from their stove to light his cigarette and they had rudely shoved him out of the house.

He had asked for a drink of water and they wouldn't give him any and turned him away.

I asked the Latvian who lived in the house and he replied that they were Old Believers. I had heard about them from my grandfather, a very religious man. It was from him and not at school that I learned to read, and not in Russian, but in Church Slavonic.[9] Despite all this he categorically refused to go to church, although we lived close to it and, when the Easter procession passed by, he would leap out, ostentatiously close the gate and let forth a stream of obscene abuse. The reason for his behaviour was that one time long ago, when my great-grandfather died, the priest had demanded some fabulous amount (in my grandfather's opinion) to bury him, which made him very angry.

In a word, my grandfather had a good knowledge of everything to do with religion and he told me who the Old Believers were in his own sweet time. I explained to the gunners that the residents of the neighbouring house were not Nazis but Old Believers and they had evicted one of our soldiers for religious reasons rather than from some national or political hostility. It was better to leave them alone, or else there would be a national scandal.

In the battle for Rēzekne our battalion effectively perished, it could be said; only twelve men survived and no officers. We were sent some young lieutenant as new commander, and that was the whole battalion. Then reinforcements arrived and the battalion was replenished.

June 24th was a day I remember well. In the early morning, when the sun was only beginning to rise, we advanced into a meadow. Before us lay a farm of the kind known in the Baltic as a *folwark*.[10] We moved towards it. It was just as well that we were dispersed, for when we drew near, the Germans opened fire. Some of our own detachments had already secured the *folwark* and the enemy were trying to drive them out. As a result, we suffered big losses.

I knew incidentally that a prisoner had been captured who said that the *folwark* we were assaulting belonged to the father of the commander of the German detachment which was defending the area. So the enemy would fight for it to the last and simply not give it up. Where I found that out, I no longer remember.

We had just reached the *folwark* when a new artillery attack began. I took refuge behind a barn and my mate hid behind a pile of bricks. But he was out of luck; whether because the Germans had deliberately damaged a bee hive nearby or it had been destroyed by blast from an explosion, but a whole swarm of angry bees descended on him. They stung him so badly that he swelled up and had to be sent to the rear.

Lying ahead was a dense field of rye, a hill and another *folwark*. We advanced through the field towards the hill, either crawling or stooped over, just making sure we were not visible above the rye. But they opened fire with mortars and again the battalion suffered losses; we remained stuck in that field till evening.

At night we moved ahead; we could already see the *folwark*'s orchard. I went back to the first *folwark*, the one with the bees, which we had occupied, and even nodded off for a bit. In the morning it turned out there were many wounded Germans there. I began to look for our own surviving troops.

The new day dawned, and we were faced with renewing the attack, but from an orchard with a forest beyond it rather than the rye field, which now lay behind us. After a while some divisional scouts came back from there. They took up a position not far from us and reported to the staff headquarters that they could not go any further because there was a German sniper ensconced somewhere there. They had been unable to uncover him and, even had they done so, their sub-machine guns, with their range of only 200 metres, would not have been able to wipe him out anyway.

The divisional commander contacted our battalion commander, and he sent me and my mate Misha Shchemelinin, who was the same age as me, to help the scouts out. Before the war Misha had lived only a kilometre and a half from me but we ended up in the same sniper company and then in the 171st Division. There were only two of us snipers for the entire battalion. In addition to us the battalion commander selected another couple of soldiers for our protection.

Misha and I crawled to the edge of the forest, which was in no-man's land, and began to keep watch on the *folwark*. It occupied an area of roughly 600–800 square metres. After a while we noticed that the branches of a tree between the house and the barn had begun to sway. Evidently a marksman ensconced up there had slipped. We began to scrutinise the tree more attentively and noticed a rope ladder on one side of the trunk; it was barely visible.

We began trying to provoke the sniper into firing, but it didn't work at all. However, we still got him; we simultaneously opened fire at that part of the tree's crown where we thought he was sitting. Following our shots something dropped from the tree. Whether we hit him or not, I don't know, but there was no more sniper fire from the enemy's direction in this sector.

At this point someone threw a cone in our direction. I looked around and saw the scouts waving at me to come back. It had become clear that the Germans had occupied the *folwark* and the commanders were demanding an explanation from the scouts. After this the battalion went into this same forest and then mounted an attack on the *folwark*.

The battalion had barely reached it before they ran up against the Germans, who were digging a new trench on the flank of the line of attack. The command 'Forward!' followed, and the Germans opened a furious hail of fire from their machine guns. I dropped down and began to keep watch. The Germans had run off somewhere to the left, and then suddenly it was as if they disappeared – apparently, they had a trench or something like that in that spot. We charged in the direction of the *folwark*.

I now realised that the trench into which the Germans had jumped led to the barn in front of us and the Germans were probably assembling in it. Running beside me was one of our machine gunners, Pakholchuk by name, and I shouted to him that he should aim at the barn. And just at that moment I saw a machine gun poking out from there.

Then I felt something burn my left foot; the sole of my foot was hot. I paid no particular attention to it at first and ran on for several metres; I thought I must have stepped on an anti-personnel mine. I raised my foot and took a look at it. It appeared to be intact; the heel had not been torn off. But then it began to give up on me; it went numb and I lost control over it. Soon I could not even walk.

It was clear that I was no longer a capable fighting soldier. I called out for a medical orderly. Our regiment had been formed from former ski battalions and therefore there were only male orderlies. On the forward line they merely bandaged up the wounded and it was up to others to take them away. But there were no medical orderlies around and I limped hurriedly into the forest practically on one leg. On the way I did bump into an orderly; we moved off a little way to the side and got into a trench, where he bandaged me up and told me I had a so-called 'blind' bullet wound – that is, a wound where the bullet remains in the body.

Having bandaged me up, the orderly left and there was no sign of those who were supposed to carry me to the rear. Meanwhile, to judge from indications, our battalion was getting ready to repel an enemy counter-attack, and I decided that it would be better for me to vacate this spot under my own steam. I took familiar paths through the orchard and then past the *folwark* as far as I was able, using my rifle as a crutch. My wounded foot by that time had almost ceased to function.

In the orchard I came across one of our troops who had been recently killed; blood was still seeping from his riddled body. Nearby was a barn built out of rough stone. I hid behind it to get my breath back and there I found our mortar squad. Also there was a cart on which the driver transported mortars and shells from the rear. He had just unloaded some stuff and was about to go back to the rear, so he took me with him. Along the way it turned out that he was from a completely different regiment, so I ended up in some other medical centre.

This marked the start of my peregrinations from hospital to hospital. Although the wound turned out not to be 'blind', it would not heal up for a long time. Then it was discovered when I returned to the front that the reason for this was a small fragment of bone left behind in it. Although the medical staff had said that the bone was untouched, this turned out not to be the case. The fragment came out of its own accord and after that I almost forgot about the wound.

After returning to the front, I no longer fought as a sniper. I was wounded twice more: a splinter passed within a centimetre of my carotid artery, but this wound healed up in nine days, and then I suffered in a shell blast. With the same 171st Division I fought my way through half of Poland, helped to liberate Warsaw and reached Berlin for the capture of the Reichstag. In the autumn of 1945, I was demobilised as a thrice-wounded veteran and did not serve in the army again.

12 Boris Godov

I WAS BORN ON 25 AUGUST 1920, into the family of a priest in the town of Vichuga, Ivanovo Region,[1] and lived there for the first fifteen years of my life. Then, at my father's suggestion, I joined the army as a trainee in a military band. The thing was that, by that time, two families of priests in the town had been imprisoned, and my father was concerned about my future. On saying goodbye, he insisted that I should never write to him and not admit to anyone what kind of family I was from, just say my parents were workers, and leave it at that.

I first ended up in the town of Kingisepp, Leningrad Region, as a member of the 31st Turkestan Rifle Regiment and played the French horn in a band. Then we were sent off for training, in which the 204th Assault Brigade was also taking part. Their musical director was a young lieutenant and I approached him to ask if I could transfer to his unit. Of course, he said; they would be glad to have me. So, in 1939, I went to Borispol,[2] where this brigade was stationed. As a member of it, I spent a month away at the war with Finland.[3] I did not see action because there wasn't any in our sector. The Finns were on some islands in a lake, while we remained on the shore. There were plans for us to liberate the islands; it is possible that our brigade even made attempts to occupy Maksimansaari and Putkisaari, but I don't remember the details. My occupation was totally non-military – playing the horn.

The Finns had a lot of sub-machine guns and their fire made it impossible to get up and attack. But it could be that our troops had no particular wish to attack – they realised that there was no point. As a result, on Red Army and Navy Day,⁴ the then General Zhukov visited our lines and ordered the air force and artillery to blast these islands to smithereens together with all the enemy forces dug in there. The planes turned up and bombed the hell of out of the islands. We arrived later, and found nothing, and no one, left – the Finns had taken them all away, both living and dead, and evacuated everything they could from the island.

As it happened, the war ended at this point and we were given 400 rubles each as a bonus and dispatched south through Belorussia – by summer we were already liberating Bessarabia.⁵ By that time our company, which comprised medical, music, quartermaster and sapper platoons, needed a deputy commander for political education. I was offered the position and eagerly accepted, graduated from a school for junior officers, and became deputy commander for political education. Because I possessed only one military skill, that of musician, I was made a health instructor as well – assault force members were supposed to have a minimum of two special skills.

My standard weapon was a self-loading SVT (Tokarev) sniper rifle with a magazine holding ten cartridges. I had attended courses for snipers back home while still at school. I had often fired rifles, only without optical sights, and I wasn't too bad at it. In the unit I was considered almost the best shot. Commanders often asked me to stand in for someone to help them out and I almost always scored nines or tens.

After liberating Bessarabia, we returned to Borispol, which stood on the eastern bank of the Dnieper, 30 kilometres from Kyiv. It is now the site of Ukraine's biggest airport, but back then it was a military airfield with the longest runway in Europe – 5 kilometres. It was constructed specially for the large four-engine Tupolev TB-3 bombers. Just before the war there were plans to lengthen it by another kilometre and a half and construction equipment was brought in for this purpose, but military action disrupted the project.

Our training was of the highest standard. An assault trooper was considered to be a self-sufficient battle unit who ought to be able to safeguard and provide for himself in any conditions. Special stress was placed on the 'safeguarding'. We spent a lot of time being taught how to fall without breaking anything; we also learned hand-to-hand combat and the art of survival. The training lasted almost two years and we were constantly occupied.

Actual parachute jumps were few and far between; I did only twenty-four. The twenty-fourth was in Bessarabia and there were none after that. We were dropped from heights between 1,000 and 2,000 metres and we jumped with both a main parachute and a spare one. We packed them ourselves in large special sheds, after which we had to sign that we had done it ourselves.

All assault troops were armed exclusively with automatic weapons: SVT Tokarev and AVS Simonov rifles, PPSh Shpagin and PPD Degtyarev sub-machine guns, and Tokarev and Simonov machine guns. We also had 37-mm spade mortars, which had to be stuck in the ground before use, as well as 50-mm company and, I believe, 82-mm battalion mortars. The brigade was equipped to the highest standard and in physical terms the personnel were impeccably trained.

I was in Kyiv when the war began – one of our lieutenants had been killed in a parachute jump and we had gone to his funeral. We stayed the night with the relatives of our musical director; they had a large apartment in Kyiv. There were about twenty of us and we probably slept on the floor. We had decided to take a stroll in the park the following day, a Sunday, and go back to Borispol in the evening. But the bombing began in the morning, our musical director got us all up, and we set off back to our unit.

The brigade was thrown into battle at the beginning of July – the Germans were hurtling along the Brest–Lithuania highway towards Kyiv. We were dropped off by army transport in the neighbourhood of the old border near Novohrad-Volynskyi.[6] Two German battalions had launched forward and left us with the problem of cutting off the highway in their rear and crushing them. We surrounded them in two hours and wiped them out. Thanks to our automatic weaponry we created a huge curtain of fire, under which the Germans began to panic. When a thousand men begin rattling away with sub-machine guns, it's a terrifying force. If we moved into a gap, we snuffed out any enemy resistance momentarily. But this advantage of ours had its drawback – we never had enough ammunition. Our shoulder packs were half full of bullets. If the machine gunners were running out of cartridges, the other troops would shed some for them – usually half their load.

In this, my first engagement at Novohrad-Volynskyi I operated both as a sniper and as a medical orderly. Under our fire the Germans began to scatter; they did not know where to run. It was an open area, with fields on both sides of the road. I would take aim with my SVT, look up, and a German would have fallen. I did not experience any particular emotions. I fired, and a German tumbled over, fired again, and another fell. Every one of my bullets resulted in a corpse or a casualty. The Germans began to put their hands up and surrender; in the first month of the war this was a rarity.

During a bombing raid near Novohrad-Volynskyi I suffered badly from blast. The general staff decided to send back to the rear but, because I was a health instructor and knew everyone in the medical unit, I got them to agree to let me stay. Then the Germans burst through and, while we were retreating, I left my sniper rifle at the brigade headquarters in Novohrad-Volynskyi.

After serving in the assault forces, I had two and a half years with divisional reconnaissance; this was from late autumn 1941. The Germans were hurtling towards Moscow and moving up their forces to Tula,[7] while we were bringing in the Far Eastern and Siberian divisions. I was assigned to the 413th Rifle Division, which was transferred in seventeen train-loads to Stalinogorsk.[8] By the time we got there, the first of our regiments was already embroiled in the battle, so the Germans knew who they were fighting and were tossing leaflets from aeroplanes offering surrender – in other words, why should we fight if the war would be over in a month in any case.

My regiment almost completely perished there. We were facing the elite Grossdeutschland Division and its mortars carpeted our positions with dense fire while their tanks circumvented us on the flanks to crush our artillery. The Germans were actively supported by their air force, while we had no such backing. When the regiment became almost incapable of fighting, it was finished off by the enemy infantry.

As a result, we had to retreat. Our artillery was horse-drawn, and therefore it all stayed where it was. I remember seeing there a large pre-revolutionary 122-mm howitzer of 1914 vintage. We left that behind. Our divisional artillery regiment had 122-mm howitzers and 152-mm guns. Our gunners fired at tanks, but discharged most of their ammunition too early. More shells were brought up, but they turned out to be the wrong calibre. They were 76-mm and by that time all our 76-mm guns were either destroyed or put out of action.

I commanded a reconnaissance group during these engagements and had eleven men under me. The entire divisional reconnaissance group number numbered twenty-nine and they reported to the head of the reconnaissance section, who was a major. We were hardly ever used to perform our basic function; rather, we acted as a reserve – we would be told that the Fritzes were pressuring a particular village and thrown in there.

There was a constant shortage of ammunition, so we had to use captured enemy supplies. As a result of that experience, I cannot stand German grenades – because of their long handles, the way they flew through the air, and their nine-second delay, it was easy to pick them up and toss them away. I tried to stock up on our own F-1 grenades. I had them packed away in all possible places; I would carry up to ten of them. But I was not keen on bottles full of inflammable liquid. We once had some delivered that did not ignite. After 1941 I did not encounter this kind of weapon.

One time in winter on the Ugra River,[9] we were assigned the job of assisting one of our own companies. We got through into the designated village to find this company already in action – the Germans were attacking it. We delineated sectors with the commander, who was a lieutenant. My men dug in on the left flank, covering a field and a wood from which the Germans were continuously attacking, while the lieutenant took care of the centre and the right flank.

We had a captured German machine gun with interchangeable barrels and it fired well. We beat off the first attack; the Germans were approaching in small numbers. On the second attack there were more of them; five Germans broke through in the centre and our lads surrounded them and took them prisoner. Then came another attack and at this point my men got up without a command for a counter-attack. Several of them were wounded, some perhaps even killed. Then someone had the idea of making the prisoners retrieve the wounded. We had only just dealt with this when there was another attack. The Germans burst into the village again.

They set up a machine gun in one of the houses. I was standing with a staff sergeant not far from its kitchen window when the Germans began to fire at us. A bullet wounded me slightly but hit him right in the forehead. I tossed an anti-tank grenade in order to keep this machine gun quiet at least for a couple of seconds; it exploded near the house. Then I dashed up and threw an F-1 grenade in the window. Three Germans leapt out and two were killed on the spot. We took the house back. Thus, in half a day we had repelled six attacks, but we had also helped the company and held the village. We began to withdraw in the twilight because there was no point in hanging on here – no reinforcements or orders were forthcoming. We rejoined the regiment; I was given a ticking off for withdrawing the detachment without instructions, but there was no further punishment.

In the winter the Germans began to retreat, and we pursued them, picking up a lot of weapons as trophies. I acquired a Parabellum pistol and Mauser sniper rifle with sights of eight-fold magnification. Nothing like the four-fold magnification I was used to. I found it in a German cart which had got stuck in the snow and been abandoned; we captured it without a fight. The lads would collect enemy sub-machine guns and cartridges and exchange them for vodka.

I also collected bullets for my rifle. There were four varieties: ordinary, armour-piercing, exploding and tracer and they had different coloured heads: green for tracers, black for armour-piercing, and the rest I don't remember, but they made a fine collection. I was curious as to what cartridges consisted of and, with the aid of a file, I carefully worked away at them – both our own and enemy cartridges. If you file away at a tracer cartridge, white phosphorous seeps out. It glows in the dark and we had fun with it, smearing our mates' moustaches while they were asleep. We were idiots; we did not realise that you could poison yourself with it.

The tracer bullets once came in handy for my Mauser. The Germans had dug in at a village and we couldn't dislodge them. They wheeled a gun into a barn, blew out a log from one wall and fired from there – we couldn't get at them. Our machine gunner fired away at the straw roof of the barn, but was unable to set it alight. So, I told him: let me have a go. I fired a German tracer bullet and the barn immediately ignited. Both the barn and the house next to it burnt down.

One of my wounds is connected with this rifle. I have four altogether: two shell splinters hit me in the hip joint, one almost reaching the bladder; another, between my vertebrae, has been with me for my whole life.

One day I noticed a German officer on the forward line, saw that he had a red stripe down his trousers and decided to take him out with my captured sniper rifle. The distance was quite normal – about 500 metres. I lined him up, took aim and fired – one shot and he was down. They all rushed towards him and I fired again, and at this point they spotted me. I began to crawl away from my position and that is when they got me.

After that I had no further contact with sniper weaponry. I had done my bit and been awarded my decorations and medals. For me the war finished on 11 May 1945 in Germany.

13

Maria Bondarenko

MY NAME IS MARIA DMITRIYEVNA BONDARENKO (née Kataieva). I was born on 23 February 1925 in the village of Kostino, in the Kirovo-Chepetsk district of Kirov Region.[1] My father died when I was only four years old, so my first childhood recollection is of his funeral and the priest and church choir singing. I have no memory at all of my father's face.

After completing six grades of schooling, I began work on the collective farm. On 22 June 1941, the war began and life became very difficult; there was real privation. We ceased to receive anything much at all for the work contributed to the collective farm: we were provided with hay and straw, and that was it. Not even a gram of bread was issued and we lived on what we grew on our own allotment.

In 1942 I went to the recruitment office and said that I wanted to train as a sniper – I was very keen to get into the Central Women's Sniper School in Podolsk.[2] At seventeen years of age of course I was not wanted by anyone. The recruitment officer told me straight: 'Go play with your dolls; there's no war for you.' But I was persistent, and went back a second and a third time. Then, on one of my visits, it fell to my advantage that, sitting next to the official was some colonel back from the front, who told him to sign my application.

It was 1943 before my call-up papers arrived. I went to see the collective farm chairman, explained what had happened and requested provisions for my family. He issued a whole pood[3] of flour. My mother was able to bake some bread at least, or else we would have lived just on potatoes. When she saw me off to the front, she gave me an icon of the Mother of God. I carried it with me through all my campaigns, carefully guarded it and, when I came back from the front, I brought it with me.

I went to the recruitment office, where girls of my age were assembled, as well as some 'real ladies' of twenty-five or so and, when the escort came, we set off for Podolsk. We were in the school's second draft of sniper cadets.

The school was located in a five-storey building in a settlement around a cement works. We arrived in September and tuition began immediately. We were taught to march, to crawl on our elbows and to shoot – standing, lying and kneeling. We were trained using Mosin rifles equipped with sniper sights. The teachers devoted a lot of time to camouflage. Finally, in March 1944, the course concluded, and we held a graduation party and set off for the front.

I ended up with the Belorussian Front; some eighty-five of us were sent there. My group of forty girls was met, shown the dugouts in which we would live, and registered for rations. During the first few days we were taken out to the forward line, so that the new arrivals could get their bearings, become familiar with the scene and take a look around. Then, when we felt completely at home, we were divided up among different units and sub-units. I finished up in the 259th Rifle Regiment within the 179th Vityebsk Red Banner Rifle Division.

My first engagement is solidly imprinted on my memory. We were advised in the early morning that an offensive was about to begin. I took up a position in an oak tree about eight metres above ground level. We were set the task of wiping out machine-gun squads when our soldiers got up to advance. After that we were simply to eliminate German manpower.

We always operated individually in our firing positions. We were armed with SVT (Tokarev) automatic rifles with sniper sights. Thanks to the self-loading mechanism we could follow up every shot with another, which increased the probability of hitting the target. It was a magnificent rifle, fired with great precision, and I had it with me right through the war.

My rifle had PU sights with a 3.5× magnification. I always fired with maximum magnification, as it enabled me to aim better. I tried to shoot from distances of less than 500 metres, but sometimes this had to be extended to 800, although this happened very rarely, most often on attack. When our units were advancing, I liked to take up a position in a tree. At the sniper school we were also taught to conceal ourselves under burnt-out machinery – under armoured cars or tanks – but I didn't like that because visibility was poor.

On an offensive we strove most of all to wipe out the enemy, and we fired with great frequency. But the most frightening thing of all was when the artillery of each side was bombarding the other; you felt you could perish at any moment. My mother once wrote to me at the front: 'You should get married, girl. Some girls are coming back from the front with babies and living in the rear, and you could get killed where you are!' I answered her: 'Mum, I won't be coming home that way. It'll be with a chest full of medals or a headless body!' She was badly upset by my reply.

I could hit an enemy soldier in the head from a distance of up to half a kilometre. Occasionally I might fire from a kilometre away, but no further than that, as it became difficult to scrutinise the target. We fought only during the day – we had no devices to enable night-time shooting. We wore the usual field uniform: tunic and trousers, with an overcoat for cold weather. In modern war films we are shown in some sort of camouflage, but that is all nonsense; that never happened.

As a rule, we used ordinary cartridges. Tracers were recommended for adjusting a rifle and correcting your line of fire, but we did not use them. Nor did I have occasion to use incendiary bullets.

I can remember my first enemy victim – he was a middle-aged German machine gunner. When I shot him, I felt no particular emotions, but later I began to cry, or rather to sob. For a long time afterwards, I smeared my tears over my dirty cheeks thinking about his children awaiting their father . . . and I had killed him. We were each issued 40 grams of alcohol, so I drank it down in one gulp and never wept again for enemy casualties. Nor did I ever drink alcohol after that. War was a dreadful thing, like the Lord's Passion; it was frightening enough just to sit on a tree stump, never mind actually fight.

After several days our forward push fizzled out – the Germans knocked out many of our infantry units and we were again placed on the defensive, awaiting reinforcements. We snipers took to stalking. It was done like this. I would go out to a forward-line trench, prepare a position in one section of it, make a gun port and camouflage it so that neither it nor my rifle was visible. Then I prepared a second and a third position. I always did at least three. Then I began to keep watch, to wait for some heedless German to appear. I would fire and immediately move over to my second gun-port, fire again and proceed to the third. The German snipers on the other side also engaged in stalking, especially against us women. They had no female snipers, just men. This *modus operandi* continued until reinforcements arrived and the front moved westwards once again.

In the autumn of 1944, I was promoted to sergeant and put in command of a platoon section of women snipers. By that time, we had almost reached the Baltic States. Fighting there was hard; the ground was swampy. It was in the Baltic that I was wounded for the first time; a German sniper sent an armour-piercing incendiary bullet through my left boot and foot. My second wound was a graze from a tracer bullet fired by another sniper. But we gave as good as we got; I personally wiped out four of them. They were spotted with the aid of binoculars. In the beginning I had the standard field glasses with six-fold magnification, and then I came across some German ones with the same magnification. But I never used a telescope for observation; they were too heavy and unwieldy. Binoculars were much better.

When you saw that you had killed an enemy sniper, you felt a particular satisfaction, because they inflicted heavy losses on us – many of our own girls perished at their hands.

My sniper section was seconded to various regiments and our objectives were set by their commanders. When we came back from the forward line, we went to the regimental command post, where everything was written up on a special board; significant landmarks, observation sectors, numbers of kills. The general staff kept constant watch on our operations through a stereoscopic telescope and recorded our successes, and then we transcribed them onto pads for ourselves. Altogether I killed twenty-eight Germans in the course of the war and this figure was confirmed by the general staff.

We often ran into the scouts near the regimental headquarters when they were going out on reconnaissance, and they would invariably come up, give us a hug and say: 'Wow, girls, I can't wait!' But the deputy political education officer would spot them hugging and kissing and call one of the scouts over: 'Come over here and sign for the donation of your salary for a tank column; tanks are needed for the front.' He was such a bastard. Because of him the lads became too scared even to give us a peck on the cheek. We would see them off beyond the front-lines with our good wishes. And often they did not come back; two might leave and only one of them return. And yet they were still just boys – eighteen- and nineteen-year-olds.

As soon as I was put in command of a sniper section, there were attempts to turn me into a so-called 'campaign wife'. One night an orderly turned up about 2:00 a.m. and the woman on duty shouted: 'Kataieva to report!' I was perplexed, wondering what urgent business there could be – it was dark outside and nothing was visible. I went out to see the orderly and he said the regimental commander was summoning me urgently. So, I went with him. We arrived at the staff dugout, and there a table was laid. I reported in as Sergeant Kataieva. The regimental commander said I could stand easy and put my weapon down.

I sat down and suggested that there must be an offensive set down for the following day, since he had summoned me with such urgency. But he laughed in reply and told me bluntly that no offensive was planned at the moment and that I should come and live with him. I then stood up and answered clearly that that was not what I had come to the front for. It wasn't for this that the state had spent resources on my training – it was my duty to kill Nazis rather than lie abed with sundry old codgers in their fifties. I was only eighteen and I would return home a virgin. The commander pointed to his head with one finger and told me I must have a screw loose. Maybe so, I replied, but when I go home to my village, my husband will be happy to carry me over the threshold.

I went back on my own, without the orderly. The girls were straight onto me as to what had happened and I told them everything, without holding anything back. Katya, a girl from Moscow, who was twenty-eight years old, said: 'You fool!' In the end she married the same commander; she didn't mind who she went to bed with. On the other hand, she did drive around in a staff car, while we were still trudging on foot.

However, when I returned home, I married Sergey Bondarenko and he really did carry me over the threshold. The people of Kostino gossiped away: you shouldn't marry her; she's back from the front with her medals, but she's probably been under a bush with someone or other. So on the day after the wedding Sergey hung out the bloodied sheet for the whole village to see.

Fighting in winter was particularly hard. The Germans were no fools and donned white trappings like us, so that it was difficult to pick them out against the snow. For the sake of camouflage their officers on the forward line tried to dress like their men. It is only in modern films that they run round in peaked caps and epaulettes. In fact, in their field dress they were barely distinguishable from ordinary German soldiers.

I was wounded for the third time while we were defending a position in East Prussia. I was observing through a gun port with my binoculars when a shell exploded next to me. A splinter hit my left cheek, knocked out my teeth and skewed my whole face. I remember being afraid at the time, thinking: who will marry me now with my mouth all squint. But I did not even have to go to hospital; in the divisional medical centre they straightened my face out and put my mouth back the way it was.

The fighting for Königsberg was particularly fierce and we had a hard time. It was here that we called a halt.

In January 1945 I was awarded the medal 'For Valour' and in March, by order of the 530th Rifle Regiment, 156th Rifle Division, I received the Order of Glory, 3rd Class. A second Order of Glory was presented to me in May 1945.

When we learnt on 9 May that the war was over, our joy knew no bounds. We had a meeting at the staff headquarters and organised a festive parade. We had just got back to our quarters when we saw the surrendering Fritzes making their way along the road – whole divisions of them plodding along. Some strode with their heads proudly held high; others were limping with their eyes on the ground. Personally, I felt enormous relief when I heard the news of victory – now I wouldn't need to kill any more.

14 Anatoly Nevara

I WAS BORN ON 3 JULY 1927, in the village of Komisssarov, in the Olkhovatka district of Kharkiv Region.[1] Interestingly enough, it was even called that before the Revolution. My parents had a big family – nine children, although two died in infancy, so that left four daughters and three sons, including me.

I learned about the outbreak of war from a radio speaker; they had been installed a year or two earlier in the main squares of all population centres. They were square-shaped objects, hanging from posts, and from them we learned the latest news. On the first day of the war Molotov spoke and announced that the war had begun.

My father was a Communist and chairman of the Party's regional executive committee. My eldest brother and sister were also Communists and had graduated from teachers' colleges. My brother incidentally left for the front as a volunteer during the very first days of the war, returned and subsequently taught in our school. By the time the Germans were approaching Kharkiv Region, we were already familiar with stories of what they did to the families of Communists on occupied territory, so my father decided not to tempt fate and to evacuate. He was given two horses and a cart, and we loaded our modest chattels and set off. True, we did not have to travel far with the horses – standing at another village was a train for evacuees; my father came to some arrangement and we travelled further east on it. As for the cart, Father handed it over to a military unit for temporary use.

We were evacuated to the village of Brabander in the Kukkus district of the Volga German Republic.[2] My father became chairman there. At first, I worked in the fields with him, gathering the harvest, and then he appointed me head of the fishing team, which at first comprised only women and old men. In actual fact the old men took no part in the fishing; they just told us how to set a net and pull it out – shared their experience.

As soon as Kharkiv Region was liberated, Father made to set off back home. My mother tried to dissuade him, saying that here at least we had a home, and there was nothing back there. But Father would not listen to her, and back we went. We returned to find everything in ruins: villages burnt, cities destroyed, gallows still standing in squares in some places. My father was appointed chairman of the district manufacturing combine – to make tables, chairs, doors, windows. I qualified as a joiner and began to work for him.

My father complained one day that there was a shortage of fountain pens in the district. He asked me to take one to pieces, find out how it was constructed and see if we could put them into production. I did so; there turned out to be nothing complex about them, and soon we were making these pens and supplying villages with them.

When I turned sixteen, I began to write to the recruitment office, asking to join the army. I was put off and put off, and received call-up papers only after I turned seventeen. I was then sent to the No. 30 regional school for top-class marksmen to undergo sniper training in the town of Piryatin, Poltava Region.[3] The recruitment commissioner was probably hoping that by the time I had finished training, the war would be over, but it continued for another whole year. The school was on the edge of the town and was quite large – several hundred cadets were taught there at the same time. Recruits trained for half a year in monthly stages, so that every month one draft graduated and another began.

The cadets were mainly soldiers who had distinguished themselves in sharpshooting at the front. There were several dozen young folk like me, of whom I was probably the youngest.

The instructors were all front-line veterans, but they drove us so hard that I can't remember any of their names. Some of them walked with canes owing to wounds; others had no arms or legs, but they all had combat experience and a superb knowledge of their field. From morning to evening we learned to shoot and dug sniper lairs big enough for two; moreover, we dug them in a horseshoe shape, so that if a shell struck, there would be a greater chance of at least one marksman surviving.

Adjacent to the school was a huge training field, where nobody had cleared up the traces of recent fighting – burnt-out tanks, wrecks of artillery weapons and vehicles. This is what we trained on.

They drove us night and day, so I can't even remember when I managed to get some sleep. The platoon commander would take us out in the dark to some area, indicate an imaginary forward line and an imaginary enemy line, and order us to set up and camouflage sniper lairs. In the morning he would walk out to his designated German lines and, if he could detect any of our firing positions from there, the culprits responsible would spend the whole day digging new ones, while the rest of us had shooting lessons. I became a very good shot. Later, as an officer, I was a member of the regional shooting team and once I even got to the Ukrainian republic competitions.

We used ordinary Model 1891/30 rifles, without bayonets but with sniper sights attached. I don't recall the degree of magnification, but from 300 metres I could easily see a man's head in full detail. With the aid of two drums, we could adjust the sights according to the wind speed and distance and we had a decent chance of hitting the target from distances up to half a kilometre.

We were well fed, but with occasional lapses. There were periods of several weeks when we ate nothing but swede. And one time an officer discovered several wagon-loads of buckwheat under an embankment, and for a certain period that is all we ate: buckwheat porridge for breakfast, buckwheat soup for dinner, and buckwheat porridge for supper. After a week of this diet, we were dreaming of swede. But, despite the disruptions, we could always rely on getting tea with sugar and a small lump of butter in the morning.

When we had completed five months of training, we were formed into a group of 280 men and sent off to the Second Ukrainian Front on probation. At that time, end of February – beginning of March 1945, there were still positional battles being fought. We were issued white camouflage gear along with our winter uniforms.

As soon as we had disembarked on arrival we were seconded to various units – roughly ten or twelve per regiment. From the regimental staff headquarters I was sent to a battalion, and from there to a company. In the rear of this company lay a village on the outskirts of a town; this was in the West Carpathian part of Czechoslovakia. We were issued weapons – brand-new sniper rifles, probably brought in specially for our probation and well calibrated. We were not accustomed to this; at the school the weapons were worn out old things.

Our sniper operations began. We would go out into no-man's land while it was still dark and make ourselves a lair. This was about 300–400 metres from the enemy lines and 50–70 metres from our own trenches. The preparation took several days but finally we completed it. After this we began to crawl out every day to our lair before it was light and take up our firing position. We took dry rations with us and sat in our lair till dark, after which we crawled back and collapsed into bed till first light. That went on for a whole month. In actual fact I spent around twenty days at the front.

We almost never spoke to the other soldiers – only at supper time – and, even then, we only exchanged a couple of words. We got very tired. It would appear that all you were doing was sitting and looking continuously through your gunsights. But in actual fact, after a day of this you were overcome by a dreadful fatigue, though you became aware of this only in the evening when you began to loosen up your numb body and crawl away.

Supper was the only meal we ate in the trenches; breakfast and dinner we took with us as dry rations. Our supplies included American canned stew, I remember this, and big lumps of sugar which we smashed with hammers. There were also American canned vegetables. These were only issued on the forward line. When we went back to the front, a field kitchen cooked borshch and porridge, but only fed us twice a day instead of three times: at dawn and in the evening.

My partner and I took turns at firing. We drew lots to determine who would take the first shot. When it was my turn, I would adjust the sights and look for a target, while my partner would just indicate significant landmarks where he might have noticed something. In order to be able to record in my sniper booklet that a target had been hit, I needed the confirmation of my partner and a lookout from the infantry, so not everything got recorded. But we were regarded as being on probation, so we did not pay much attention to this.

We took very few shots in the course of a day – one or two, three at the most. There were days when we didn't fire at all. According to my calculations, in twenty days at the front I wiped out nine Germans – that is for certain, disregarding the dubious hits. My partner Boris scored roughly the same. But I was credited with only the three kills that were actually confirmed by infantry lookouts. Their attitudes to probationers were dismissive, and only changed when I 'bagged' an officer.

We only moved position once. When bullets began to whistle over our first lair, which was under an oak, it became clear that we had been spotted. Then we dug a new lair in a different place – this time beside a tank.

Our probation period was already coming to an end when we went out into no-man's land one more time. It was sometime after midday and it was my turn to shoot, when my partner called out in an agitated voice: 'Tolya, an officer.' I spotted him; his peaked cap had a sort of high crown. I was just about to press the trigger when the target disappeared. My partner was sympathetic: 'Not your day.' But then the officer re-appeared, this time with a pair of binoculars, and began to look beyond our forward line. There was no distance between us – 300 or 400 metres. I aimed between his eyes and fired. I saw him fall, and the binoculars too.

We quietly cried: 'Hurrah!' under our breath. My partner almost jumped up with joy: 'You got him, Tolya. You got an officer. Now it's just up to the infantry to confirm it.' At this point the Germans began to pummel our forward line with their artillery, firing for around half an hour. One shell exploded beside my partner, burying him and deafening me.

I crawled along the trench to my partner, dug him out and bandaged him up. He was still breathing. I don't remember where he was wounded, except that it was in the chest. 'Vanya! Vanya!' I called but he did not hear me and did not come to. I unscrewed the top from my flask and tried to get him to drink, but more of it was spilled than went into his mouth. In the evening, with darkness falling, a few infantrymen crawled over – back in the trenches they had guessed that something was wrong. We pulled Vanya out, but he was already dead. The infantry helped me to drag him and his weapons back to our lines. To a large extent they dragged me as well. I saw no more action after that and only a few days remained to the end of my probation period. By the time our group set off back to Piryatin, only about half of us remained; some had been killed and others ended up in hospital.

I went back to the school. Graduation plans were made: a shooting test was organised and exams on tactics and several other subjects under battle conditions. Graduates were fitted out in new uniforms, issued new *kirza* boots and sent off to a transit camp, with the front as their final destination.

There I slept for a few days on a three-layer bunk. One time I woke up because I felt someone removing my boots, looked down and saw that some beanpole with a nasty look about him had already got one boot half off. I told him to lay off and he replied that they wouldn't take a milksop like me to the front anyway; I had been lying there for three days and they weren't sending me off. So, I didn't need new boots, while for him, a front-line veteran and hero, they would come in handy. He was prepared to give me his worn-out pair. I took a look around, but the other troops were either asleep or pretending to be asleep. I cried out, but the thief had almost pulled one boot off.

At this point a sergeant with two decorations on his chest – the Order of Glory and the Red Star – emerged from a bottom bunk. 'Cut it out,' he told the beanpole. Then somebody else got up. The beanpole let go of my boot, but grabbed a knife and attacked the sergeant. But then somebody else jumped on him from a top bunk, another sergeant with front-line experience. The others also pounced on the beanpole, wrestled him to the ground, tied his hands and took him to the head of the transfer point. It turned out that he was no front-line veteran but a real criminal. He had engineered the whole thing at the transit camp and intended to sell the boots later. He was arrested and I got to know the front-liners who had come to my rescue: Sergeant Lunin and Senior Sergeant Yudin. We were joined later by Ignatyev, another graduate from my sniper school.

We all asked we be sent to the front, but we ended up at the Kharkiv general military college for infantry and, when that was disbanded, we were all, except Ignatyev, transferred to the No. 2 Kyiv general infantry college named in honour of the Communists of the Zamoskvorechye district.[4] We had been studying for some time when the alarm went off at five in the morning. We rose quickly; all officers were with their detachments and gave the command: 'Form up without weapons!' We ran out and fell in on the parade ground, and then the school principal, a front-line general, ordered the head of staff to read out the command: 'On the occasion of the conclusion of the Great War for the Fatherland,' he read, 'the gates of the college are being opened and all cadets are granted two days of leave to celebrate Victory Day.'

Outside machine-gun bursts could be heard here and there, flares were leaping up into the sky, and there was noise all around. Dawn had broken. We sewed on clean undercollars to go with our uniform, which was still new, and went into town. There the residents were all out on the streets, shouting, crying, hugging and kissing, especially the women. That was how I celebrated victory.

15 Mikhail Budenkov

MY NAME IS MIKHAIL IVANOVICH BUDENKOV. I was born into a peasant family on 5 December 1919, in the village of Slavtsevo, Vladimir Region.[1] After completing seven grades of schooling, I worked on a collective farm. In 1936 I enrolled in a course in naval mechanics near Moscow and, after graduating from that, I spent two years on the Moscow canal on the diesel vessel *Busygin*. In 1939 I went back home and worked as a tractor driver.

In November 1940 I was called up into the army. I ended up serving on the western border of Belorussia in the 15th Rifle Regiment within the 49th Rifle Division. In the winter our 2nd Rifle Battalion was fully transferred to the 84th Rifle Regiment in the 6th Oryol Red Banner Rifle Division and stationed at the Brest fortress.[2] My platoon section stood out for its high level of firing readiness. In February 1941 a competition was organised for us. I fired at three targets: a chest-high target at 100 metres, a disappearing target at 200 metres, and a moving target at 300. We were issued three cartridges for each and every one of my nine bullets hit the target. The company commander, Mikhail Tuzikov, voiced his personal appreciation to Nikolay Klopov, Mikhail Morozov and me. This was the first award of my entire military career. Apart from that we were given a leave pass for the city of Brest.

My high degree of accuracy was the reason why I was sent off to the 30th Special Sniper-Training Company, in which all detachments of the 84th Regiment were involved.

Exercises in the sniper company began in March 1941. They were conducted by Lieutenant Belikov, who subsequently lost his life during the first days of the war. Much attention was paid to selecting the right firing positions, both basic and reserve, and camouflaging them, moving swiftly and invisibly between them, and developing the ability to measure distance by eye – being able to estimate the distance to the target is very important for a sniper. Our topics of study included 'The sniper on attack', 'The sniper on defence', 'The role of the sniper in repelling enemy counter-attacks', 'Firing at tanks and aircraft' and 'Eliminating enemy snipers, observers, spotters, and reconnaissance and signalling groups'.

We also had constant shooting practice. After three months each of us could land all three issued bullets within a circle of two centimetres diameter from a distance of 100 metres, which exceeded the expectations of our commanders. The best shots could hit a cartridge case from the same range.

The training was meant to finish on 1 July, but the outbreak of war forced adjustments. On the last Saturday of peace-time, 21 June, the skies were sunny over Brest. We spent the day estimating distances to targets and camouflaging positions. It never occurred to us that we had only a few hours of peacetime life ahead of us.

On returning to our units, we put our weapons in order, sang as we marched in formation to dinner and began to prepare for a free afternoon in the city. I polished my boots till they shone, ironed my trousers and tunic, sewed on a fresh under-collar, washed my foot wrappings and handkerchiefs and wrote a letter home. The following day I was due to pick up some photographs in Brest and I mentioned this in the letter. But I was not destined to pick them up.

In the evening after supper the company watched a film. It was a lengthy screening and as a result we went to bed significantly later than usual. In the early morning we were wakened by the rumble of artillery salvos beyond the Bug[3] and shells exploding on our unit's grounds. The earth was shaking from the explosions, walls were wobbling and huge columns of smoke and dust were rising into the sky above the Brest fortress and the southern military township. They formed such a dense shroud that the sun could barely shine through – we greeted the war in darkness.

The sniper company responded to the alarm. Soon Lieutenant Belikov appeared. He looked confused and he was not wearing his tunic – he was just in his boots, riding breeches and shirt. He said the Germans were directing a massed artillery attack at the southern military township.

We were almost unarmed. On the previous Wednesday we had been told that for each pair of snipers the appropriate weaponry would be a Three Line magazine rifle and an SVT (Tokarev) automatic. Consequently, half our rifles had been collected and there had not been time to issue new weapons. Besides this, we had very few cartridges and not a single grenade. We armed ourselves while battle was already raging, after shooting the locks off depots which the enemy had already set fire to.

We took up an initial battle position in the old training trenches by the highway leading to the southern gate of the Brest fortress. We could hear the sounds of rifle fire; it came from the border guards and soldiers who were building pillboxes in the fortified district. By that time the Germans had already managed to drive the border guards from their posts and were drawing close to us. At first their scouts decided to burst through at a rush, on motorbikes with side-cars, each of which seated two infantrymen. But after running into our accurate fire, they turned back. It was in this engagement that I killed my first Nazi. Meanwhile Belikov had sent two signallers to the divisional headquarters, but they never returned; there were no orders with regard to further action.

The Germans continued to reconnoitre our positions; three scouts appeared on the right flank. They crept under cover of the fumes and dust, aiming to create panic by penetrating through to our rear. I happened to be the closest to them, discovered them in time, and aimed at one of our uninvited guests. A muffled shout followed and one of the Germans fell to the ground. I kept the two others pinned down with my rifle fire; we needed to capture a prisoner to interrogate. In the end they abandoned their rifles, got up and raised their hands. Under interrogation these gentlemen in high boots with iron-capped soles and uniforms with cuffs folded back behaved quite arrogantly, told us nothing and just bellowed: '*Russe kaput, Moskau kaput, Heil Hitler!*' We had to dispose of them.

Soon after that a real hail of fire descended on our sector; we were the target of artillery and mortars, and bombs were falling from above. After dropping their loads, the enemy planes blanketed us with fire from their machine guns and cannon. Then enemy tanks appeared to the north of the fortress; they surrounded us and by the end of the day we were in an encirclement.

The retreating forces formed a detachment around which those escaping encirclement gathered – infantry, gunners, tank crews, airmen, sappers and medics. At first it was a disorganised rabble, but then commanders emerged. By day we mounted a circular defence and at night we began to move eastwards. All those fit and able assisted the wounded, carrying the serious cases on waterproof capes. Along the way we overran small detachments of enemy marauders and troops from the rear, and soon we were almost fully equipped with German weapons and ammunition. But there were cases where we too bore heavy losses in these night-time engagements. Exploiting their crushing advantage in air power, artillery and armoured vehicles, the Germans dispersed our detachment along the way. Near Kalinkovichi[4] I emerged from encirclement with several dozen chance companions, who had also been cut off. From there we were directed back to Gomel[5] for re-formation.

I was wounded for the first time during the initial weeks of fighting as I was escaping encirclement. An enemy mortar splinter got wedged in my heel bone and has remained there to this day. During the fighting on the River Sozh,[6] where we were sent from Gomel, a German bullet drilled a hole in my hip. The lads made a dressing and helped me back to the rear, where my lengthy peregrinations from hospital to hospital began.

The next time was when I had ended up at the front in winter, as part of reinforcements to the 2nd Guards Division led by Colonel Porfiry Chanchibadze. Its objective at that moment was to cut off the Minsk highway between Yartsevo and Safono, join up with General Belov's cavalry and encircle the Vyazma[7] German grouping.

On arrival I was very keen to acquire a sniper rifle, but there weren't any and instead I got a 50-mm mortar. I was familiar both with mortars and with this particular weapon and knew that it had a range of 800 metres. So, it didn't cause me any difficulties.

It so happened that, at the end of February 1942, my friend machine gunner Vasilyev and I were dug in on a hill in the area where the Minsk highway connection with the city of Dnipro had been cut off and in fact defended it for several months, till the beginning of April. The approaches to our position were mined and therefore we felt secure. We were occasionally sent reinforcements, several men at a time, but the battalion by that point scarcely amounted to a platoon and the reinforcements quickly drained away while we continued to fight.

Finally, on 5 April, I was wounded for the third time while repelling yet another enemy attack; an explosive bullet hit my thigh bone and tore away a lump of flesh on its way out, leaving a wound 9 × 7 centimetres across. This time I was out of commission for a long while and only returned to the forward line in November.

I ended up among reinforcements for the 21st Guards Division and was designated a mortarman in the 59th Guards Regiment, where I took part in the Velikiye Luki[8] offensive, which lasted from 24 November 1942 to 20 January 1943. Our division formed part of the 3rd Shock Army, which was allotted a principal role in this operation. At the beginning of December, the River Lovat was well in our rear and we emerged to the south of the Chernozyom railway station on the Velikiye Luki–Nevel railway line, thereby fulfilling the objective set by the commanders. Now the Germans were no longer able to use this highly important transport link to supply their 7,000-strong Velikiye Luki grouping.

On reaching the designated line we were ordered to dig in there and prepare to defend it. On our sector the Germans were holding on to the village of Sedurino, in which only a single house was still standing, and that had lost its roof. Our forward line ran through the village of Leskovo, which the Germans had completely burnt down. As we dug trenches and made dugouts, we had no idea that we would be dug in there for a long time – a whole year.

Although the commanding officers were quite happy with me as a mortarman, in March 1943 they acceded to my request and transferred me to a rifle company, where I became a sniper once again. I had continually bombarded the general staff with applications for a transfer because I considered that I would be more useful on the forward line as a sniper; after all, I had undergone lengthy training for this special role. I was aware that I had more chance of surviving as a mortarman but, given the knowledge and experience I possessed, I could not just calmly spend my time sitting in a bunker; I was irresistibly drawn back to the forward line, and they finally took note of my views.

The commander of our mortar platoon, Lieutenant Eduard Ermel, a Tartar by nationality, was very upset at my transfer. He liked the way I fought and we had become friends. One day I gave him a graphic demonstration of my shooting prowess. Even before my transfer I had equipped a firing position, from which I kept watch on the Germans. One day I took Ermel to it and he gasped in amazement. I was about to tell him where and how I had acquired my sniper skills when a Fritz suddenly appeared. Pointing him out to the lieutenant, I got my rifle into position and began to wait for a suitable moment. The rifle was a standard Three Line; I did not have one with optical sights at that time.

With a knapsack packed to the brim on his back and a sub-machine gun across his chest, the German emerged from some bushes and began to make his way along a gully towards a rise known as Height 190. I caught him in my sights and fired. He stood there for a second, swayed to one side and fell into the snow. It was my twelfth victim. Ermel looked at the enemy's body and said that now he understood why I was keen to join the snipers, but still remarked that I had a greater chance of surviving the war as a mortarman.

Finally, on 22 February 1943, on the eve of Red Army Day, I was presented with a sniper's record booklet, in which it was noted that on this day, while still a mortarman, I had wiped out nineteen Fritzes with my sniper fire. At the personal initiative of our divisional commander new sniper rifles were brought into the division. He presented me personally with rifle number 1661; I remember it to this day.

On our regiment's defensive sector, to the right of Leskovo, stood Height 190 and behind it, the Chernozyom railway station. Slightly to the south-west of the village, beyond the railway line, was the village of Sedurino, which now comprised a single dilapidated house. When I was a mortarman, I was not very interested in this building; I merely knew that behind it, further on towards the forest, there were enemy mortars. Now this house in no-man's land drew my attention. I was confident that the Germans had set up a firing point under it. The food cans scattered around nearby pointed to this. I decided to make my way into no-man's land with my partner Vasiliy Shkrablyuk and wipe out the Germans who were trying to get into this house. If nobody showed themselves, we would simply set fire to the house and shoot those who leapt out. At night, under cover of darkness, we moved out. The soldiers in the trenches had been warned that, if we fired, they were immediately to let off several machine-gun bursts to prevent the enemy from spotting us.

By first light we had prepared a lair 150 metres from the enemy forward line and camouflaged it. The house in Sedurino with the suspected enemy firing position seemed to be quite close. Vasiliy went to ground about fifty metres behind me. He was supposed to cover me in case of necessity.

The sun had long been up but no movement was observable on the part of the Germans. My back was getting very warm and my mouth had been dry for a long time. I spotted a heap of dry rubbish in the attic of the house and fired an explosive bullet. The rubbish caught fire. Several machine-gun bursts resounded behind me, intermingled with the sharp crack of uncoordinated Three Line shots.

The seconds slowly ticked by; the fire spread, fanned by the wind. I waited patiently to see if Germans would leap out of the house or not, whether my calculation was correct or if I was mistaken. In the event it was vindicated many times over. The first German appeared, a shot was fired, and he fell. Behind him appeared another. A second shot and he bit the dust beside the first one. Then the Germans crawled out one after another and I barely had time to reload my rifle. All in all, the fire drove out seventeen of them, and not one escaped alive.

The fire grew even stronger. Finally, there was a powerful explosion as the ammunition inside detonated. It demolished the house and tore the German bodies to shreds. It was only possible to leave no-man's land by night and therefore I waited till late in the evening and only then crawled back to join Shkrablyuk. Together we returned to our trenches, where we were given a triumphant welcome by our comrades in arms.

In the sniper company at Brest, it was not explained to us that no-man's land is the best place for a sniper. I worked it out for myself while I was crawling along the forward line by the Chernozyom railway station: the enemy were liable to search for you in the trenches and the pillboxes behind them, but not right under their noses in no-man's land, from where you could strike at him invisibly from what was for a sniper a short-range distance of 200–250 metres.

The more actively our snipers operated in the spring and summer of 1943, the deeper the enemy dug in and broadened his network of trenches. But we learned how to select for our firing positions sites from which at least a small sector of the enemy's communication trenches was visible. In other words, you could look and fire. Thus, the Germans could only feel completely secure against our fire in the dead of night.

Of course, there were cases when a sniper went out stalking and came back without having taken a single shot. In such cases our snipers joked about it, referring to the 'culprit' as a 'loafer' and his barren day as 'idling'.

We kept waiting for the enemy snipers to come after us. We knew that they existed and that their rifles were just as good as ours and fitted with the remarkable Zeiss optics of 8× magnification as opposed to our 4× Soviet sights. Because of this we constantly camouflaged our firing positions very carefully. And then one day it did happen.

On this day we made a sortie into an ambush set on the sector of the 69th Regiment of our division. When we got back, the company commander, Captain Surkov, said that an enemy marksman had drilled a helmet lying on the parapet of one of our trenches. We were set the task of eliminating an enemy sniper.

Overnight we questioned soldiers in all sections of the company, but neither the riflemen nor the machine gunners had the slightest idea where this dangerous foe could have dug in. Then we decided that two sniper pairs should make a sortie and try to provoke our enemy into action. However, this proved fruitless; the German sniper did not take the bait and react to our false targets and that meant that the man facing us was no novice.

As the sun was declining one evening, I glanced through its last rays at the slopes of a hill lying significantly north of Sedurino and spotted a barely noticeable pall of smoke, which instantly dispersed in the swiftly darkening blue haze. Lengthy observation of this sector enabled me to detect in time the narrow strip of a gun-port skilfully concealed from our eyes by grass. Apparently, the enemy marksman had lit up, and I had fortuitously espied the smoke of his cigarette.

I continued my observations. A small pillbox low to the ground had been built 10–15 metres in front of the enemy trench and was most likely connected with it by an underground passage. It was less than 200 metres away from us. We convened a small council of war and decided to strike the enemy from no-man's land at first light, when he would be blinded by the rising sun. We circumspectly dug niches near our firing positions in the expectation that the Germans would respond with concentrated mortar fire to the loss of their sniper.

In the morning, an unaccustomed, almost dead, silence reigned on the forward line. One might have thought there was no war on at all. And then I took aim at the enemy gun-port and fired a tracer bullet at it. My shot was covered by several more from the trenches. Meanwhile my mates began to fire bullet after bullet at the gun-port of the enemy pillbox, preventing its occupant from even raising his head. At the same time, I trained my sights on a machine-gun post a few metres to the south, where the Germans were setting up a gun.

My calculation was fully vindicated. Frustrated by our fire, the enemy sniper went back via the underground passage to his trench, emerged at this gun site, laid down and raised his rifle . . . but he did not get time to fire it. I riddled his body several times, so that no doctors would get him back on his feet again.

I had a hunch, though, that it would be better not to take my eyes off this louse's body, and I continued my observations. An hour went by, and a second, and then another Fritz appeared. He dragged away the dead body, but he could not reach his rifle; it was too far away from him. It seemed that he was very keen to grab that rifle. First, he tried to reach out to it with his hand, but could not do so. Seeing that no one had fired at his hand, he crept out into the machine-gun site at full height... That was what I was waiting for. At night we crept back from no-man's land and reported to Captain Surkov that the objective had been achieved.

June 22nd, 1943, marked two years since the outbreak of war, and on this ill-fated day I was wounded yet again. It happened like this. Along with my sniper mate Stepan Petrenko I had gone out, while it was still dark, to our earlier prepared firing positions at the junction of the 59th and 64th Regiments in our division. By midday the sun was baking down and it was very humid, but we kept up our patient watch on an enemy trench, a small part of which we were able to observe lengthwise. The exits of two enemy dugouts looked directly out on it and it was the occupants of these who were the object of our 'undertaking'. We notified our soldiers in the trenches behind us of the operation; as usual, they were supposed to muffle our shots with their own and, where necessary, cover us with their fire.

Petrenko and I were quite some distance from each other but, if required, we were able to cover each other. However, thanks to this position we were able to view through our sights a more significant sector of the enemy trenches than if we had been right up close to them.

The hours went by agonisingly slowly, sticky perspiration dripped into my eyes and insects tormented me, but all these hardships were soon rewarded; almost simultaneously a Fritz emerged from each dugout and approached the other. When they met in the trench, one stood at attention before the other, who was bald and presumably an officer. I instantly shot him through his denuded skull. He waved his arms as if he was threaded on a string and fell dead. I had not had time to reload before the other nipped into his dugout. But as an experienced sniper, I realised that someone would most likely attend to the body.

I did not have to wait long; about ten minutes later another German looked out of his dugout. He quickly glanced around like a gopher and made a lively dash for the long, weighty body of the dead German. He began to run his hand over his tunic, feeling the pockets; evidently, he was collecting documents and suchlike. It appeared that this Fritz had decided that his senior officer had been killed by a stray bullet, a regular occurrence at the front, rather than a sniper's bullet, or else he would have acted more cautiously. At length, the German finally grasped the nettle and knelt beside the dead man – and that second, he became a dead man himself. His body writhed around for several seconds in a death agony, but then it straightened out again and lay still.

The presence of two corpses now left no doubt that there was a Soviet sniper operating in this sector, and the Germans hunkered down in their dugouts. Over an hour went by, and then an enemy mortar battery opened fire along no-man's land. Their squads did not know where we were and were firing at random. The first salvo fell quite a distance away from Petrenko's and my positions, but subsequent explosions churned up the earth much closer; one mortar detonated almost beside me and I felt something strike my leg.

In an attempt to tease out the German battery, our mortar crews responded to the enemy bombardment. This resulted in a duel and, as a result, the enemy forgot about us for a while, which was what I needed. I quickly crawled over to my reserve firing position and took off my boot, which was filled with blood. Stepan soon made his way over. He was all in one piece and that showed we had got off lightly. My partner helped me to bandage the wound. It turned out that my leg had been penetrated by splinters in three places. We waited for the cover of night and I limped over to our own side.

This time I spent three months in hospital. At the beginning of October, I managed to get myself transferred to a battalion of recuperating troops attached to the 153rd Reserve Regiment. I had simply decided to escape back to my own unit, but to carry out this plan in pyjamas would be tricky; uniforms were not issued to the recuperating. Having received my boots, tunic and riding breeches, I did not of course go to any reserve regiment, but headed towards the forward line. I was detained by a barrier detachment[9] but when its commander, a lieutenant, learned that I was not deserting but, on the contrary, heading for the front, and received confirmation from my regiment that I really was a sniper wounded on 22 June, he almost gave me his blessing. Soon I was back amongst my own lads and literally two days later our division liberated Nevel.[10] We took the town easily, seizing around forty caches of enemy ammunition and other military supplies, but we still had to hold it: fierce battles raged. Nevel suffered severely from shelling and bombing, but at least we held it.

By the end of the week the battle intensity had eased and the Germans began to dig in. While keeping watch on their forward line one day, I discovered a lone sniper lair on a hill across a highway; most likely the enemy had set up an advance post in it for the night. Before first light I made my way out to our forward trench, found a convenient position there and began to keep watch. Soon I caught a glimpse of a helmet above the lair. It looked as if a Fritz was gathering something up and would emerge any minute. And indeed, he soon crawled out, but instantly froze, pinged by my bullet. At first, he thrashed around in a weird fashion, raised his legs and sluggishly moved his hand, and then he lay still. I shot him a second time and waited, but nobody else came during the entire day. This was the twenty-seventh Fritz I had killed during the operation to liberate Nevel and by 25 December my overall tally came to 158.

The best place for a sniper during an offensive is ahead of the main line, but in this case, it was necessary to use all means of covert movement. Then, if you could remain unnoticed, you could easily strike at an enemy observer and wipe out a machine-gun squad. I was able to attest to this during the battles for the Maievo Heights, as a result of which almost our entire company perished in the middle of January 1944.

The Fritzes had hidden access to the top of the hill via a river bed, along which they were able to lead up reinforcements while remaining outside our field of vision. We had to walk 800–900 metres across an area exposed to fire with snow up to our waists. Thanks to a dense system of trenches and pillboxes supplied with water from snow, the hill was converted by the enemy into a well-fortified strongpoint. Several earlier attacks had been smashed to pieces before us.

When our company commander, Lieutenant Mikhail Goryunov, explained the battle orders, he said that the regimental command had decided to draw the entire battalion together into a single force for the attack. True, we did not have much manpower left, but orders were orders.

I proposed that before the attack I should take up a position in no-man's land and support our troops through my rifle fire. Covered by the din of battle, I would be able, unnoticed, to quell the enemy machine guns and artillery observers. Goryunov agreed with my proposal and so, donning a white camouflage suit, I set off for no-man's land. Although the weather was frosty, by the time I had reached the position I had mapped out for myself, a small shell hole, I had worked up quite a sweat.

I had barely taken a good look around before two flares shot up and our mortarmen opened fire on the hill. Simultaneously the company attacked. I began to knock out the enemy machine guns with my rifle fire. Magidov, one of our soldiers, fell into my shell hole as an uninvited guest and immediately sustained a light splinter wound in the head. It was not life-threatening but it tore off a solid strip of skin. I had to take a break in order to bandage him up, after which, under the cover of the descending gloom, he made his own way to the rear. While I was occupied with that, our attack finally conked out.

Goryunov leapt down into my lair and the company ascended to the middle of the hill, but went to ground, barred by enemy mortar fire. We began to wonder what to do next; there was no possibility of help. At this moment the Germans sent up a series of flares, opened fire in a desultory fashion, and let off several salvoes of mortar bombs. During this bombardment our company commander was killed and responsibility for commanding the remains of the company fell to me, because there were no officers left and I had been made Party organiser literally the day before.

I realised that night time was the right time to attack and this was our only chance. I gave orders for the lads to sneak up as close as possible to the enemy trenches, toss their grenades and burst into the enemy fortifications. They did so, and as a result my reliance on the suddenness of our attack was fully vindicated. A few surviving Fritzes fled in panic, leaving behind an MG 34 machine gun, which I was well familiar with by then, and some cartridges and their long-handled grenades. I took over the machine gun and laid my sniper rifle down on the parapet.

At first the Germans unleashed a squall of shells and mortars on us. The fire was so dense that the hill seemed to be seething like a volcano. Because there were very few of us left and we were highly dispersed, the company suffered only odd losses here and there. The bombardment continued for half an hour, after which the first lines of the enemy infantry came forward. A lone machine-gun round served as a signal for the assault.

We decided to let the enemy within slaughtering distance and only then to open fire. I pressed the trigger when they were only about a hundred metres away. The captured machine gun proved superb at mowing down rows of its former owners. This was repeated by the sub-machine gun rounds and rifle shots of my comrades in arms. The dead Fritzes fell like stacks of straw and the wounded attempted to crawl away. The few survivors finally proved unable to hold out and took to flight. Soon there was barely a single living German on the hill. I discovered only one, about 25–40 metres away. I took up my rifle. Through the sights he appeared to be only an arm's length away. I fired right at his helmet. The bullet knocked it off his head and the Fritz flopped down, stunned by the blow. With a second shot I finished him off.

The enemy tried to make a second attack with the support of five tanks. Fortunately, they were hindered in approaching the hill by the steep banks of the nearby river, thanks to which the Germans had until quite recently been able to take reinforcements up the hill unseen. The tanks supported their thinning advancing ranks with high-explosive and machine-gun fire but, even so, it proved impossible to capture the hill. Soon the whole slope was paved with enemy corpses. During an interval between attacks, I noticed four Nazis who had incautiously emerged from behind a bush and bunched up together. I grabbed my sniper rifle and fired, then again – two of them immediately fell into the snow; the rest quickly evaporated.

Finally, towards evening the attacks ceased; there were hardly any Germans left. There were only eight of us, practically all wounded and needing medical assistance. But it was only at night, when it was pitch black, that we were relieved by a company of sub-machine gunners and the regimental reconnaissance group. On the following day the battalion was taken away to rest in the rear.

Our battles in the winter of 1943/44 cost us dear. We bore losses. I myself was twice wounded by shell splinters and the second wound took two months to heal. But by spring the division had arrived at the Belorussian border. As a reward for my heroism and achievements the commanders sent me on leave. Being able to see the familiar sights of home again after almost four years was for me a very precious reward.

However, my leave quickly came to an end and I returned to my company, which had been substantially reinforced, and 22 June 1944 saw the beginning of Operation Bagration,[11] which resulted in the liberation of Belorussia and much of the Baltic region.

On 6 July 1944, 1st Company of the 59th Guards Regiment crossed the River Drissa.[12] I was entrusted with the command of an advance detachment. The Germans only discovered us when we were climbing out of the water on the bank we had captured. One of their machine-gun squads opened fire, but it presented no danger to us; by that time, we were in the 'dead zone'. To the sound of machine-gun rounds I scrambled up the steep slope and silenced the enemy with a couple of grenades. We got through to level ground and quickly expanded the bridgehead. The resultant enemy counter-attacks failed to drive us back into the river; we withstood the pressure. Having crossed to the west bank, our units moved forward of their own accord, and our Baltic offensive began.

We now made occasional stops during which we consolidated on the territory we had gained. Here we frequently withstood several enemy counter-attacks before moving forward again.

The next enemy onslaught on our lines took place on 27 July 1944. We made a long march overnight and by morning we had already secured the Daugavpils–Livani highway. The severely thinned ranks of our battalion took the lead and the remaining regimental units followed. We had no problems capturing the road. But it turned out later to be an enemy trap; they had decided to blanket us with machine-gun fire and then wipe out the survivors.

The principal German forces were concentrated on a farm to one side of the road. On a hill to its left was an enemy pillbox. The main body of the company gathered in a pit from which earth had been taken for road repairs. I went up, noticed a foxhole there and occupied it.

By that time the enemy mortars had opened fire on previously designated landmarks. Apparently, the Germans had worked out beforehand where our forces would gather and were now shelling those areas, inflicting palpable losses on us. These were indeed the most significant losses our company suffered in the course of our progress through Latvia. Our company commander Nikolay Ponomar, my old friend Kolya Korotkov, and many others were wounded.

I remained safe and sound and kept watch. I noticed some ranks of Nazis preparing to attack. They were advancing at full height under the command of three officers; one was in the centre and two on the flanks. I shouted to our own troops that we were under attack and trained my sights on the first of the enemy officers, who was striding along on the left flank. The shot resounded and the officer spread his arms as if clutching at the air, swayed and hit the ground – followed by the officer on the right. It was now the turn of the officer in the centre. He waved his arms as the bullet hit him and flopped down flat on the earth.

I was joined by the rest of my comrades-in-arms. Although I had now fought for over three years, this was the first time that my fury and hatred had reached such a boiling point. I dispatched bullet after bullet at the German soldiers and failed to notice two enemy tanks crawling out from behind some bushes and supporting their infantry with fire. I sobered up when fountains of earth rose before me, stirred up by the tank machine gunner. I immediately rolled into a shell hole and that saved me. The tank switched to another target – the squad manning a medium machine gun. It fired a shell at them and wiped out the entire crew, after which the enemy tank crawled away again. In spite of our losses, we still repelled the enemy attack.

In the evening an order came for the company to capture the farmstead. But how could this be done when we had only nine men left? However, orders were orders. As Party organiser, I took command and suggested that we employ reconnaissance tactics. Under cover of darkness, we crept up towards the enemy trenches, which had been dug out on a hill next to the farmstead and then charged them. Before jumping down into them we waited for our grenades to explode in the communication trenches. This daring assault was successful; we wiped out the enemy and occupied the hill, dug in there, and began to think how to seize the farmstead, but it turned out that the Germans had abandoned it themselves.

In the morning I counted up the enemy losses. In their counter-attack on our positions, when I killed the three officers, they numbered just short of thirty or so. But there were only five left from our company; as a result of the assault on the hill occupied by the Germans, we had lost another four wounded. The commander of the reconnaissance detachment from the next unit discovered to his surprise that the farmstead and the hill, where he had been ordered to reconnoitre the enemy lines, had already been liberated. He mentioned that that day, 27 July, our troops had liberated Rēzekne and Daugavpils and suggested where we should look for our own division, whose zone of attack now lay in a different direction.

By 20 August we were already in the area of Ergli, a large Latvian village only 100 kilometres from Riga. Here the Germans halted our company with massive firepower, by one of the farmsteads. Our platoon commander, who was standing in for the recently killed company commander, lost his life and once again I had to take over.

The only solution was to take out the enemy machine gunners. I took advantage of a hold-up which occurred with an enemy machine gun, which was pinning the company to the ground. It looked as if the Germans were changing the belt and I crawled into a less dangerous position. From there I crawled on my elbows to the foot of the rise on which it was set up. The slope was so steep that I remained unseen by the Germans. However, I had a good view of them. Following some muffled shots from my rifle the machine gun fell silent. I got up but could not see anything except discharged shells – neither machine gun nor machine gunners. Seemingly, the rest of the crew had dragged their bodies away.

I went to ground on the hill, but then I noticed another trench covered with drying twigs. It was situated 80–100 metres closer to the farmstead, from where they were still firing at our company, which had gone to ground there. I quickly moved over there and, three minutes later, I caught sight of a German running with a machine gun over his shoulder about seventy metres away. One shot and he hit the turf. Then another one came near carrying boxes of ammunition; he ended up lying next to the first one.

I was now quite cut off from my own forces and situated to the right of the farmstead. If the Germans had discovered me and attacked, it could have been an awkward situation.

Meanwhile time was elapsing and evening drawing in. At this point I spotted a gathering of Germans, as many as half a company. I almost lost it; apart from a rifle and grenades I had nothing, and they were heading in my direction. Given the weapons I had, it looked like curtains for me and there were only minutes to think my way out. Then I made a decision; I crawled towards the two machine gunners who I had killed several hours earlier. Approaching the body of the first German, I pulled his MG 34 towards me and then the box containing the machine-gun belt, which turned out to be unused. I occupied a firing position among some stones, set up the machine gun, loaded it and looked around. The Germans were still forming up right in front of me. They were gathering around their officer, waiting for something or someone. Having checked my weapon once again, I let off an initial long burst, then a second one and then fired without a pause.

The dumbfounded Germans dashed into the bushes in panic, shouted, and dropped down, while I fired and fired. Later the lads worked out that, not counting the four machine gunners I had killed with my sniper rifle, I had laid low some sixty-seven Fritzes with the machine gun that day. When I stopped firing and came to myself, it turned out that, thanks to my fire support, the company had entered the farmstead.

I fought in the Baltic until the middle of September 1944, after which the commanders sent me to study at the Moscow Lenin Double Red Banner Military–Political College. Then my name was put forward for the title Hero of the Soviet Union; my overall combat tally by then amounted to 449 dead Nazis. The order was signed off on 24 March 1945, and a month and a half later the war finished. I celebrated that notable date, 9 May, in Moscow. Another six weeks later, on 24 June, I joined in the victory march through Red Square in the ranks from our college, having already taken part in the legendary Victory Parade. For me that was the end of the war, which I had left home for almost exactly four years earlier on the western boundary of our country, in the hero-city of Brest.

Notes

Chapter 1

1. Now Lomonosov, near St Petersburg.
2. The regiment became better known as Major-General Fedorov's 'automatic' company, as it had been issued with a selection of prototype self-loading rifles – the work of the Russian rifle designer Vladimir Fedorov, who subsequently did much to set up a Soviet designer school.
3. A voluntary paramilitary organisation set up to support the defence, aviation and chemical industries by training reserves for the armed forces.
4. 'Shot' in English: the name given to officer-training courses in the Soviet armed forces.
5. Near Moscow.
6. The qualification *modifitsirovanniy* ('modernised') is not universally accepted as having official sanction, though now widely used to distinguish the two types of sight.
7. 'Three Line' alluded to the rifle's calibre (7.62-mm or .30-inch using traditional measurements): 'line' was a term used for one-tenth of an inch.
8. Prior to the adoption of the Tokarev rifle, Degtyarev and Simonov rifles had undergone evaluation. Operating manuals confirm that at least a few examples of the Simonov-designed AVS, adopted in 1936, were equipped with optical sights to serve as sniper-rifles.
9. Tsentralniy Arkhiv Ministerstva Oboroni Rossiyskoy Federatsii ('TsAMO RF', Central Archives of Ministry of Defence of the Russian Federation), Chest 217, group 1221, case 226, inventory sheet 151.
10. TsAMO RF, Chest 1119, group 10803, case 336, inventory sheet 101.
11. TsAMO RF, Chest 376, group 10803, case 336, inventory sheet 101.
12. A spelling discrepancy in the original Russian text gives the second mention as 'Buzolin': both surnames exist.

13. TsAMO RF, Chest 6525, group 7461c, case 2, inventory sheet 267.
14. Also known as the Young Communist League, the Komsomol organisation acted like a Communist Party youth division.
15. A system for compulsory military training of civilians, Vsevobuch was originally established in 1918.
16. TsAMO RF Fond 235, Opis' 2074, Delo 1065, List nachala dokumenta v dele: 27.
17. TsAMO RF Fond 239, Opis' 2224, Delo 193, List nachala dokumenta v dele: 69.
18. TsAMO RF Fond 841, Opis' 1, Delo 140, List nachala dokumenta v dele: 97.
19. TsAMO RF Fond 500, Opis' 12451, Delo 407.
20. In Chudovo District, north-west Russia – T.N.
21. TsAMO RF Fond 1359, Opis' 1, Delo 12, List nachala dokumenta v dele: 41.
22: 'Double claiming', where more than one person claimed the same kill, is a common phenomenon – for example, claims made by RAF pilots during the Battle of Britain often proved to be overstated when compared with actual German losses.

Chapter 3

1. Central Ukraine.
2. Mid-Siberia. During collectivisation of agriculture – from 1929 – many of the more prosperous farmers were driven off their properties and exiled to Siberia or Kazakhstan.
3. Dyachenko appears to have been sent on an extraordinary journey – 1,500 km north to Norilsk, whence his call-up papers emanated, and then 1,500 km south to Kansk for training!
4. West of Moscow.
5. Just over 200 km east of Leningrad/St. Petersburg.
6. A locality just south of Leningrad.
7. A war-cry which seems to have arisen from an English or Dutch naval warning to watch out below, as something was about to fall on the deck – 'Fall under' or *'Von anderen'*.
8. The name given by Soviet troops to the Focke-Wulf Fw 189 reconnaissance plane on account of the quadrangular shape of its unusual twin-boom layout.
9. Up to his death in 1948, Zhdanov was regarded as Stalin's most likely successor.
10. Just south of Leningrad.
11. A heavy engineering works originally founded by Peter the Great.
12. A reference to Collectivisation and the practice of seizing the assets of the so-called *kulaks*.

13. A southern tributary of the River Neva, which it joins south-east of Leningrad.
14. German hand grenades with long handles.
15. 'Navoz' in Russian means 'manure'.
16. A massive tank battle 500 km south of Moscow in July–August 1943, in which the German Army unsuccessfully attempted to surround a salient bulging out westwards from the Soviet front.

Chapter 4

1. About 600 km up the Volga from Stalingrad.
2. Another 150 km upriver.
3. Followers of the Ukrainian nationalist Stephan Bandera.
4. North-west of Warsaw.
5. Also known by the German name Soldau.
6. The contemporary German names for these places are shown in the table. Modern names are: Deutsch-Eylau = Iława; Saalfeld = Zalewo; Mewe = Gniew; Starogard = Starogard Gdański; Königsberg = Kaliningrad; Danzig = Gdańsk.
7. Belorussian towns near the capital, Minsk.

Chapter 5

1. About 85 km east of Moscow.
2. A federal republic inhabited by a non-Russian nationality who speak a language distantly related to Finnish.
3. A type of multiple-rocket artillery usually mounted on ordinary trucks.
4. A lieutenant-general decorated for his role in the defence of Moscow, Vlasov was subsequently captured by the Germans and agreed to lead a so-called Russian Liberation Army (ROA) comprising mainly Soviet POW, to fight on the German side. In the event, the ROA saw little action and Vlasov was executed by the Soviet authorities in 1946.

Chapter 6

1. A street in central Moscow.
2. Connecting the south bank of the Moscow River with Bolotny Island.
3. In the Urals.
4. About 400 km south-east of Moscow.
5. Just south of Moscow.
6. Near Podolsk, south of Moscow.
7. Now Wascz.

Chapter 7

1. In the Urals area.
2. A city now on the border with Kazakhstan.
3. Half-way between Orenburg and the Volga.
4. Over the Vistula River.
5. In south-east Poland.

Chapter 8

1. Close to the Latvian border.
2. Now the site of St Petersburg Airport.
3. Site of the high school attended by Russia's greatest poet and renamed in his honour in 1937.
4. About 150 km south of Leningrad.
5. Siestarjoki in Finnish.
6. Snipers hidden up trees, who reportedly caused immense damage during the Winter War.
7. Literally 'butchers', a term used to refer to the White Finns in the Finnish Civil War of 1918.
8. A Yiddish gangland song which seems to allude to the disposal of stolen property.
9. Seemingly a mixture of sulphur and phosphorous named after its inventor, Koshkin: the full name *Koshkina smes* meant 'Koshkin mixture'.
10. Usually translated as senior lance-corporal.
11. In the Russian enclave of Kaliningrad.
12. Also in the Russian enclave of Kaliningrad.

Chapter 9

1. At the top of the Caspian Sea.
2. A city captured by the Russians from the Turks in 1790 and now in Ukraine.
3. A Turkic-speaking ethnic minority occupying their own republic north-west of the Caspian Sea.
4. A city in the North Caucasus region, nearly 300 km south of Stalingrad.
5. A large city on the north-east of the Black Sea.
6. A village to the west of the Volga.
7. A town about 300 km north-east of Rostov.
8. The Red Army had suffered heavy losses in two earlier attempts to penetrate it.
9. A city on the Sea of Azov.

Notes

Chapter 10

1. Now the Bashkortostan Republic, whose residents speak a language related to Turkish.
2. 7,000 square metres.
3. Capital of the Bashkir republic.
4. Now Samara.
5. A largely forested area embracing parts of Poland, Belarus, Ukraine and western Russia.
6. Now the city of Oral in Kazakhstan.

Chapter 11

1. In south-west Russia close to the Belarusian border.
2. Resisting the forces of General Anton Denikin, who attempted to capture Moscow from the south.
3. November 1939 to March 1940.
4. Now Dimitrovgrad.
5. Russian towns close to the Latvian border.
6. The river flows north roughly parallel to the Latvian and Estonian borders and into a lake just past the Russian city of Pskov.
7. Members of a sect which broke with the Russian Orthodox Church over doctrinal matters in the seventeenth century and established their own communities in remote places.
8. Eastern Latvia.
9. A language based on Old Bulgarian into which the scriptures were translated for propagation among the Slavs.
10. A type of large privately owned farm found in the Baltic region.

Chapter 12

1. 300 km north-east of Moscow.
2. Now Boryspil, a small city close to Kyiv.
3. November 1939–March 1940.
4. February 23rd.
5. Romanian territory which had previously been part of the Tsarist empire; under a secret protocol to the August 1939 Nazi–Soviet Pact Germany agreed not to interfere with Soviet actions against Romania.
6. Roughly half-way between Kyiv and the Polish border.
7. About 200 km south of the capital.
8. Just south-east of Tula, renamed Novomoskovsk in 1961.
9. A northern tributary of the Oka, which it joins near Kaluga.

Chapter 13

1. Several hundred kilometres north-east of Moscow.
2. Some 20 km south of Moscow.
3. About 16 kg.

Chapter 14

1. Eastern Ukraine.
2. An autonomous Soviet republic populated mainly by the descendants of Germans who had been encouraged to farm the lower Volga area under Catherine the Great. Its German population of around 370,000 was deported to Siberia and Kazakhstan in September 1941 for fear they would collaborate with the advancing Nazis.
3. 150 km east of Kyiv.
4. An area of central Moscow south of the river.

Chapter 15

1. North-east of Moscow.
2. Formerly known as Brest-Litovsk, right on the Polish border.
3. A river rising in the Ukraine and running through Brest before joining the Polish River Narew, which flows into the Vistula.
4. A town 400 km from the border.
5. Second-largest city in Belorussia.
6. A tributary of the Dnieper flowing through Gomel.
7. City 230 km west of Moscow.
8. City in north-west Russia.
9. Charged with blocking deserters trying to leave the front-line.
10. Close to the Belorussian border.
11. Named after a distinguished general in Russia's Napoleonic campaigns.
12. Tributary of the Dvina or Daugava, flowing westward through Belarus.